CAMBRIDGE LIBRARY COLLECTION

Books of enduring scholarly value

History

The books reissued in this series include accounts of historical events and movements by eye-witnesses and contemporaries, as well as landmark studies that assembled significant source materials or developed new historiographical methods. The series includes work in social, political and military history on a wide range of periods and regions, giving modern scholars ready access to influential publications of the past.

A Catalogue of the Medieval Manuscripts in the University Library, Aberdeen

M. R. James (1862–1936) is probably best remembered as a writer of chilling ghost stories, but he was an outstanding scholar of medieval literature and palaeography, who served as Provost of King's College, Cambridge, and later as Provost of Eton. His detailed descriptive catalogues of manuscripts owned by colleges, cathedrals and museums are still sought after by scholars today. This catalogue, originally published in 1932, describes just over 80 medieval manuscripts. Thirty of them, mostly later medieval works on canon law or the history of Aberdeen, came to the library from King's College. The remainder, many from the twelfth and thirteenth centuries, and regarded as more important by James, belong to the Marischal College collection, which originated in a 1624 bequest and contains several manuscripts formerly owned by St Paul's Cathedral, London. James describes their structure, content, provenance and decoration, and the book is illustrated by 27 plates.

Cambridge University Press has long been a pioneer in the reissuing of out-of-print titles from its own backlist, producing digital reprints of books that are still sought after by scholars and students but could not be reprinted economically using traditional technology. The Cambridge Library Collection extends this activity to a wider range of books which are still of importance to researchers and professionals, either for the source material they contain, or as landmarks in the history of their academic discipline.

Drawing from the world-renowned collections in the Cambridge University Library, and guided by the advice of experts in each subject area, Cambridge University Press is using state-of-the-art scanning machines in its own Printing House to capture the content of each book selected for inclusion. The files are processed to give a consistently clear, crisp image, and the books finished to the high quality standard for which the Press is recognised around the world. The latest print-on-demand technology ensures that the books will remain available indefinitely, and that orders for single or multiple copies can quickly be supplied.

The Cambridge Library Collection will bring back to life books of enduring scholarly value (including out-of-copyright works originally issued by other publishers) across a wide range of disciplines in the humanities and social sciences and in science and technology.

A Catalogue of the Medieval Manuscripts in the University Library, Aberdeen

Montague Rhodes James

CAMBRIDGE
UNIVERSITY PRESS

CAMBRIDGE UNIVERSITY PRESS

Cambridge, New York, Melbourne, Madrid, Cape Town, Singapore,
São Paolo, Delhi, Dubai, Tokyo, Mexico City

Published in the United States of America by Cambridge University Press, New York

www.cambridge.org
Information on this title: www.cambridge.org/9781108027885

© in this compilation Cambridge University Press 2011

This edition first published 1932
This digitally printed version 2011

ISBN 978-1-108-02788-5 Paperback

A CATALOGUE

OF THE

MEDIEVAL MSS. IN THE
UNIVERSITY LIBRARY
ABERDEEN

LONDON
Cambridge University Press
FETTER LANE

NEW YORK   TORONTO
BOMBAY   CALCUTTA   MADRAS
Macmillan

TOKYO
Maruzen Company, Ltd

WILLIAM ELPHINSTONE 1431—1514
Bishop of Aberdeen, and Founder of the University
From the portrait at King's College

A CATALOGUE

OF THE

MEDIEVAL MANUSCRIPTS IN THE UNIVERSITY LIBRARY ABERDEEN

BY

MONTAGUE RHODES JAMES, O.M., Litt.D., F.B.A.

F.S.A., Hon. D.C.L., Oxford, Hon. Litt.D., Dublin, Hon. LL.D., St Andrews

PROVOST OF ETON

CAMBRIDGE

AT THE UNIVERSITY PRESS

1932

CONTENTS

LIST OF PLATES

[The photographs of MSS. were taken by Mr G. Aubourne Clarke, F.R.P.S., F.R.Met.Soc., of the Observatory, King's College.]

PREFACE

THE collection of manuscripts described here falls into three divisions, those namely of King's College, Marischal College and the University.

In the following pages something will be said of the character and provenance of the medieval portion of the two older sections, each of which has a complexion of its own. The 'University' division, consisting of recent acquisitions, may be left out of account.

The King's College books, of which there are thirty, are of late date (only one—no. 155—is as old as the thirteenth century) and their predominant 'note' is local. Some (nos. 12–17, 184, 198, 222) are the gifts of Bishop William Elphinstoun, and all but one of these are portentous Canon Law books: another (239), written at Aberdeen, is of like character. More interesting are the volumes (22, 247–250) which come from the Cathedral of Aberdeen and tell of its constitution, endowments and furniture: in these, naturally, much local history is contained, which cannot be adequately dealt with in a catalogue, and has indeed been worthily enshrined in Cosmo Innes's two volumes of the *Registrum Episcopatus Aberdonensis* issued in 1845 by the Spalding Club. Nevertheless I have ventured on short descriptions of the volumes, and have reprinted (I must confess, in ignorance of the earlier publication) certain inventories. Lastly, the Orosius (214), once owned by that ancient worthy Hector Boece, must not be forgotten.

It is the Marischal College section which contains well-nigh all that is important to the learned and artistic world in general. The nucleus of the section is the bequest made by Thomas Reid, Latin Secretary to James Sixth and First, in 1624. This consists of some twenty-five manuscripts, apart from printed books.

It will not be out of place to give in full the list of them as drawn up and attested by Patrick Dune, the Principal and first Librarian of Marischal College.

1. The Hebrew bybill, perg.
   Not described here.

2. Augustin de Ciuitate dei, perg.
   Now bound with no. 8, as it seems.

There is a remarkable fact regarding the provenance of the majority of these books; namely that sixteen of them certainly and four more almost certainly come from the Cathedral library of St Paul's in London. The 'certain' instances are Reid's 2, 3, 5, 6, 7, 8, 9, 10, 13, 15, 16, 17, 19, 21, 22, 23: the 'almost certain' are his 11, 12, 14, 20; his 18 is lost: his 4 is from another library: of his no. 1 I can say nothing: his 24 and 25 were written for private persons.

The St Paul's provenance of one volume (no. 137) had been noted long ago by Dr Sparrow Simpson on the strength of an unerased inscription (see Savage, *Old Engl. Libraries* p. 120); and I was led by this to speculate on the possibility of Reid's having procured more than this one book from the same source. The inquiry was not hopeless, for there exists in print (in Dugdale's *History of St Paul's* p. 392) a catalogue of the Cathedral library made in 1458, about which I will be somewhat diffuse. Dugdale took it from "an ancient roll in the Hatton Library." It is in the form of an indenture "between Dean William Say and the Chapter of St Paul's and Roger Mersh an executor of the late Walter Shyrington Chancellor of the duchy of Lancaster to Henry VI and Canon Stagiary of St Paul's of the first part, and Masters John Raven and David Hampstede, perpetual Chaplains of the chantry of the said Walter founded in his chapel situate near the north door of the said Church of the other part—being an Inventory of all and singular the books and their contents existing in the new library late begun by the said Walter and fully built by his executors over the cloister of the cemetery of the same Church, called Pardonchirche-Hawe, and delivered to the said Chaplains as custodians of the said Library the 25th day of March a. d. 1458."

The catalogue is a full one, divided into classes lettered from A to U, and enumerating somewhat more than 160 volumes, for each of which it gives the opening words of the second leaf. This useful practice (a common one in the later medieval period) enables us to identify with certainty any MS. of which the second leaf has survived; and in this particular case it has been of signal service, as a glance at the descriptions of Reid's MSS. will show. Besides those which certainly occur in the catalogue of 1458 there are a few (present nos. 10, 219, 240, 244) which contain the name

T. Graunt: a reference to Le Neve's *Fasti Eccl. Angl.* under St Paul's shows that this was Thomas Graunt who died Treasurer of St Paul's in 1474. With him I also associate nos. 7 and 218, the latter of which belonged in the xiv[th] century to a fellow of Oriel College, Oxford.

One or two other volumes I attribute to St Paul's on mere grounds of general probability, which in this case are fairly strong.

Very few books from St Paul's exist in other libraries: I can only point, at present, to the Radulphus de Diceto at Lambeth (MS. 8) and a Suetonius in the British Museum (Royal 15. C. iii).

The only other book of Reid's to which a certain provenance can be assigned is the Bestiary (present no. 24) which has on its flyleaf the Old Royal Library press-mark, and is identifiable in the inventory of that Library made in 1542.

Nearly all of Reid's books have a uniform binding, the precise date of which must be determined by experts. The letters $\overline{ABD}$ (for Aberdon.) have been stamped on the covers.

One other medieval English provenance can be noted: no. 154, which may have been acquired as late as 1756, is from the Carthusian house of Hinton in Somerset.

Bishop Burnet figures as the giver of the most beautiful of the manuscripts next to the Bestiary. No. 25 is a Psalter and Hours, with many miscellaneous devotions, bequeathed by him in 1714. That it was done for an English owner early in the xv[th] century is certain: equally certain that that owner was a person of quality interested in the Brigittine order. But at present his identity cannot be determined. The book is remarkable both for its decoration and its contents, and further light on its history would be most welcome.

Passing over a few gifts of the Governors of Gordon's Hospital and others, we come to the last important benefactor, Dr Guise, the giver of nine volumes, whereof the present numbers are: 106, 107, 138, 156, 161, 216, 242, 275, 276.

They are largely foreign books. No. 106, the oldest of the whole collection, is partly in the Beneventane hand and contains a letter hitherto unknown, by one Berengar, directed against his more famous homonym of Tours; 107 is a late French book, 138 late Italian; 156 is from Ourscamp near Noyon; 161 very likely also French; 216

seems to be English; 242 is from North Italy; 275 French; 276 English.

In date the manuscripts range from cent. xi (to which may belong 9 and 106) to xvi; a majority of Reid's books belong to cent. xii and xiii. In respect of decoration nos. 24 and 25 far excel the rest; to them may be added 11, in view of some fine initials.

The literary contents comprise few rarities; the letter of Berengar in 106, the miracles of the Virgin in 137, and the notes by Thomas Gascoigne in 241 are certainly remarkable, but the patristic texts are nearly all copies of very well known works. Of the classics all are late save 152 and 165, and these are not earlier than cent. xiii.

A certain number of manuscripts were brought to my notice after the printing-off of pp. 1–105: these, therefore, are treated as a supplement, but are inserted in their proper places in the Short List, and marked with an asterisk.

This supplement is followed by a Note on the History of the Library, and a hand-list of the manuscripts not included in my descriptive catalogue: both contributed by Dr Douglas Simpson.

Of the method of cataloguing it is perhaps enough to say that I have not deviated here from the practice followed by me for many years; material, dimensions, date, structure, contents and decoration of each volume are noted, and short texts of interest (as in the case of Gascoigne's notes) are transcribed. Many references to the *Patrologia Latina* of Migne are borrowed from Schenkl's *Bibl. Patr. Lat. Britannica.*

It has been a real pleasure to study a collection hitherto little known: not less pleasant is the recording of my gratitude to the authorities of the University for the facilities accorded to me, and in particular to Dr W. Douglas Simpson, Librarian, for the very great pains he has taken in arranging the despatch of the manuscripts to Eton and in answering my many importunate queries. Professor A. Souter, F.B.A., has also very kindly looked through the proofs.

M.R.J.

July 1932

NOTE ON THE ABERDEEN CATHEDRAL
REGISTERS, ETC.

IN the publication of the Spalding Club, 1845, *Registrum Episcopatus Aberdonensis*, 2 vols., 4to., edited by Cosmo Innes, the manuscript sources are described in vol. i, lxvii–lxxiii, and lettered from A to H. Their contents are arranged in order of date; and dispersed throughout the two volumes.

A, the Registrum Album, and **B,** of Bishop Dunbar's time, are in the Advocates' Library, Edinburgh.

C=no. **247.** The Charters, etc., are inserted in order of date in vol. i.
The Statutes, etc., are in ii. 59 *sqq.*
The Inventories in ii. 127–153, 162–174.
The Obits in ii. 200–207.

D=no. **248.** The Anniversaries are at the foot of pp. 1–25, vol. II; a later series ii. 207–228.

E=no. **249.** Deeds, etc., in vol. i.
The Inventories are in ii. 154–162.
Rentalia, etc., ii. 229–235: 283 *sqq.*

F=no. **250.** The whole text in ii. 179–199.

G Not described here. Documents in vol. I.

H=no. **22.** The Epistolar, of which there is a full recent edition. Documents from it are in ii. 236 *sqq.*

Facsimiles of the script and decoration are given

from **C** : vol. ii, plates 6, 7.
,, **D** : ,, pl. 10.
,, **E** : vol. i, pl. 4; ii, pl. 8.
,, **F** : vol. ii, pl. 1, 9.
,, **G** : ,, pl. 5.
,, **H** : vol. i, pl. 1; ii, pl. 1, 11, 12.

SHORT LIST OF MSS. DESCRIBED.

NOTE : The MSS. marked with an asterisk are described in the Supplement, p. 106.

	Short title	Provenance	Date	Library
1.	Gregorii Moralia xxiii–xxxv	[Reid 7] St Paul's	xii	Marischal Coll.
2.	Isaias, etc. glosati	[Reid 13] St Paul's	xii	,,
3.	Gregorii Registrum	[Reid 3] St Paul's	xii–xiii	,,
4.	Aug. in Ps. i–l	[Reid 9] St Paul's	xii	,,
5.	Aug. in Ps. ci–cl	[Reid 6] St Paul's	xii	,,
6.	Aug. contra Julianum	[Reid 16] St Paul's	xiii	,,
7.	Aug. opuscula	[Reid 11]? St Paul's, Graunt	xv	,,
8.	(1) Aug. de ordine, etc.	[Reid 15] St Paul's	xiii	,,
	(2) Aug. de Ciuitate dei	[? Reid 2] St Paul's	xiii	,,
9.	Aug. de verbis domini	[Reid 10] St Paul's	xi or xii	,,
10.	Gregorii Pastoralis etc.	[Reid 5] St Paul's, Graunt	xiv and xv	,,
11.	Hieronymi Epistolae	[Reid 14] ? St Paul's	xii	,,
12–16.	Nic. de Tudeschis	W. Elphinstoun	1470	Coll. Reg.
*17.	Dominicus de S. Geminiano	W. Elphinstoun	1469	,,
*21.	Polychronicon in English	J. Gordon	xv early	,,
*22.	Epistolare (H)	Gavin Dunbar	1527	,,
24.	Bestiary	[Reid 4] Old Royal Library	xii and xiii	Marischal Coll.
25.	Psalter, Horae, etc.	Bp. Burnet	xv early	,,
*105.	Albertus Magnus	Germany	xv	Coll. Reg.
106.	Aug. de doctr. christ. etc.	Dr Guise, Italy	xi	Marischal Coll.
107.	Georgius de Sclavonia	Dr Guise, France	1411?	,,
*108.	G. de Cayoto	Alex. Galloway	xv	,,
119.	Patrick Dune, Notebook		1595	,,
137.	Gregorii Homiliae. Miracula B.V.M. etc.	[Reid 19] St Paul's	xiii	,,
138.	Ubertino de Casali	Dr Guise, Italy	xv	,,
139.	Biblia	Governors of Gordon Sch.	xiii–xiv	,,
148.	Cato. Boethius	Governors of Gordon Sch.	xvi	,,
152.	Martialis		xiii	,,
154.	Sermones	Carthusians of Hinton, Somerset	xiv	,,
155.	Summa Raymundi		xiii	Coll. Reg.
156.	Bernardus	Dr Guise, Ourscamp Abbey	xii	Marischal Coll.
161.	De Sacramento	Dr Guise	xii	,,
163.	Cicero de Oratore	W. Laurence	xv	Coll. Reg.
164.	Pomponius Mela	J. Gordon	xv	Marischal Coll.
165.	Ovid. Metamm.	David Guthrie	xiii	,,
184.	Hen. Bohic	W. Elphinstoun	xv	Coll. Reg.
*198.	N. de Tudeschis, etc.	W. Elphinstoun	xv	,,

Short title	Provenance	Date	Library
205. Seneca etc.	[Reid 23] St Paul's	xiv and xiii	Marischal Coll.
214. Orosius etc.	Hector Boece	xv	Coll. Reg.
215. Aug. de Concordia Evang. etc.	[Reid 20] ? St Paul's	xii–xiii	Marischal Coll.
216. Beda etc. in Apocalypsim	Dr Guise	xii	,,
*217. Biblia		xiii	,,
218. Bernardus	[Reid 12] Oriel Coll. ? St Paul's	xiii	,,
219. Aug. in Johannem	[Reid 8] St Paul's, Graunt	xii	,,
222. Laur. Valla	W. Elphinstoun	xv	Coll. Reg.
223. Super Organon		xv	,,
239. Gul. Hay Quaestiones		1535	,,
240. Legenda Aurea	[Reid 22] St Paul's, Graunt	xiv	Marischal Coll.
241. Ric. de S. Victore	[Reid 21] St Paul's, Th. Gascoigne	xiii	,,
242. Comm. in Ps. LXXI–CL	Dr Guise, Italy	xii	,,
*243. R. Hampole on the Psalter		xv	,,
244. Rufini Hist. Eccl.	[Reid 17] St Paul's, Graunt	xii	,,
*247. Aberdeen Cathedral Inventories (C)		xv and xvi	Coll. Reg.
248. Aberdeen Cathedral Register (D)	P. Leslie	xvi	,,
249. Aberdeen Cathedral Register and Inventory (E)		xv–xvi	,,
250. Aberdeen Cathedral Inventories (F)		1549	,,
253. Ric. de Media Villa		xv	Marischal Coll.
254. Aristotelis Politica	R. Irving	xv	,,
255. Bernardus de Gordonio		1462	Coll. Reg.
*256. Medica (Philonius)		1461	,,
*258. Medical Receipts in English		xv	Marischal Coll.
*259. Avicenna		1469	Coll. Reg.
260. Alex. de Villa dei		xv	,,
261. Super Organon		xv	,,
262. P. de Ancharano		1484	,,
263. Boethius etc.	Jo. Vaus	xv	,,
271. Psalter, Horae. Sarum	[Reid 24 or 25]	xv	Marischal Coll.
272. Horae. Sarum	[Reid 24 or 25]	xv early	,,
273. Horae. Amiens		xv late	Coll. Reg.
274. Horae. Flemish	Jac. Fraser	xv	,,
275. Biblia	Dr Guise	xiii	Marischal Coll.
276. Horae. Sarum	Dr Guise	xv	,,
*278. Aberdeen Grey Friars. Obits		xvi	,,
364. Ptolemaeus	S. Maximin, Treves	1426	,,
686. Hieron. in Matth.	? Bamberg	xii	University
687. Hilarius Pictav.	Italy, Phillipps	xv	,,
688. Historia Scholastica	Fr. Edmond	xii	,,
*984. Ps.-Athanasius, etc.		xv	,,

No. 6, folio 53, recto (lower half)

No. 11, folio 75, recto (lower half)

CATALOGUE OF MANUSCRIPTS

1. GREGORII MORALIUM
LIBB. XXIII–XXXV.

{ Old marks
  D². 5. 31
  H. I. 2

Vellum, 15 × 10¼, ff. 224, double columns of 37 lines. Cent. xii, in a magnificent hand, black and rather rounded.

Binding, stamped leather (xvi) over wooden boards. Clasps gone; lettered on sides A B̄ D̄.

Collation: 1⁸–28⁸.   2 fo. maior sit.

No. 7 in the list of T. Reid's MSS
Liber Acad. Marischall. Abredon.

From St Paul's Cathedral, London. Entered in the catalogue of 1458 under letter O.

Tertia pars Moralium Gregorii continens xiii libros 2 fo. maior sit deus homine.

In Reid's list the entry is 'Gregorius in Iobum duobus voluminibus,' but no second volume appears to exist.

f. 1 a blank.

On 1 *b*–5 is the text of the Book of Job from xxxii to the end, divided into sections, each corresponding to a Book of the Moralia: headed in red:

Liber primus quinte partis libri Iob   .   .   .   .   . f. 1 *b*
Finita sunt uerba Iob. Omiserunt autem
—senex et plenus dierum.
The lower half of col. 2 of 5 *b* is filled with a title in splendid
   red and blue capitals (in alternate lines).
Incipit liber / Primus quin/te partis / Moralium / Beati Gre/gorii
   pape / urbis Rome / in librum Iob.
f. 6 has a headline (xiv). Lib. 23 tocius operis.
Prefationem huius operis   6
Magnificent initial P, 9 in. high, the main framework in orange
   with foliage insertions and convolutions in red, blue and
   green. The ground of the head of the letter blue with white
   dots: the original green (silk?) guard remains.
The text of the Book is in red.

J. A. C.   I

Lib. II quinte partis (=XXIV). 21 *b* initial in fine red outline.
,,   III (XXV). 35 *b* similar.
,,   IV (XXVI). 47   ,,
,,   V (XXVII). 68   ,,
Lib. I ultime partis (XXVIII) 87. Title in red and blue capitals
         and fine red outline initial.
,,   II (XXIX). 99 *b* similar initial.
,,   III (XXX). 117 *b*   ,,
,,   IV (XXXI). 136 *b*   ,,
,,   V (XXXII). 162   ,,
,,   VI (XXXIII). 177   ,,
,,   VII (XXXIV). 198   ,,
,,   VIII (XXXV). 211 *b*   ,,
ending 224 *a*: pro me lacrimas reddat deo et d. n. I. C. cui cum
      patre et sp. s. honor et imperium per eterna sec. sec. Amen.
Expl. moralia b. Greg. pape urbis rome in librum iob, in xxx.
      quinque libros divisa. 224 *b* blank.

The book is a very fine piece of work: chapter numbers have
been added throughout by a hand of cent. xiv, but otherwise it
shows few traces of use.

2. ISAIAS JEREMIAS THRENI BARUCH   Old marks
GLOSATI.   D². 5. 32
                                         H. I. 5
                                         7. 23. xvi

Vellum, 15 × 10¾, ff. 154, double columns of text and gloss:
text has 33 lines to page, gloss 66 or more.

Cent. xii late in a very beautiful hand, large of course for text,
and small for gloss, both exquisite.

Binding as for no. 1, etc., lettered A $\overline{\text{B D}}$ on sides. Chainmark
at foot of f. 1.   2 fo. (3) Ieronimus.

Lib. Acad. Marischall. Abredon.

No. 13 in the list of Reid's MSS. From St Paul's, London.
Entered in the catalogue of 1458 under letter M.

Textus Isa. et Jer. gl. et intitulatur super Is. et. Jer. 2 fo.
Ieronimus.

Collation: 1² 2⁸–20⁸.

f. 1 *a* blank. On 1 *b*, 2 *a*, in the hand of the gloss is a table of
the kings (and prophets) of Israel and Judah, with brief historical
notes, ending with Neemias,

              partem templi perficeret.

This is in a number of narrow columns.

On 2 *b* in the text hand
    Inc. Prefacio S. Ieronimi Presb. in librum Ysaye prophete . f. 2 *b*
    Nemo cum prophetas—insultarent. Expl. Pref.
Isaias glosatus   3
Gloss begins. Ieronimus. Sic exponam ysaiam
The initial to the Book cut out.
Headlines in red and blue capitals, counterchanged.
Ieremias glosatus .   .   .   .   71 *b*
Gold initial to prologue remains. Initial to text cut out.
The gloss is in many places arranged in curious patterns when
    it reaches the lower margin. Thus on 96 *b* it imitates a snake:
    see also 107.
Threni glosati   132
Here the historiated initial remains: letter in blue on gold
    ground: Jeremiah beardless nimbed sits on *L.* with hands to
    face: the city on *R.* The chapters have initials in colour:
    there are six columns to the page here.
Baruch (without gloss)   150
Inc. prefaciuncula S. Jeronimi Presb. in librum Baruch.
    Liber iste qui Baruch
The upper *R.* corner of 150 cut out, with the initial
—que est ex ipso. Expl. liber Baruch.
Exemplum epistole quam misit Ieremias etc.   153
ending 154 *b* in rather smaller script.
—longe ab opprobriis. Expl. exemplum ep. Ieremie prophete.

A very fine example of writing. The remaining historiated
initial is of excellent execution.

3. GREGORII REGISTRUM.

$$\left\{ \begin{array}{l} \text{Old marks} \\ \text{D}^2. \ 5. \ 33 \\ \text{H. I. 3} \\ \text{3 B. xvi} \\ \text{II. 2. 11} \end{array} \right.$$

Vellum, $14 \times 10\frac{1}{4}$, ff. 162, double columns of 48 lines. Cent. xii
late—xiii early in an excellent regular hand, rather pointed.
                               2 fo. (table) ad sancta loca.
Binding as for nos. 1, 2: lettered A $\overline{\text{B D}}$ on sides.
Collation: 1^8 (wants 8) 2^6 3^8 (+ 1) 4^8–11^8 12^6 13^{10} 14^8–20^8 21^4.
Liber Acad. Marischall. Abredon.
No. 3 in the list of T. Reid's MSS. From St Paul's, London.

Entered in the catalogue of 1458 under letter O as: Gregorius in Registro continet xv libros 2 fo. ad sancta loca.

1. In triple columns and two hands.
   Capitula epistolarum S. Gregorii . . . . . . f. 1
   1 Symbolum fidei
   (Lib. xiv. Ep. xiii)—pacto potest obligare.
   Most of 7 *b* blank.

2. Symbolum fidei dictatum a b. Gregorio papa . . . 8
   Credo in unum deum
   —laxari peccata in nomine patris et filii et sp. s.

3. Title in red and blue capitals 8
   Registri b. Gregorii pape urbis Rome liber primus inc.
       Mense Septembre Indictione viiii Gregorius episcopis per
       siciliam constitutis
           Ualde necessarium esse
   A magnificent initial in shaded pink set on dark blue ground
       containing convolutions and two animals (white and blue) on
       gold ground: within square frame, half orange, half green.
       The style is the marked one seen in Canterbury books of
       this date.
   Lib. ii. 23, iii. 29 *b*, iv. 40 *b*, v. 48, vi. 62 *b*, vii. 73 *b*,
       viii. 84 *b*, ix. 92 *b*, x. 112, xi. 120, xii. 131 *b*, xiii. 134 *b*,
       xiv. 143. Ep. xiii ends: nulla unquam ratione sustineat.
   Col. 2 of 146 *a* blank.
   Epistole que pretermisse sunt de superioribus indictionibus 146 *b*
   1 (Sabiniano). De causa maximi
   xxxiii. Episcopis per galliam etc.
           Diuinis preceptis
   —memores nostri custodiat fratres karissimi.

4. In a more beautiful and smaller hand 155
   Canons of certain Councils, viz.:
       Romanum of 826. 15 Nov.
   In nomine...imperantibus ludowico...et lothario...presidente...
       eugenio...
   Ut episcopus honus et approbatus operis ordinetur Beatissimi
       pauli discretione
   40 canons, ending: ut sacerdos loci considerauerit. Expl.
       conc. Eugenii pape.
   Capitula in synodo actaque apud meldensem urbem...anno
       incarn. dom. dccc. xlv. (17 June) . . . . . 156 *b*
   Salubre et decens esse cognoscitur
   Canons numbered to xxxiii (but only 32) followed by extract
       Greg. Ianuario karalitano Inter querelas multiplices
   Then 26 unnumbered canons. 158
   Ut nemo episcoporum quemlibet sine certa et manifesta peccati
       causa [causa] communione priuet, etc.

The 18th is a recapitulation of enactments against Jews, the
    19th also against them.
The last: Hec autem constituimus non preiudicantes—ultione
    plectatur.
Of Toul (or Savonieres) 14 June, 859   160
Headed: Karolus contra Guenilonem archiep. (of Sens, 840–
    865).
    Libellus proclamationis karoli regis aduersus guenilonem.
14 Articles ending: adiutorium aliquid prestitit.
Epistola Synodalis gueniloni archiep.   161
Dilecto et uen. gueniloni...Remigius lugdunensium metropoli-
    tanus ep. etc.   .   .   . ·   161
De instauratione pacis
—sententias a maioribus institutas excipias. Expl.
Si quis accusatur episcopus quemadmodum sit euocandus.
    Ex conc. Carthag. cap. xix .   .   .   .   .   .   161 *b*
Aurelius ep. dixit. Quisquis episcoporum,
    followed by other extracts, ending :·
Ex conc. etiam sardicensi c. xxxii ac ex conc. toletano.

The initials of Books are large and flourished but not very
remarkable. Those of Epistles alternately red and blue. All the
execution is good.

4. Augustinus super Ps. i–l.

⎧ Old marks
⎪ D². 5. 34
⎨ II. 2. 1
⎪ H. 1. 8
⎩ 8. B. xv

Vellum, 13¾ × 10, ff. 204, double columns of 42 lines. Cent. xii
(first half) in a very fine hand perhaps of the Canterbury school.

2 fo. quid superbit.

Binding as for 1, etc.
Collation: 1¹⁰–19¹⁰ 20⁸ 21⁶.
Liber Acad. Marischall. Abredon.
No. 9 in the list of T. Reid's MSS. From St Paul's, London.
Entered in the Catalogue of 1458 under letter M as: Aug. super
1ᵃᵐ quinquagenam Psalterii 2 fo. quid superbit terra.

At top of f. 1 is an inscription (xii) carefully disguised with
    hatching
        Liber Ricardi episcopi, most likely Richard de Belmeis,
    1108-1127.

Also a xivth-cent. title (as in no. 1) Aug^{us} super prima in
partem Psalterii. On last page at top: liber sci pauli london.
Title in red and green capitals occupying col. 1 :
  Aurelii Augustini Doctoris Eximii Expositionis super psalmos
  prima pars incipit.
Space of half a column for an initial (Beatus vir) qui non abiit
in consilio impiorum (red and green capitals)
    De d. n. I. C. hoc est homine dominico.
Each psalm has a decorative initial: red and green are the
favourite colours. They form a remarkable series. Notable
are those to ps. vii, ix, xiii–xvi, xviii, xix, xxxvi (3), xli, xlii.
A good number are quite plain.
Ends 203. —deus de illo exiget suam. Colophon in red and
green capitals: Aur. Aug. doct. eximii expositionis super
psalmos prima pars expl.
On 203 *b* an addition : Imperatorum constitutionem frustra
obicitis Catholicis—Priuati enim dicuntur qui publicis non
sunt dignitatibus implicati. 204 blank.

The text of the Psalter written in red throughout.

5. Augustinus super Psalmos ci–cl.

⎧ Old marks
⎪ D². 5. 35
⎨ II. 2. 2
⎩ H. 1. 9

Vellum, 13¾ × 9½, ff. 353, double columns of 36 lines. Cent. xii
early in an admirable hand : like that of no. **4**, but not perhaps
identical with it.

  Binding as for no. 1, etc.   2 fo. patrem quod autem.
  Collation : 1⁸ (wants 1) 2⁸–22⁸ (wants 5) 23⁸–44⁸ 45⁶ (wants 4–6).
  Liber Acad. Marischall. Abredon.
  No. 6 in the list of T. Reid's MSS. From St Paul's, London.
Entered in the Catalogue of 1458 under letter M as: Aug. super
3^{am} quinquagenam Psalterii 2 fo. patrem quod autem.
  Number of psalms added at top in cent. xiv.

The text of the Psalter written in red.
Augustinus super Ps. ci (no title) .   .   .   .   . f. 1
Ecce unus pauper orat et non orat (blue, red and green capitals)
in silentio
Initial in red outline: above, an angel in air, horizontal;
below, a beardless tonsured man kneeling, hands stretched
upward: draped altar and chalice on *R*. Some of the subsequent initials are decorative, but many plain.

Ending 353 *b.* Et quia sapere secundum carnem mors est. *omnis spiritus laudet dominum.*
Aur. Aug. ep. tract. de ps. centes. quinquages. expl. (blue, red and green capitals).

Both this and no. 4 are very fine examples of writing.

6. AUGUSTINUS CONTRA JULIANUM.
EIUSDEM EPISTOLAE.

$\left\{\begin{array}{l}\text{Old marks}\\ \text{D}^2.\ 5.\ 36\\ \text{II. 2. 3}\\ \text{x. B. xv}\\ \text{H. 1. 12}\\ \text{MSS. 4. 7}\end{array}\right.$

Vellum, 13¾ × 8¾, ff. 4 + 144, double columns of 60 lines. Cent. xiii in a very good regular close pointed hand.

Binding as no. 1, etc.   2 fo. ret episcopus. Ideo.
Collation: a^6? (wants 3, 4?) 1^{12}–4^{12} 5^{10} | 6^{12}–12^{12} 14 (two).
Liber Acad. Marischall. Abredon.

No. 16 in the list of T. Reid's MSS. From St Paul's, London. Entered in the Catalogue of 1458 under letter M, as: Aug. contra Julianum 2 fo. ret epus ideo *in uno vol.* cxxxix Epp. Aug. ad Volucianum et ad alios et aliorum ad Aug. *in eodem vol.*

On the four prefixed leaves is writing in various hands.

On i *a* rudiments of a tabula super 6 libros Aug. contra Iulianum. i *b* blank.

On ii extracts from or synopsis of the six Books against Julian, closely written. After this, two leaves perhaps lost.

On iii *a* in the same hand the end of a similar analysis of a work in 20 Books: part of xviii, xix and xx remain.

On iii *b* extracts from the Epistles of Augustine.

On iii *b*, iv, pencil notes, much rubbed.

    1. Augustini contra Julianum libri sex (no title) . . . . f. 1
        Contumelias tuas et uerba maledica
      Lib. II. 7, III. 12 *b*, IV. 19 *b*, V. 29, VI. 36 *b.*
      Ending 46 *b*: tenere qua uinceris.

    2. Epistolae Augustini cxxxix (no title) 47
      Inc. capitula uoluminis huius numero centum triginta nouem
      i. Ep. Aug. ad uolusianum.
      cxxxix. Item ep. eiusdem ad Probam de orando deo.

The text ends unfinished in 138 ad Paulinum et therasiam
    Qui autem de littera per repromissionem
On the same page (f. 148 *a*) is a pencilled list of names and
    payments (xiii–xiv) :
            Mag^{ro} Th. 4 solid.
            Ricard (?) pauperi xvi*d.*
            Joh^{ni} de humley xii*d.*
            d^{ns} Rogerus 2 sol.
            Ricardus capellanus socius eius xvi*d.*
                     etc.
On 148 *b* a table in the hand of i *a*.

Initials are in red and blue, well done but not remarkable. The
writing however is notably regular, close and good.

7. AUGUSTINUS.

                                Old marks
                                D^2. 5. 37
                                II. 2. 7
                                H. 1. 14

Vellum, 13 × 10¼, ff. 257, double columns of 44 lines. Cent. xv,
not late, in a good clear English hand, rather florid.
    Binding : stamped leather (xvi) over wooden boards : lettered
A $\overline{B\,D}$: two clasps gone.
    Collation : 1 flyleaf 1^8–28^8 | gap | 29 (four) gap 30 (three) :
original foliation.
    Liber Acad. Marischall. Abredon.
    It is no. 11 in the list of T. Reid's books.   2 fo. satis est.
    The recto of f. 1 (flyleaf) blank :. on i *b* table of contents headed
        In hoc volumine continentur opera subscripta. Numerus
        contentorum Augustinus 42.

     1. Augustinus de pastoribus   .   .   .   . f. 1
         Spes tota nostra (sermo 46. xxxviii. 270).
         At top : Augustinus ego do normas presbiterorum
              Impleo quos morum quos et honore rego
         —ad unitatem. Expl. etc.

     2. Sermo eiusd de ouibus .   .   .   .   8 *b*
         Verba que cantauimus (S. 47 : xxxviii. 295)
         —deus noster.

     3. Aug. de fide et simbolo (xl. 181)   15
         preceded by Retractation. Quoniam scriptum est
         —intellegant. Expl. etc.

Ends 257 *b*; most of a column blank.

The Table adds

Liber Senece de formula vite honeste siue de 4 virtutibus
cardinalibus fo. 258,

but this is gone.

Our knowledge of the provenance is gone with the irrecoverable inscription on 251 *b*. St Paul's is most probable, though the book is not found in the catalogue. It may well be one of Th. Graunt's books : cf. no. **10**, etc. There is a fine initial in blue, pink and green on gold, and partial border of good English style on f. 1. The several tracts have small initials in gold on blue and pink grounds, flourished. The book is clean and well preserved.

8. AUGUSTINUS.

⎧ Old marks
⎪ II. 2. 4
⎨ H. 1. 13
⎩ D². 5. 38

Vellum, 12¾ × 10⅝, ff. 116, double columns of 79 lines. Cent. xiii in two hands : the first rather larger : both admirably clear and regular.

Binding : stamped leather (xvi) over wooden boards ; stamped A $\overline{\text{B D}}$: two clasps gone.

Collation : 1¹² | 2¹²–9¹² 10⁸.

Liber Acad. Marischall. Abredon.   See below.

It is no. 15, and possibly also no. 2, in the list of T. Reid's books. From St Paul's, London.

I. 1. Liber S. Augustini de perfeccione iusticie hominum ad eutro-
pium et paulum (contra Coelestium) .   .   .   .   . f. 1
Sanctis fratribus et coepiscopis eutropio et paulo (xliv. 291)
ending unfinished 4 *a* : odiosissimum
Most of 4 *a* and all 4 *b* blank.

2. Augustinus de ordine (xxxii. 977)   5
prefaced by extract from Retractations. Per idem tempus—
capitales.
Text : Ordinem rerum.
Lib. II. 7 *a*, ending 11 *a* : lumen fuisset illarum.

3. In another fine hand.
Capitula to Libb. 1–x of De Ciuitate dei   .   .   .   .   11 *b*
Unfinished, 12 *b* blank.

II. 4. Augustinus de Ciuitate dei (xli)   13
     Extract from Retractations : Interea cum roma—sic incipit.
     Text. Gloriosissimam ciuitatem dei
     Lib. II. 16 *b*, III. 20, IV. 24, V. 27 *b*, VI. 32, VII. 34 *b*, VIII. 38 *b*,
       IX. 43, X. 46, XI. 51 *b* (with capitula, as have the following
       Books), XII. 58, XIII. 60, XIV. 63 *b*, XV. 68, XVI. 73 *b*,
       XVII. 79 *b*, XVIII. 84 *b*, XIX. 92, XX. 96 *b*, XXI. 102 *b*,
       XXII. 109 *b*.
     Ending 116 *b*: gratulanter agant. Gloria et honor deo patri et
     filio et sp. sancto omnipotenti deo in excelsis in sec. sec.
     Amen.

The book has been carefully read, numerals affixed to chapters and headlines added in cent. xiii–xiv: and in the former part are many marginalia and some grotesques and diagrams.

Initials in blue and red, indented, and flourished.

An inscription has been cut off the foot of f. 1, but I do not think it was a note of provenance, and I see no other trace.

The entry in the St Paul's Catalogue of 1458 under letter M is: Aug. de Ciuitate dei 2 fo. *curramus credendo in alio volumine.*

Aug. de perfectione justitie		
de ordine		
de vera religione		
contra mendacium	de mendacio	
in Iponosticon	de ii animabus	*in eodem*
de penitentia	de agone Christiano	*volumine*
de bono coniugali	de bono virginali	
ad Inquis. Ianuarii	Contra advers. legis et prophetarum	
In libro Retractationum	de fide et legibus	

Whence I gather that Vol. I of this MS. is but a fragment of a larger collection, and Vol. II has been bound with it.

9. AUGUSTINUS.

Old marks
II. 2. 5
H. 1. 7
D². 5. 39
Oldest mark, 3. B. xv sc.

Vellum, 12⅞ × 9½, ff. 1 + 137, 34 lines to page. Cent. xii early, mainly in one large clear hand with a distinct slope, but at first in somewhat smaller script. The slope might suggest a German origin, but I believe the hand is English.

Binding: old stamped leather (xvi) over wooden boards: stamped A B̄ D̄: two clasps gone.

Collation: 1 flyleaf 1⁸ 2⁸ (4 and 6 canc.) 3⁸–9⁸ 10⁶ 11⁸–18⁸ (wants 6–8).

Liber Acad. Marischall. Abredon.

It is no. 10 in the list of T. Reid's books.   2 fo. Eiusdem.

From St Paul's, London.

> f. 1*a* is blank. On 1*b* in a good xii^th-cent. hand, rubrics; some in capitals.
>
> Extracts on the salvation of Solomon.
> De Salomone Augustinus. Salomon inquit uir tante sapientie
> Ieron. in xviii° libro super Ezech. Quamuis peccasse
> Ambr. Salomon ille mirabilis
> Item Ambr. in Apol. dauid. Quid de dauid dicam
> Aiunt libri hebrei. Salomonem quinquies tractum
> —a se ipso depositus est REGNO.
> These extracts occur with some frequency.
> Inc. capitula S. Augustini de verbis domini (xxxviii. 636)   . f.   1
>   Agite poenitentiam etc.
> The last Eiusdem de scripturis ueteribus ac nouis contra arrianos.
> Text. Evvangelium audivimus et in eo dominum .   .   .   2
> Sermo lv (last in the Table) ends 135*b*:
>   sed erunt aequales angelis dei. Per XP̄M. DN̄M. NR̄M.
> Expl. sermo beati ⟨augusti⟩ni episcopi lv.
> Like all explicits, in red capitals.
> Item eiusd. de uerb. d^ni in euang. sec. Ioh. Ego sum uitis etc.   136
> Inc. sermo lvi
> De sancto evangelio presente tempore (xxxviii. 530)
> —non uidetur ab eis qui foris sunt.

I am not sure that there is a real change of scribe. The large hand is well set in by f. 22. Initials are fairly plain, in blue and red.

Schenkl dates the MS. at 1090: he may be right; it is at latest very early xii^th-cent.

The entry in the St Paul's Catalogue of 1458 is, under letter N, Aug. de verbis domini 2 fo. *eiusdem de verbis domini.*

10. GREGORII OPERA.

$$\left\{ \begin{array}{l} \text{Old marks} \\ \text{D}^2.\ 5.\ 40 \\ \text{II.}\ 2.\ 12 \\ \text{H.}\ 1.\ 4 \end{array} \right.$$

Vellum, $12\frac{1}{2} \times 9\frac{1}{8}$, ff. 3 + 210, double columns of 42, 45, 46 lines. Two volumes, (1) of cent. xiv early in fine round hand, (2) of cent. xv rather late, in clear but not beautiful script. Flyleaves xv late, in double columns of 50 lines.

Binding: stamped leather (xvi) over wooden boards, clasps gone, lettered A $\overline{\text{B D}}$ on each cover.   2 fo. Sic saul.

Collation: 3 flyleaves 1^8–3^8 4^{12} (wants 12) | 5^4 | 6^8–18^8 | 19^8–25^8| 26^8 27 (three).

This is no. 5 in the list of T. Reid's books. Like others, it belonged to T. Graunt (see below). From St Paul's, London.

Liber Acad. Marischall. Abredon.

The three flyleaves are from a late MS. in clear, rather current hand, probably from a book of Homilies. The only beginning is on f. iii.

Erexit salomon columpnam etc.

legimus salomonem in ingressu templi duas columpnas tam magne selcitudinis quam mire pulcritudinis erexisse.

On iii *b* at top, in red, is the title, rather cut

Contenta huius libri $\left\{ \begin{array}{l} \text{(Pastoralia)} \\ \text{Omelie} \\ \text{libri dialogorum} \end{array} \right\}$ Gregorii cum eorum tabulis,

and on *R.*, scribbled over, the name Graunt.

> I. 1. Inc. prol. b. Gregorii in libro pastorali (lxxvii. 13) .   .   . f.   1
> Pastoralis cure—repellantur. Expl. prol.
> Inc. 1. liber. b. Gregorii pape urbis rome qui pastoralis dicitur
> scriptus ad Iohannem ep. Rauenne*n*. ne imperiti ad magis-
> terium uenire audeant.
> Nulla ars
> Headlines in red added by Graunt.
> Lib. II. 11 *b*—manus leuet.
> Expl. lib. q. d. past. editus a b. Greg. papa.
> 35 *b* blank.
> 2. Table of cent. xv. (by Graunt?)...Abstinentes—Zizannia   36

II. 3. In a decent hand of cent. xv not early: with changes.
         Inc. regula b. Augustini (xxxii. 1337)   40
         Ante omnia fratres—non inducatur. Expl. regula.

     4. Exposicio eiusdem edita ab Hugone de S. uictore (clxxvi. 881) .   42
         Hec precepta que subscripta sunt
         —non refrigescat ab spiritualibus. Expl. expos. regule.

     5. In nomine dei summi inc. epistola S. Gregorii...in libro
         omeliarum ad Secundinum. ep. Taurom(en)itanum (lxxvi.
         1075)   57
         Reuerentissimo ... Secundino coep. Gregorius ... inter sacra
         missarum solempnia—certiores fiant.
         Capitula   .   .   .   .   57 _b_
         Leccio etc....In illo tempore...Erunt signa .   .   .   58
         Omelia habita ad populum in basilica S. Petri ap.
         Dominus ac redemptor
         —in nostris mentibus loquatur. Qui uiuit etc. per omn. sec.
         sec. amen.
         Expl. liber Omeliarum B. Greg. pape etc.
         Et diuiditur in duas partes et quelibet pars continet viginti
         omelias.

     6. Hec inc. tabula super omelias B. Greg. pape .   .   .   .   136 _b_
         Abrahe—Xpianos. Expl. tabula etc.

     7. In nomine d. n. I. C. inc. dialogorum liber Gregorii pape
         urbis rome (lxxvii. 149)   144
         Quodam die nimiis—distinguo. Expl. pref.
         Inc. primus liber. Petrus.
              Non valde in ytalia
         Capitula on 144 _b_. Lib. II. with capp., 154, III. 165 _b_, IV. 181 _b_.
         Ending 199 _a_: hostia ipsi fuerimus.
         Exp. dialogorum liber quartus a S. Greg. editus.
         199 _b_ blank.

     8. Inc. omnes materie istius libri per modum Alphabeti   .   .   200
              Abbas—Ursi.   Ihesus. Amen.
         Expl. tab. super IIII^or libros Dial. Greg. pape.
         Sunt odiosa tria Christo testante sophia
         Sordida uita senis. dis mendax. fastus egenis.
         The name Graunt scribbled over.
         210 _b_ blank.

The xiv^th-cent. portion has some nice initials in blue and red;
the rest are not remarkable.

Thomas Graunt, the owner of this and several other MSS., was
Treasurer of St Paul's, London, from 1454 to 1474, when he died.
His books are not in the Catalogue of 1458.

11. HIERONYMI EPISTOLAE.

$$\left\{ \begin{array}{l} \text{Old marks} \\ \text{D}^2.\ 5.\ 61 \\ \text{II.}\ 2.\ 8 \\ \text{6. B. xvi} \\ \text{H.}\ 1.\ 6 \end{array} \right.$$

Vellum, $13\frac{1}{4} \times 9\frac{5}{8}$, ff. $122 + 2$, double columns of 58 lines.
Cent. xii in a very beautiful, close, upright hand.
Binding as for no. 1, etc.   2 fo. Epistola.
Collation: $1^2\ 2^8$–16^8 . b^2.   3 fo. mans curiositatem
Liber Acad. Marischall. Abredon.

No. 14 in the list of T. Reid's MSS. Probably from St Paul's, London, but not to be found in the catalogue of 1458.

On i *b*, otherwise blank, is a xvth-cent. title:

Jeronimi epistole, followed by an erasure of several words (perhaps an inscription by T. Graunt, of St Paul's).

f. 1 blank.
Hec sunt capitula libri huius. Numero cxxvj .   .   .   . f.   2
     i. Epistola Damasi pape ad Ieronimum.
     ii. Ep. Ieron. presb. ad papam Damasum de septem uin-
         dictis Cain.
     iii. De egressione filiorum israel ex egypto ad eundem.
     iv. It. ad eund. de ignorantia ysaac.
The last six are:
         cxxi.   Jer. ad Occeanum de morte Fabiole.
         cxxii.   ,, ad Marcellam de exitu Lee.
         cxxiii.   ,, ad Marcellam de uita aselle.
         cxxiiii. ,, ad Innocentium de septies percussa.
         cxxv.   ,, ad Principiam de uita S. Marcella(-e).
         cxxvi.   ,, ad Pammachium de morte pauline.
Text.
     Ep. Damasi pape ad Ieron. presb.   3
     Dormientem te
Ends 122 *a*: primum sequeris patriarcham loth.
     Expl. lib. epistolarum b. Ieron. presb.
A note (xiv): Multis ignotum est de saul et Ionata
—ubi (Bernardus) lamentacionem videtur facere de girardo
     fratre suo nuper defuncto.

The collection is almost exactly identical with that in the Cambridge University Library MSS. Dd. 2. 7, Kk. 2. 14, and there are many copies of it of the same date, *e.g.* Royal MS. 6. C. XI, 6. D. I, II, III.

No. 22, folio 12, verso
(arms of Bishop Gavin Dunbar)

No. 17, folio 2, recto

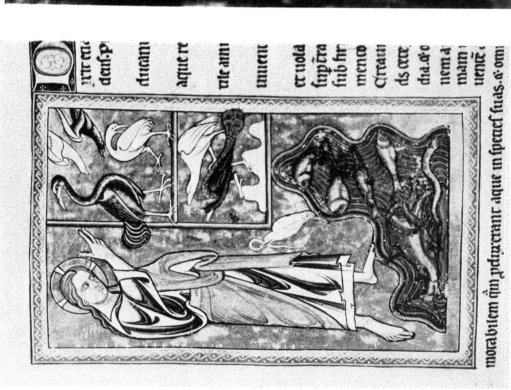

Two leaves at the end of the volume are from a well-written xiiith-cent. copy of the Decretales Novae (?).

    Inc. lib. III de uita et honestate clericorum.
                Clerici arma portantes
with glosses.

There are some admirable initials, especially that on f. 3, a D in blue, with inner ground of gold filled with convolutions in blue and pink, and small animals. Outer ground pink, framed in gold edged with green. A long panel down the side of the page. It might be Canterbury or St Albans work.

12. N. DE·TUDESCHIS, I.

$\left\{\begin{array}{l}\text{Old marks}\\ \text{D}^2.\ 5.\ 62\\ \text{O. I. I}\\ \&.\ 2.\ 3.\ 4\end{array}\right.$

Paper, 14$\frac{5}{8}$ × 10$\frac{3}{4}$, ff. 187, double columns of 59–60 lines. Cent. xv (1470) in an ugly pointed hand, probably Italian.

    Collation: A^{12}–P^{12} Q^8 (wants 8).
    Liber Coll. Reg. Aberdon.
    On f. 1: Liber Willelmi de Elphinstown.
    At end: Liber Mag. Wilelmi de Elphinstoun hic finit.
    Binding: modern paper boards, half backed.
    No headlines or initials.
        N. de Tudeschis super Decretales Novas
        Gregorius episcopus
        Quoniam omnis racio superne creature vel terrene
The last section commented on is *Hiis quibus.*

Ending: vide tamen omnino quod dixi. inc. ex parte S^n de consti.

13. N. DE TUDESCHIS, II.

$\left\{\begin{array}{l}\text{Old marks}\\ \text{D}^2.\ 5.\ 65\\ \text{O. I. 2}\\ \&.\ 2.\ 3.\ 5\end{array}\right.$

Uniform with **12.**
Collation: 1^{12}–19^{12} 20^{10} 21^{10} 22^6, ff. 254.
The name of Will. Elphinston at each end.

Coloured initials and rubrics inserted in this volume.

At foot of f. 1 the initials V. E. in blue, connected by a red cord.

Rubrica de iureiurando

   quia in defectum probacionum.

Last section, *Tua nobis*, ends:

deus aperiat intellectum studencium in hac compilacione ad honorem ipsius. Amen.

Expl. tercia pars super 2do decretalium lecture Reuerendiss. d. Nicolai Abbatis de cicilia decretorum doctoris alias Panormitani.

14. N. DE TUDESCHIS, III.

{ Old marks
  D^2. 5. 66
  O. 1. 3
  &. 2. 3. 6

Uniform with **12**.

Collation: A^{12}–Z^{12} 2^{12} con^{12} Aa^{10} Bb^{10} (wants 9, 10), ff. 318. No headlines or initials.

   Redemptoris postulato suffragio ut ostendat originem

Last section. *Super specula.*

Ending: dirigat per suam ineffabilem clemenciam. Amen.

Expl. lectura d. pa(normitani) super tercio decretalium.

      Parisius/anno lxx°/Iunii xxii°.

The work was printed by Jenson, Basel, 1477. This copy has been little used. There are two more volumes of it, nos. **15** and **16**, which are not described here.

24. BESTIARY.

{ Old marks
  D^2. 6. 34
  II. 3. 9
  H. 2. 7
  O. 4. 6

Vellum, 12 × 8¼, ff. 1 + 103, 29 lines to page. Cent. xii (and xiii) in a fine hand, noticeably narrow and upright.

Binding: new.

Collation: 1 flyleaf: a^8 (wants 2, 8) b^8 (wants 4, 5) c^8 (wants 4, 8) d^8 (wants 4, 5) e^8–l^8 (wants 1) m^8 n^8 o^6 p^4 (wants 4). ff. 56 and 93 are double leaves.   2 fo. gone.

From Marischal College.

It is no. 4 in the list of T. Reid's MSS. Before he acquired it, it was in the Royal Library : on f. 1 is the number 'no. 518,' and the book is recognizable in the Inventory of 1542.

It is an extremely fine copy of the Bestiary, a sister book to the Bodleian MS. Ashmole 1511, corresponding exactly in text and pictures (though not illustrated by the same artist): the Ashmole MS. is however complete, whereas this has lost ten leaves with pictures, and a few pictures have been cut out of the text.

It is a MS. of the Second Family (as distinguished by me in *The Bestiary*, Roxburghe Club, 1928). This means that the order of beasts begins with Lion, Tiger, Pard, Panther.

A description of it is given in the volume just cited (p. 55): an illustrated article on it appeared in the *Aberdeen University Library Bulletin*, no. ˙36, 1928.

The flyleaf has a late title.

Text. In principio fecit—ab omni opere quod patrarat .   . f.   1
   (Gen. i. 1–ii. 2) : a leaf gone after 7.

Omnibus animantibus—caprarum et ouium 5*b*
   (Isidore *Etym*. xii. 1. 1–8) : f. 6 blank, and a leaf gone after
    it with pictures of the Lion.

Inc. liber de naturis bestiarum   7
   Leo fortissimus—occursum. Prov. xxx. 30.
Rubric. *De leonibus et pardis et tigribus lupis et wlpibus
   canibus et simiis.*
   Bestiarum uocabulum—eo ferantur. Isid. xii. 2. 1, 2.
   Leonis uocabulum ex greca—omnium bestiarum...xii. 2, 3.
Rubric. *De generibus luporum* (!)
   Cuius genus tripharium—consortium. Ambr. *Hexam*. vi. 14.
The two rubrics, which are incorrect, occur also in Ashmole.
   De tribus principalibus naturis leonis.
     Phisici dicunt—pedum uiribus. From Physiologus, Isidore,
      Solinus, and Ambrose.
We continue with the text on beasts : Tigris etc. The list will
   be given when we come to notice the illustrations. After
   f. 9 two leaves are gone with the end of Pantera, the
   sections on Antalops, Unicornis, Linx, Grifes, and part of
   Elephas.
After Leucrota 15*b* a leaf is gone with Cocodrillus, Manticora,
   Parandrus.
After f. 18 a leaf is gone with pictures of Canis (detection of
   murderer).
The homiletic passage beginning Quocienscumque is appended
   to Canis. This occurs in many copies : the reason is obscure.

After f. 21 two leaves are gone, with Bos, Camelus, Drome-
darius, Asinus, Onager, Equus (part).

The section on Beasts ends with Formica: reuocauerit.

Hic. inc. de auibus   25

Unum autem nomen—uocarentur. Ambr. *Hexam.* v. 47 and
Isid. xii. 7, 1–9.

On 25 *b*–63 is a great part of the text of a tract by Hugo de
Folieto called *Aviarium* (*P.L.* clxxvii. 15). This is also in
Ashmole and in a good many other copies.

The text begins *De pennis deargentatis columbe.*

Columbam cum pennis—pauperibus presentatur.

26. *De columba et accipitre.*

Cum scribere illiterato

26 *b. de tribus columbis.*

Si dormiatis etc.

Birds end with Aquila—conformem reddit.

De apibus—preponderant   63

De arbore que dicitur perindens—et periit . . . .   64 *b*

De serpentibus . . . .   65 *b*

Anguis omnium (Isid. xii. 4. 1)
—hominis morte serpens.

Inc. de uermibus—agitatus prolabitur (perl-)   72

Inc. de piscibus. Pisces dicti (Isid. xii. 6. 1) . . . .   72 *b*

Only six lines left: a leaf gone after 72.

The section on fishes ends: luligo et huic similia.

De arboribus. Arborum nomen (Isid. xvii. 6, and 7 with
omissions) . . . .   77 *b*
—scribe in buxo.

Ysidorus de natura hominis   80

Natura dicta (Isid. xi. 1)
—mortuis prebentur.

Ysidorus de membris hominis (*ib.*).   89

Pulmo—subiungamus.

De etate hominis (Isid. xi. 2. 1–37)   91

Gradus etatis—humum inicere.

De lapidibus igniferis—debachatur . . . . . .   93 *b*

From Physiologus 37.

With this the original hand ends. On 94 a late xiii^th-cent.
hand continues.

De lapide adamante.

Phisiologus dicit. Est lapis qui dicitur adamas et in quodam
monte
—sine ipso factum est nichil.

Adamas lapis paruus—genera eius sex . . . . .   95 *b*

De lapide qui dicitur mermecoleon   96

Item lapis est in mari qui latine dicitur mermecoleon grece
conca sabea
—Ecce ancilla domini...secundum uerbum tuum.

A tract on the Twelve Stones　.　.　.　.　.　.　96 *b*

Fundamenta muri ciuitatis—iuxta illud Prudentii

Versus. Prima petit campum dubia sub sorte duelli Pugnatura
　　fides. Et quia sine fide...dicit ergo.

Rubric. Primus lapis in fundamento muri est iaspis.

Each section has verses appended. The 12th ends
　　—locum decimum meruit possidere.

It is not the text printed with the works of Hugh of St Victor.

A Lapidary follows: in the order of Marbod's poem, with a few
　　omissions　.　.　.　.　.　.　.　.　.　100

De effectu lapidum.

Diamas lapis est inter omnes lapides durissimum etc.

Adamas siue dyamas—inuenitur similiter in arabia.

101.	Acates.		Cornelinus.
	Electrum.	103.	Ethites.
	Sernatides (? Haematites).		Celnites.
101 *b*.	Iaspis.		Sagatromen.
	Saphirus.		Ceraunius.
	Smaragdus.		Eliotropia.
	Sardonius.		Epistites.
102.	Sardina.		Ematites.
	Crisolitus.	103 *b*.	A(s)bestos.
	Topazius.		Sadda.
	Iacinctus.		Modus in terra turcorum.
	Amatistus.		Selaor.
	Celidonius.		Exacontalitos.
	Lapis rubeus.		Dionisia.
	Gagates.		Eris electrus.
102 *b*.	Magnes.		Diadocos.
	Corallus.		Pirites.
	Alemandina.		Chelonites.

Ending: hic lapis non tenet ignem.

So much for the text. The pictures are as follows:

f. 1. Full page. First Day. A column on *R.* of picture has the text
　　In principio—terram in capitals, white, on pink and red, on
　　blue.

　　The Creator full face, blessing, cross-nimbed, stands on four
　　mountains. A circle of three concentric bands of gold and
　　colour about Him.

1 *b*. Second Day. The Creator stands on green water; a band of
　　blue and white cloud across top: the rainbow about Him as
　　before.

　　Leaf gone with Third and Fourth Days.

　　Fifth Day. The Creator faces *R.* On *R.* are birds in compart-
　　ments. Below is water with fish. *Bulletin*, fig. 1.

　　Sixth Day. Similarly arranged with beasts in compartments:
　　elephant, lion, hare, squirrel, cat. Others below are
　　damaged.

f. 3. The Creation of Eve : has been scraped : Adam is seen slumber-
        ing on rock on *R.*

    3 *b.* Full page, perhaps the Seventh Day. The Majesty of God seated
        full face, with book, blessing : bow below His feet. The
        Evangelistic emblems at the corners.

    3 *b,* 4 *a* blank.

    4 *b.* Full page. Adam naming the animals. He is throned, robed,
        in upper *L.* portion. The animals are arranged in compart-
        ments on *R.* and below his feet. *Bulletin,* fig. 2.

    6. Blank. Leaf gone with pictures of Lion, probably two full pages.

    8. Tiger, blue. A tree : a man in mail and helmet with nasal,
        throws down a glass ball : he has the tiger's cub, also blue.

    8 *b.* Pard, red.

    9. Panther, followed by deer, camel, goat, lion. Dragon hides itself
        in red hill on *R.* Two leaves gone, see above.

    11. Castor, two hunters. The bitten-off glands lie on the ground.
        Ibex, red, leaps down from rock.
        Hyena, red and white, serrated back : corpse in sarcophagus.

    12. Bonnacon, red, pursued by two mailed men.
        Simia : *L.* man with spear ; *R.* two monkeys, each with two
        young.

    13. Satyr, horned, tufted body, holds a sort of green mace : kneels
        on one knee.

    14. Caper, blue, scratches head with hind foot.
        Capreae : two, back to back, on hind legs in circle.

    15. Monoceros, red and white, gold horn.
        Ursus licks a red ball, its whelp.
        Leucrota, red, goes to *R.*
        Leaves gone, see above.

    16. Vulpis on his back. Six cubs look out of a green hill below ;
        four or five birds perch on the fox, four more in air.
        Eale, blue, faces *L.*
        Lupus, dark and shaggy. Shepherd sleeps on hillock : sheep
        in arched doorway. Dog on top of porch barks.

    18. Canis. Three dogs chained by their necks to a tree.

    18 *b.* Two scenes of the capture and rescue of King Garamantes.
        Bull., fig. 3.
        One leaf gone after 18, with picture of dog detecting his
        master's murderer.

    19 *a.* Three pictures of dog with meat in his mouth ; dog in water,
        perhaps the reflection of the first, and dogs licking themselves.

    20 *b.* Sheep, picture gone.

    21. Ram, blue.
        Lamb, in a circle.
        Pigs, red and blue.
        After 21 two leaves gone ; see above.

f.   23 b. Cats, **three,** two blue and one yellow, licking itself.
         Rat eating cheeses?
         Weasel, red.

  24. Mole, viewed from above.
      Hedgehogs, seven, under red and blue tree : they have fruits
          on their spines.
      Two lines of white ants : pink anthills on *R*.

  25. Here begins the *Aviarium*.

  26. Dove and hawk, facing, under domed roofs.

  27 b. Silver dove, facing *R*, in a circle.

  28. Pictures cut out.

  29 b. Bluish hawk, flying up.

  30. Another looking to *L*.

  31 b. Two turtle doves on conventional tree.

  32. Two more on a knot of foliage in a circle.

  32 b. A cross with a dove in medallion in *C*.

  34. The Virgin in a mandorla holding a dove on a disk : six doves
          in the ring of the mandorla, white, on blue disks : spandrels
          trellised.

  35. Picture containing three lozenge-shaped compartments :
          (*a*) young pelicans peck their parent ; (*b*) she kills them ;
          (*c*) she revives them with her blood. They are red, with blue
          wings.

  35 b. Nycticorax in a circle, black, and owl-like.

  36. Epops in circle, with 4 internal lobes and central medallion.
          Four young pluck out their parent's feathers. *Bull.*, fig. 4.

  37 a. A man shoots upward at four magpies in a conventional tree.
          Corvus, in circle, black.

  39. Cock, picture cut out.

  41. Ostriches, one arranging eggs with beak, the other looking up :
          there should be a star, but there is none. They are many-
          coloured, and hoofed.

  44 b. Two Vultures in a circle, back to back.

  45 b. Six Cranes, dark coloured : one holds a stone.

  46 b. Milvus, in circle.

  47. Green parrot on tree.
      Ibis, dragon in claws, stoops to feed young in nest.

  47 b. Swallow, in circle.

  49. Two Storks, one eating a frog : in a circle.

  49 b. Merula in coloured circle.

  50. Owl, horned, in a circle.

  50 b. Blue hoopoe in coloured circle.

  51 b. Bat.
        Gracula cut out.

  52 b. Nightingale on nest in coloured circle.

f. 53. Two Geese in circle.

53 *b*. Two Ardeae (bitterns).

54. Partridge cut out.
Partridge, stealing eggs from a full nest.

54 *b*. Halcyon, green, in coloured circle.

55. Fulica, red, preening itself.

55 *b*. Phoenix in air between two conventional trees plucks a branch. Sun above.

56. Phoenix in nest: flames. Sun above.
This is a double leaf.

57. Crowned man in bed, head to *L*. White Chaladrius on his feet looks at him.

57 *b*. Quail on green hillock: in double circle.

58. Cornix in coloured circle.

58 *b*. Swan.

59. Six coloured Ducks in circle.

59 *b*. Peacock.

61 *b*. Large Eagle. (*a*) in air with fish; flying up; a piece cut out of upper margin perhaps contained the sun; water below. (*b*) smudged: eagle plunges headlong into well between two trees.

63. Three curved lines of white bees flying down to three hives.

65. The tree Perindens, large. Five doves perched on either side. Two blue dragons back to back look round at the doves on the lowest branches.
Here begin the Serpents.

65 *b*. Blue dragon coiled about a red and white elephant.

66. Basilisk, red, crested: a weasel on its back bites its neck.

66 *b*. Two Vipers mouth to mouth. Three young burst out of the mother's body.

67 *b*. Man in hat and tunic with shield points his staff at a blue two-legged winged Asp, coming down from a tree on *R*, and vomiting fire.

68 *b*. Scitalis, two-legged, winged.
Amphisbaena, one head biting the other: legged and winged.
Hydrus, blue, penetrating a red and white Crocodile with serrated back.

69. Boas, in circle, legs and wings.
Jaculus, silver on gold.

69 *b*. Siren, snake with legs and wings, white.
Seps, blue.
Lizard, red and white, blue head.

70. Large. (*a*) Six salamanders on branches of tree: a dead man poisoned by their venom on the fruit lies in front. (*b*) A salamander plunges into a well. (*c*) Six salamanders rise out of flames.

f. 70 b. Saura passes through an arch towards the sun on *R*.
   Stellio, blue with white spots.

71. Serpent, blue with red wings, squeezes through a little tower:
   its old green skin (on *L*) is scraped off. In a coloured circle.

72, 77 b. Fine initials.

81. Under a round arch, blue and red turrets above, a young man
   in blue over brown-red writes (*ysid*)*orus* (*de n*)*atura hominis*
   on book on desk. On the desk, partly obscured by green
   paint, is a word ...*hane*.

93 (a double leaf). Lapides igniferi: two scenes: (*a*) nude man and
   woman holding stones, stand apart; a mountain in *C*. with
   tree; trees *R*. and *L*. (*b*) They embrace, and the mountain
   bursts into flame. *Bull*., fig. 5. Cf. plates 16 (Ashmole,
   1511) and 18 (St John's College, Oxford) in my *Bestiary*.

94. Later picture of Adamas, stone lying on hill.

96. Later picture of pearl in water, rays or dew dropping on it.
   These are poorly done.

The pictures are on burnished gold grounds, and have variously
patterned frames.

25. Psalter, Hours, etc.

$$\left.\begin{array}{l} \text{Old marks} \\ \text{O. 4. 4} \\ \text{II. 4. 2} \\ \text{D}^2.\ 6.\ 38 \end{array}\right.$$

Vellum, 12 × 8½, ff. 1 + 10 + 311, 21 lines to page. Cent. xv
early in a fine hand, French-Flemish, for English use.

Binding: brown calf, xvii–xviii.

Collation: 1 flyleaf a^{10} | 1^8 2^8 (+ 1) 3^8–14^8 (+ 1) 15^8–26^8 (wants 3)
27^8–40^8 (wants 8). Foliation on lower corners, very incorrect.

Bequeathed in 1714 by Bp. Burnet to Marischal College.
Flyleaf blank.

I. The Kalendar is a gathering of 10 leaves, every page bordered.
   On i *a* are these memorial verses:

(*a*) Cingula blandorum glosat ficus esca dolorum (*Jan.*)
   Bellat aquis grifo fera dura sincopa ballo (*Feb.*)
   Arbore firmauit ea donet ceruus aquauit (*Mar.*)
   Gutis fetus eum: celebrat rasis ancora gressum (*Ap.*)
   Exultat docilis: carnis bona gliscere festis (*May*).
   Extollens dirum: balat accola gens fugitiuum (*June*).
   Dormit clam borias alias facit ergo dietas (*July*).

Curuus agit gemitum furantis ei cape boscum (*Aug.*)
Ang(e)licis gladiis extorquet dira cohortis (*Sept.*)
Bina gerit flores escis decies boat aures (*Oct.*)
Gummifere frondis: detur cortex bidualis (*Nov.*)
Hanc fouet exiguum: dape circiter appeto gustum (*Dec.*)
One line to each month: another form doubtless of Cisio ianus,
but not known to me.

(*b*) Sep sequitur Sulpi: xl. post crasque uedasti.
Pas benedic marcique roga pen preuia gordi.
> (Of the movable feasts, Septuagesima, Lent, Easter, Roga-
> tions, Whitsunday.)

(*c*) Adam degebat ergo cifos adrifex.
Sur confles adam flebis egens coeas.
Evidently these 12-syllabled verses also refer to the months.
Also the following dates:
> Magna pestilencia, 1349.
> Insurrectio communis populi, 1381.
> Magnus uentus, 1361.
> Bellum de cressy, 1346.
> Capcio regis francie, 1356.
> Capcio regis scocie, 1346.
> Terre motus, 1384.

Table showing the Signs and age of moon, for the several
months . . . . f. i *b*
Kalendar, blue, red, black: few entries ii
Each month has 17 tables, in about 27 columns,
viz. plan of Zodiacal sign, sunrise, sunset, Cycle 2 cõ (= con-
junction), Cycle 2 opp(osition) and the like for Cycles 3, 4, 5.
Tables of eclipses, viz.:
> Solar for 2nd Cycle from 1046 (*sic* for 1406) to 1424 . . viii
> Solar for 3rd Cycle from 1425 to 1443.
> Solar for 4th Cycle from 1444 to 1462.
> Lunar for 2nd Cycle from 1406 to 1424 . . . . viii *b*
> Lunar for 3rd Cycle from 1425 to 1443.
> Lunar for 4th Cycle from 1444 to 1462 ix
Note of Sunday Letter, 1381, etc., and a memorial distich.
Tabula ad sciendum festa mobilia temporibus preteritis et
futuris (for 19-year cycle) . . . . . ix *b*
f. x blank.

II. The next division of the book consists of a large number of
miscellaneous devotions: to f. 113. Not every prayer will be
indexed here, but the groups will be described.
Rubric on the virtues of the prayer following, viz. . . . 1
D. d. omnipotens pater etc. Da mihi famulo tuo N. uictoriam.
Prayer of St Augustine. Deus propicius esto 4
Verses of St Bernard. Illumina and Collect . . . . 4 *b*
Memoriae of SS. Michael . . . . . . 5 *b*

Guardian Angel.	. f.	6	Anthony.	. .	13
John Baptist .	.	7 *b*	Anne .	. .	13 *b*
John Ev.. .	.	8 *b*	Mary Magd.	. .	14
Thomas of Canterbury		9 *b*	Katherine	. .	15
George .	. .	10 *b*	Margaret.	. .	15 *b*
Nicholas .	. .	11	Barbara .	. .	16 *b*
Christopher	. .	12			

Prayers of St Bridget (Birgitta). Gaude eternaliter benedictum
    corpus dei . . . .   17 *b*
followed by ten other prayers, and ending with a Memoria 21 *b*.
ff. 22-24 ruled, blank. These are not noticed in the foliation
    in the lower corner, which therefore is incorrect from this
    point, but will be used if convenient.
The Prayers that now follow begin with

Salutations to the Trinity in rhythm   22
    Ave pater immortalis. rex regum et domine

Thirteen prayers to the Son . . . .   22 *b*

Rhythm. Salue mundi redempcio. Ihesu sine principio . .   27
Twenty-two more prayers. Several on rising: on 29 *b* one
    invokes the Apostles. On 30-35 *a* is a long one:
        Domine exaudi or. meam quia iam cognosco quod tempus
            meum prope est, invoking all orders of saints. Hardly
            any rubrics.

Ten more prayers, most with rubrics; two of St Augustine .   41
ending with the rhythm
        Iuste iudex Ihesu criste, 44 *b*.
The Fifteen Oos of St Birgitta with preliminary rubric
    Misericors mundi redemptor . . . . . .   45 *b*

followed by Gracias ago tibi d. I. C. qui passionem . .   50 *b*

Rubric in French: Saint leon le pape de rome . . .   51
introducing a series of prayers of the names of Christ.

Prayers of the Cross and Passion. O crux gloriosa . .   53 *b*
Prayer of Bede of the Seven Words, 54 *b*.
The Holy Face, 57 *b*. Salutations to the Wounds, 58.
In honore armorum d. n. I. C., 58 *b*.
Ad ymaginem Christi crucifixi, 59.
Passio sec. Iohannem (short), 62.

Sequitur de sacramento . . . .   62 *b*
Prayers ending with: Dum conturbata fuerit anima mea D. d.
    meus in hora exitus mei, 68.

Devotions to the Virgin (73-113) 69 (73)
beginning with Rubric:
Has uideas laudes qui sacra uirgine gaudes etc. and Salue
    regina farced with rhyming quatrains:
        Salue uirgo uirginum stella matutina.

O intemerata (two forms), 72 *b*. Obsecro te . . . .   75 *b*

Rubric. Quicunque hec. vii. gaudia .   .   .   .   77 *b*
    Uirgo templum trinitatis
Te deprecor sanctissima, 79 *b*.
Psalterium b. v. m. Aue mater saluatoris (in rhythm) .   .   80
Veni creator, 81. Gloria in excelsis, followed by salutations to
    the Virgin, 81 *b*. Prayers with Aves follow.
A series of prayers, some in rhythm, 17 in all   85
Rubric. Legitur quod b. Thomas cantuar. .   .   .   .   96 *b*
    Gaude flore uirginali and collect.
Five Joys. Gaude perpetua uirgo and collect .   .   .   .   98 *b*
Hec sunt nomina b. m. v.   99
    Diua uirgo. uirga. flos. nubes.
Rubric to prayer Missus est angelus   100
Te ergo deprecor, 104.
Litany 104 *b*, followed by ten prayers, the last of SS. Michael
    and All Angels, beginning
      O Maria piissima stella, 109 (113) *b*.

III. The Psalter 110 (114)
Cantica 218. Litany 228 *b*.
With 19 Collects.

IV. Inc. officium b. Marie uirginis sec. usum et consuetudinem
    Sarum 237 (241)
Psalms not repeated in full.
Memoriae in Lauds: Holy Ghost, Trinity, Cross, Michael,
    John Baptist, Peter, Paul, Andrew, John, James, Bartholo-
    mew. All App., Stephen, Laurence, Thomas Cant. (lined
    through), Blasius, Christopher, Edmund, George. All MM.,
    Germanus, Nicholas, Martin, John of Beverley, William (of
    York), Leonard. All Conf., Anne, Mary Magdalene,
    Katherine, Margaret, Etheldreda, Fides. All VV., All SS.,
    Peace.
Hours of the Cross and of Compassion of the Virgin inter-
    calated in Lauds and the other Hours.
Inc. vii. psalmi penitenciales .   .   .   .   .   .   256 *b*
    Only beginnings of Penitential and Gradual Psalms.
Inc. uigilie mortuorum   257
Inc. commendaciones animarum .   .   .   .   .   .   263 *b*
Rubric and Prayer for Psalter of St Jerome   265
Sequitur psalt. b. Jeronimi   266
Hours of the Compassion of the Virgin (title gone) .   .   .   273 *b*
In commemoracione sancti angeli custodis. ad vesp. .   .   285
A complete set of Hours, Vespers to None.
Rubric. Iste sequentes oraciones dicende sunt in honore
    sollempnitatum et profestiuorum .vii. dierum principalium
    d. n. I. C. tam stando quam genuflectando in quacunque
    tribulacione uel angustia homo fuerit uel amicus eius releua-
    bitur ab hiis prenominatis si fuerit sine mortali peccato hoc
    sine dubio probatum est .   .   .   .   290 *b*

Short prayers on the Passion, each followed by a Psalm, *e.g.*:

    De eo quod dominus noster in agonia positus...

    Usque quo domine obliuisceris

    De eo quod a discipulis solus relinquitur...

    Deus deus meus

Seven in all.

Letania sanctorum .   .   .   .   300 *b*

Not the ordinary form: begins after Kyrie

    Pater de celis deus qui pro salute nostra

Few saints are invoked of each Order: see below.

Eight collects follow: the last

    Omnip. sempit. deus mestorum consolacio

ending 306 (311) *a*: 306 *b*, 307 (312) blank.

The Kalendar is remarkable not only for the wealth of astronomical matter but for the paucity of feasts, *e.g.*:

Jan. has only Circumcisio, Epiphania, Mauri, Anthonii, Wlstani ep., Agnetis, Conv. Pauli.

In other months the English saints are:

Ap. Ricardi ep. Alphegi archiep. Erkenwaldi ep.

May. Dunstani. Aug. ep. Cantuar. (both red).

June. Willelmi ep. eboracens. Albani (red). Etheldrede.

July. Transl. thome (blue).

Aug. Helene matris constantini (red).

Oct. (Francis in red). Etheldrede (Hillarionis).

Nov. Edmundi archiep. (red). Edmundi regis.

Dec. Thome archiep. (blue).

Lists of the *Memoriae* have been given.

The main Litany has a distinctly Flemish flavour.

Martyrs. Thoma (Cant.) erased...Adriane Blasi Kelme (*sic*) Kenelme Georgi Christophore Lamberte Lebuine[1] Leodegari Iuliane Quintine Edwarde Eadmunde.

Conf. Cuthberte...Swithune Ceade...Botulphe, Amande Trudo Bauo Uedaste Nicholae Leonarde Eadmunde Oswalde Maxime Augustine (Cant.) Germane Paule Bertine Anthoni Remigi Cuthberte (again) Egidi Eligi Francisce Dominice Willelme (of York).

VV. ...... Brigida Katherina...Fredeswida Tecla Editha... Clara Ursula Dorothea...Walburgis Etheldreda Cuthburga Sexburga Ermenilda Milburga Mildreda Redagundis Elyzabeth Helena...Ositha Batildis...Ghertrudis (last).

In the second Litany a few of each Order:

MM. Steph. Laur. Thoma, Iohannes et Thoma.

Conf. Martine Nicholae Benedicte Augustine Iheronime.

VV. Agatha Agnes Katherina Margareta Elizabeth Gheretrudis Lucia Aldegundis Appollonia.

---

[1] meant for Livine?

Besides these indications, the evident interest in St Bridget
(Birgitta) of Sweden must be noted. The connexion of this saint
with England dates from 1406, when Philippa, daughter of
Henry IV, married Eric, king of Norway, Sweden and Denmark.
She visited the mother house of Wadstena, and Henry Lord
Fitzhugh, who was in her suite, promised to endow the Order in
England with his manor of Hinton, near Cambridge. Envoys were
sent to England on the business of founding a house in 1408 and
1415. The house of Syon was founded by Henry V in 1416 (near
Twickenham). Its later site at Isleworth was granted in 1422,
and the convent moved thither in 1431. (Bateson, *Syon Library
Catalogue*, p. xii.)

All this has a bearing on the date of our book, which nevertheless is not easy to fix with certainty. The eclipse-tables are for
cycles of which the earliest begins in 1406, but this fact must not
be pressed.

The selection of saints, apart from the obvious Flemish insertions, shows a certain interest in Ely. Etheldreda's two feasts are
among the few entries in the Kalendar, and she, with Sexburga and
Ermenilda, figures also in the main Litany, and has a Memoria in
Lauds of the Virgin.

This, I think, must be significant: more so than the mention of
William of York (in Kal. and Lit.) and John of Beverley. It may
not be without meaning, too, that we find St Helen in red in the
Kalendar.

It would be easy and pleasant to connect the book with the
Lord Fitzhugh mentioned above who owned land near Cambridge:
but a definite piece of evidence causes a difficulty. This is the
shield in the border of f. 2, which bears barry nebuly of four *or* and
az: on a chief *az* three stars (of four main points and eight sub-
sidiary rays) *or*. These do not resemble the Fitzhugh bearings
at all.

There is, again, a picture of the owner in the border of f. 69 (73)
kneeling in a scarlet mantle lined with white over scarlet belted
gown: a pink hood thrown over *R.* shoulder: rather narrow white
collar. This suggests to me a legal dignitary, but I await con-
firmation.

Decoration. This is very sumptuous: clearly foreign in my

opinion. It should, I suppose, be classed as French-Flemish. It consists of (1) borders, full or partial. Every page on which a prayer or psalm begins is partially bordered, and every beginning of an important new section has a full border. One of the most elaborate of these is at the beginning of the Psalter, where we have a broad frame of gold filled with pairs of triangular leaves in blue and pink, bordered with white, which form shield-like devices. From this springs conventional foliage, with ivy leaf in gold and—what is a particularly favourite theme with our artist—dragons with slender arched bodies and pairs of wings, standing upright. Every page of the Kalendar quire has a border containing these dragons. Grotesques and birds (*e.g.* green parrots) are also found. (2) Initials are always in gold, and consist of red and blue foliage, heightened with white. (3) Pictures, of excellent style. (Three have been removed, but most survive.) These are mostly in the text or in initials; none are as large as full page. The grounds are commonly of a full red (or blue) with gold flourishing.

The following remain:

1. f. 2. The Trinity. The Father in pink robe over green, tiara on head, seated on blue cloth on broad pinnacled white throne, supporting the crucified Son before Him over whose head is a minute dove. Ground red, flourished: spandrels, blue angels. Floor of orange tiles. Grotesques in border including old man with open book, and rabbit. The shield is in the lower border.

2. 5 *b*. St Michael. Golden hair, blue wings, scarlet surcoat, plate armour, pierces devil with spear (cross-hilted): the devil brown-black with single horn and red tongue. Ground red flourished. Tree on *L.* like those in the early xv^th-cent. Paris books.

3. 6 *b*. Guardian angel. On *L.* Gabriel robed with scroll (*Aue— tecum*). On *R.* Raphael (?) dressed for travelling, red tunic, scarlet hose, high black shoes, holds a javelin. In air three red six-winged cherubim. Ground dark blue flourished.

4. 7 *b*. John Baptist in rocky landscape, with stream, bridge, castles and trees: he is in pink robe over skin tunic, and holds blue book with lamb on it.

5. 8 *b*. John Evang. sits writing in wooden chair: a circular two-tiered desk by him with books. The chair is on a patch of orange tiles set in grass. Tree on *L.* Ground red flourished.

6. 9 *b*. Thomas of Canterbury. In blue chasuble: he kneels at red altar on *R.*, on which is chalice with white corporal: blue

retable with gold Virgin and Child : green riddles. Grim
watches at N. end of altar. Two knights in plate with mail
gorgets, surcoats green and scarlet. One draws sword, the
other drives a knife into the saint's scalp. Ground red,
flourished.

7. 10 *b*. George in plate, mail gorget, bascinet, white surcoat red
crossed : grey horse with pink housings. A pink guard for the
front of the leg is part of the saddle. He pierces the jaws of
a small green dragon on *R.* The princess in scarlet, lamb by
her, on *L.* Rocky landscape and trees.

8. 11 *a*. Nicholas as bishop in blue chasuble, with crosier, stands
blessing : floor, orange tiles : pale purple low wall, three-
sided, behind. Ground red, flourished : spandrels blue.

9. 12. Christopher, child on shoulder, wades to *R.* through rough
water : rocky shore and trees. On *R.* hermit in door of cell
holds out lantern. Child in purple has orb.

10. 13 *a*. Anthony, white beard, black skull-cap, darkish slate
habit over purplish robe with girdle : fire about his feet. He
holds in *R.* hand book and bell ; in *L.* crosier. A pig crouches
on *L*, another advances on *R.* Rocky landscape and tree.
Ground red, flourished.

11. 13 *b*. Anne, seated in chair, on orange tiles : low wall behind.
Her robe is green : she holds an open book inscribed *aue
maria gra*, which the Virgin, crowned in blue robe on *L.*,
stoops to read. On *L.* oblong walled enclosure with tree.
Ground red, flourished.

12. 14. Mary Magd in scarlet over blue, long gold hair, holds
palm and casket. Rocks and trees.

13. 15. Katherine crowned in blue over scarlet holds green book
and sword, and stands on Maxentius, who lies crowned with
hand to face, and scimitar. On *R.* the wheels on their stand :
they have no knives in them, and are not broken. Trees
on *L.*, rocks on *R.* Ground red, flourished.

14. 15 *b*. Margaret in blue over scarlet, red wreath on head,
emerges, holding long cross, from the back of the dragon :
her skirt-end in his mouth. God in blue in cloud on *L.*
Tree on *R.* Ground as before.

15. 16 *b*. Barbara in blue over scarlet holds book, and lays *L.* hand
on the turret of the outworks of a tower on *R.* (which ought
to be much further off by rights). Tree on *L.* Ground as
before.

16. 17 *b*. Brigitta (Birgitta). In white hood or wimple, blue mantle,
ermine-lined over purplish gown, she stands in the attitude
of counting on the fingers—evidently dictating—by a desk,—
round base, screw, angled stem—with book on it. Amanuensis
in green with blue cape sits on *R.*, writing in book. God in
blue in cloud on *L.* Low wall behind, with angles in it.
Floor, orange tiles and grass. Ground as before.

No. 24, folio 36, verso

No. 24, folio 18, verso

No. 25, folio 2, recto

No. 24, folio 93, verso

17. 46. **Fifteen Oos.** Initial. On *R.* St Brigitta in wooden throne with green back, desk before her, reads to two nuns who sit on a seat on *L.* with a single open book. All three are habited in black with white wimples. In *L.* upper corner God, in blue in a cloud. Green floor. Ground as before.

18. 55. **Prayer of the Seven Words.** Initial. Christ on the cross, with title. On *L.* John supports the Virgin, on *R.* three soldiers, one white-bearded : another holds scroll *vere filius dei erat iste.* Ground as before.

19. 59. **Prayers to the Wounds.** Christ on the cross laid obliquely on the ground : a man nails the *L.* hand, another stretches the arms: a third nails the feet: a fourth digs a hole for the cross. Above, the Virgin and John seen half-length watching. Ground as before.

20. 69. **Devotions to the Virgin.** This page must be by a fresh artist. The border is of wholly different character, having on *R.* a cylindrical shaft (greenish) with large knops of foliage : grotesques, including pelican in piety.
    Initial. The Virgin crowned in blue and the Child, rayed, sit on square, tasselled, pink cushion. On *L.* an angel sits and plays the harp, on *R.* another with viol and bow: a ring of angels' heads above.
    In left margin the owner as described above: he has a scroll *o mater dei memento mei.*

21. 77 *b.* **Seven Joys.** Initial. The Virgin crowned in blue with the Child, on a seat on a gold carpet set on grass. An angel in scarlet on *L.* with basket of scarlet flowers kneels and offers one to the Child. Ground as before.

22. 110. **Psalter.** *Beatus vir.* David, old, in pink and ermine mantle over purplish robe kneels with harp to God (blue in cloud) above an altar on *R.* (blue frontal, green riddles, gold retable with seated figure of God?): low wall on *L.*, foot-pace of altar pink, floor green tiles. Ground as before.

23. 126 *b.* *Dominus illuminatio.* David, habited much as before, kneels and points to his eye. God in cloud on *L.* (blue). Hills and tree. Ground as before.

24. 137. *Dixi custodiam.* David in blue cape and scarlet, leaning with both hands on staff, plods to *L.* God as before in sky. Rocks and tree. Usual ground.

25. 146 *b.* *Quid gloriaris.* David in blue robe over scarlet, with sceptre, on green canopied throne. Before him on *R.* stands a Fool counting on his fingers: his habit party per pale, half scaled, half horizontally striped in black and white: hung with gold grelots: three-peaked cap with grelot on middle peak : scarlet bauble. This is not the right subject: it is a doublet of the next.

26. 147. *Dixit insipiens.* The Fool riding to *L.* on scarlet hobby horse (stick with ass's head) and playing on a pipe. He has a tight habit, half pink, half blue, and tall hood standing up and ending in dragon's head : scarlet shoes. Rocks and tree. Usual ground.

27. 156 *b. Salvum me fac.* David nude, crowned, lies on his back in mud-coloured water, rough, with joined hands : rocky banks. God above (blue with gold nimbus and orb).

28. 169. *Exultate.* David in scarlet over blue, in round-backed wooden chair on green tiled floor, plays with two hammers on six bells hung on wooden ring from gallows-shaped stand. Usual ground.

29. 179 *b. Cantate.* Seven coped clerks in two rows (four and three) facing *L.* sing from book on broad wooden sloping desk hung with blue cloth, on two wooden legs. The copes are scarlet, green, blue, lake. Green-tiled floor : low wall : usual ground.

30. 181. *Domine exaudi.* David in scarlet and ermine robe over blue kneels and points to his mouth, facing *R.* God as before in blue. Rock and tree : usual ground.

After 192 a leaf with *Dixit dominus* has been removed.

31. 197. *Beati immaculati.* David in pink and ermine over slate-blue kneels facing *R.* : in a gold sphere above Moses horned half-length holds the tables. Rocks and tree. Ground blue, flourished.

In the lower margin, partly cut off, is a bit of a note for the artist, in French or Flemish :

       Moyses vnt' (*or* viit. i.) comm⟨andements⟩.

Evidently the subject was chosen because the Psalm deals with the Law.

32. *Horae.* 237 *Matins.* Initial. Annunciation. Gabriel kneels on *L.* with scroll (*aue—tecum*) and points up to God in gold sphere on *L.* sending the dove on a ray. The Virgin kneels on red tiles, under green canopy : book on table with gold cloth. Lily pot in *C.* Usual ground.

33. 239. *Lauds.* The Visitation in rocky landscape with the Virgin on *L.* with book. Usual ground.

34. 248 *b. Prime.* Cut out. The Nativity.

34. 249 *b. Tierce.* Angel (half-length) in air with scroll (*Gloria— deo*). Two shepherds, one seated, in consternation. Sheep, rocks and trees.

35. 250 *b Sext.* Adoration of the Magi (none is black). Virgin (in chair) and child, on *L.* Star in blue cloud. Usual ground.

36. 251 *b. None.* Presentation. Broad altar with gold frontal and white cloth. Simeon and another behind it (*L.*). Virgin, maid, and Joseph. Usual ground.

37. 252. *Vespers.* Massacre of Innocents. Herod with scimitar (green and ermine mantle over blue, scarlet shoes) stands on *R.* with courtier. One soldier in plate mail, gorget, lake surcoat and gold skirt, stabs a swaddled child in a woman's arms. Low wall: usual ground.

253 b. *Compline.* Cut out. ? Coronation of the Virgin.

38. 256 b. *Seven Psalms.* Last Judgment. Christ in scarlet mantle showing the wounds, on rainbow, feet on globe: on *R.* and *L.* two trumpet angels (blue, half-length) with scrolls *Surgite mortui* and *venite ad iudicium.* Below, on *R.*, Hell-mouth. Heads of rising people emerge from the earth. Usual ground.

39. 257. *Office of the dead.* Funeral in choir. On *R.* a mass of black mourners. Coffin with gold pall, and candlesticks. Three coped clerks singing at sloping desk.

40. 263 b. *Commendations.* Two angels in air bear up four souls in a linen cloth to God, seen above as a bust encircled by ten scarlet cherubim on blue ground. Rock, tree, and four graves below. Usual ground.

41. 266. *Psalter of St Jerome.* Robed as cardinal he sits in seat hung with green, desk before him, and lances the paw of the lion on *R.* On *R.* a pink piece of furniture, at top of which is a square opening with books in it. Ground blue, flourished.

42. 273 b. *Hours of the Compassion of the Virgin.* Picture cut out above. Initial. The Entombment. Joseph and another support the head and feet. The Virgin supported by John, and Nicodemus with casket, stand behind the (purplish) tomb. Usual ground.

43. 285. *Hours of the Guardian Angel.* In a landscape with rock and tree stands a young man in scarlet cap, blue tunic trimmed with fur, white and scarlet hose. On his *R.* shoulder a small angel with scarlet wings, on his *L.* a small devil. Usual ground.

The number of handsome decorative initials and partial borders is, of course, very great; the execution does not seem to deteriorate throughout the book.

106. Augustinus etc.
$\left\{ \begin{array}{l} \text{C}^2.\ 3.\ 63 \\ \text{II.}\ 5.\ 1 \\ \text{O.}\ 4.\ 40 \end{array} \right.$

Vellum, $8\frac{5}{8} \times 5\frac{5}{8}$, ff. 2 + 110 + 1, 40, 45 lines to page. Cent. xi, in several exquisite hands: Italian: some ordinary minuscule, some Beneventane.

Binding, modern.

Collation: a^2 | 1^8–8^8 | 9^8–13^8 14^6 | 1 flyleaf.

2 fo. nosse gaudent.

Acad. Marischal.

From Dr Guise.

On i *b* is an old numbering, no. 44, and on 1 *a* the number 26, which latter I connect with a roughly scrawled (Italian?) list of contents on·the last flyleaf. A like number is in **242**: so this MS. also may be from the monastery of S. M. de Caritate.

The two flyleaves at the beginning are from a MS., probably of cent. x, in a very pretty rounded minuscule: i *b* obscured by the modern bookplate. The text seems to be patristic and not very interesting: the chief subject is sin. De talibus ait salomon qui letantur cum malefecerint et exultant…(ii *b*).

The first portion is in good minuscule by several scribes: sometimes with a slope.

I. 1. Ratio S. Augustini ep. de doctrina christiana . . . . f. 1
   Inc. prephatio. Libros de doctrina christiana
   —sic incipit. Sunt precepta quedam. Expl. preph.
   Inc. liber primus S. Augustini ep. de doctrina christiana.
   Sunt precepta quedam (xxxiv. 9)
   Initial of white branch-work with interstices of red.
   Lib. II. 11. Initial in gold and white branch-work.
   Lib. III. 25 *b*. In the margin of the last lines of Lib. II. is drawn a cross in gold with the words Latitudo altitudo Longitudo about it.
   Initial to III. has branch-work, white, blue, green, on gold ground, rather coarse.
   Lib. IV. 38. Initial in gold.
   —quantulacunque potui facultate disserui.
   Throughout are many marginalia, in schematic form, in a delicate hand of the same age as the text.

   2. Rubric in Beneventane script.
   Domino sancto ac uenerabili $\overline{G}$(regorio) summo pontifici Berengarius seruus eius . . . . 55 *b*
   Nouiter ad uos beatissime pater de corpore et sanguine domini exorte questionis allata relatio sic totam subito hanc terram repleuit ut non solum clerici et monachi quorum intentio in talibus inuigilare debet uerum etiam ipsi laici de hoc inter se in plateis confabulentur aiunt enim beringarium quendam turonensem magni ingenii profundeque scientie uirum romam aduenisse qui eam cui quondam abrenuntiauerat sententiam uelit c. iterum renouare. Asserens ut dicunt quod in sacramento nostre redemptionis nec panis in carnem nec uinum

mutatur in sanguinem quod quantum catholice fidei con-
trarium sit norunt illi quorum cibus est lectio sacra. Vnde
factum est ut patres et confinitimi nostri qui me ut ita dixerim
sepe mihi preponunt ad hoc meum animum excitarent
quatinus quod de his potissimum sentiam eis propalarem.
Collegi igitur has sanctorum patrum que in hoc libello continentur sententie pluribus tamen pretermisis ne silentio
prolixa foret (!) animum lectoris fortasse grauaret. Volui autem
non prius hec illorum infundere mentibus quam tibi legata
qualiacunque sint tuo examine iudicentur quoniam autem de
sacramento locuturi sumus, prius quid sit ipsum sacramentum
audiamus. Est autem sacramentum ut ysidorus ait etc.

Extracts follow, sometimes named in the margin. On 62 _b_ a
very distinct change of hand, and the text seems to be
unfinished. There is no concluding formula, and after a comment on 1 Cor. xi. 27 and on xii. 3, 4, follow miscellaneous
precepts and definitions, ending: Predestinatio est preparatio
gratie solum ordinatio et in bonis et in malis

This tract I find to be unpublished : work on it has been under-
taken by the Rev. Dr A. J. Macdonald and by Dom G.
Morris: the latter attributes it to another Berengarius of
Italy.

3. Exposition of the Lord's Prayer   63
    Pater noster...hoc nomine et caritas excitatur.   Quid enim
        carius filiis esse debet quam pater
    —Reliqua uero IIII° ad temporalem uitam pertinere uidentur.

4. AMBROSIUS   64
    Symbolum quod continetur breuiter propter eternam salutem
    —inde uitam eternam. amen.
    On 64 _b_ a note from Augustine.·

II. 5. In Beneventane script, very small and beautiful at first, growing
        larger on 90 _b_.
    Inc. sirasirm. i. cantica. c. salomonis   65
    In hoc libro qui de canticis canticorum conscriptus est quasi
        amoris corporei uerba ponuntur
    —qui sponso thalamum construat.
    Salomon inspiratus diuino spiritu composuit hunc libellum...sic
        liber incipit.
    Osculetur. (Text of the Book throughout written in capitals.)
    ending 90 _a_: Christi tamen bonus odor sumus in omni loco.
    Possibly by the author of art. 2.

6. Parabole salomonis filii dauid regis israhel   90
    Audi fili mi disciplinam patris tui etc.
    ending 105 _b_: huius uite uicem ocius transire satagunt.
    Schenkl points out that this is Bede's comment, but neither
        incipit nor explicit are those of the full text (in _P.L._ xc).

7. On mulierem fortem quis inueniet (Prov. xxx)   .   .   .   105 *b*

Mulierem etc. A diebus salomonis usque ad partum uirginis inuenerunt

ending 108 *b* : non hominum fauores superuacui. sed opera ipsa que....

? Bede.

8. The last two leaves, in another hand, are part of a comment on 1 Cor. xi. 17 sqq. Hoc autem precipio etc.

Non solum supradictis modis non esse faciendum ostendo

ending on xii. 1. —ubi non scisma sed pax et concordia maneat inter uos et in uobis.

107. GEORGIUS DE SCLAVONIA.
$\left\{\begin{array}{l}\text{Old marks}\\ \text{C}^2.\ 3.\ 64\\ \text{II.}\ 6.\ 7\\ \text{O.}\ 4.\ 43\end{array}\right.$

Paper, $8\frac{3}{8} \times 5\frac{3}{4}$, ff. 2 + 88 + 2, 31 lines to page. Cent. xv (1411?) in a decent, rather current hand.

Binding, modern.

Collation: $a^2 \mid 1^{12}$–7^{12} $8^4 \mid b^2$.

Acad. Marischall.

From Dr Guise.

1. Inc. Epistola mag. Georgii ad sanctimonialem   .   .   . f. 1

Filiole mee in Christo amantissime d^{ne} yzabelle de villa alba religiose de conuentu dominarum de bello monte (prope turonis *marg.*) Georgius de sclauonia magister in artibus et doctor in theologia Canonicus et penitenciarius ecclesie Turon....

Nosse velis carissima quod rogatur a quibusdam venerabilibus viris

The preface ends with a list of the subjects

de virginis sacrate preminencia et generositate

......

ultimo connectitur patrini cordialis exhortacio cum seriositate.

Cap. 1. *Filia.* Filiola mea precarissima. In primis et ante omnia considera et recognosce nobilitatem tuam

There are many corrections, linings out of portions of text, and marginal additions.

—mei memoriam facias in orationibus tuis sicut et ego tui facio

Gracia d. n. I. C. sit semper tecum. Amen. Expl. epistola.

2. At top.

Cest la premiere minuce de lepistre qui nest pas corrigee ne si bien ordonne comme celle qui fu faite apres ceste cy .   .   33

A ma filiole en I. C. tresamee dame yzabeau de villeblanche
Religieuse du couuent de dames de biaumont empres tours
George de esclauonie maistre ez ars et docteur en theologie
Chanoine et penitencier de leglise de tours....Vueille sauoir
que ie fu prie daucuns venerables seigneurs....

It is a French version of no. 1, ending 82 *b*

—memoire de moy en tes prieres comme ie faiz de toy. Et la
grace de n. s. I. C. soit auec toy pardurablement. Amen.

Escript a Tours le darrenier iour de decembre lan mil iiijᶜ et xj.
(I do not feel sure that this is the date of the MS.)

Two prayers 'comment ma filiole se doit recommander a dieu'
and 'quant ma filiole mettra le voil sus sa teste a matin'   .   82 *b*, 83

3. Lepistre de ma filiole Georgette de taille se commence ainsi .   83 *b*

A ma treschere filiole en I. C. et tresamee dame Georgete de
taille (of the same convent as before).

Ma treschiere filiole Puis que n. s. nous a lie ensemble
—Et par ceste presente epistre ie mentes (?) dacquitter etc.

On 85, 86 are two passages meant to be inserted in the text of
no. 2 : on 86–7 a passage in Latin, probably to be inserted
in no. 1.

The book has the appearance of being the author's autograph.

119. NOTEBOOK OF PATRICK DUNE.
$$\left\{ \begin{array}{l} \text{Old marks} \\ \text{C}^2.\ 3.\ 77 \\ \text{H. iii. ii} \end{array} \right.$$

Paper, 7¼ × 5½, ff. cir. 100. Irregularly written. 1595.

Contains very rough copies of various texts, from printed
books, viz.:

Cicero *pro lege Manilia.*

Extracts from Pauline Epistles in Greek, interlined.

A few pages of English and miscellanea.

Horatii *Ars Poetica.*

Senecae *Hercules Furens* et *Thyestes.*

Isocratis *Nicocles.*

Part of the Epistle to the Galatians.

Extracts from Cato's *Disticha*, and many notes and verses.

The name of Patrick Dune often occurs. Doubtless it was
written by him when a student : otherwise it is of little interest.

<table>
<tr><td></td><td>Old marks</td></tr>
</table>

137. GREGORII HOMILIAE.
MIRACULA B. V. M. ETC.

Old marks
C². 4. 79
II. 5. 2
H. 3. 2

Vellum, 8¼ × 5¾, ff. 1 + 156, 37, etc., lines to page. Cent. xiii, for the most part early, in a close black hand: a quire at the beginning in double columns of 35 lines.

Binding, old wooden boards covered with brown leather: incised lines: clasps gone: on each cover A $\overline{B\,D}$.

Collation: 1 flyleaf, a^8 | 1^8 2^8 (wants 8) 3^8 (wants 1) 4^8–11^8 | gap | 12^{10} 13^{10} 14^8 15^8 16^{10} 17^8 18^8.

Lib. Acad. Marischall.

From St Paul's, London: at bottom of f. 9 in a hand of cent. xv: liber datus noue librarie ecclesie sci pauli apostoli londoniis. Not in the catalogue of 1458.

The provenance is noted by Simpson, *Reg. S. Pauli,* and from him by Savage, *Old English Libraries,* p. 120.

It is no. 19 in the list of MSS. given by Thomas Reid.

I. f. 1. Has theological notes and 'distinctions' of no special interest.
    2. Another hand, beginning in single lines and changing to double columns on 2 *b.*

      Hec sunt statuta Mag. Alexandri de stauenesbi episcopi de Couentr' et Lichesfeld .   .   .   .   .   . f. 2
      Cum penitentia consistat in tribus
      Instructions to confessors, ending 4 *b*: hec omnia sunt preiudicio sentencie sanioris. Amen.
      Vniuersis archidiaconis per couentr' diocesin constitutis Alexander...salutem. Et sic uigilias noctis super gregem uobis commissum custodire etc.
      Injunctions of all kinds, ending:
      Item inhibemus sub pena dimid' marc' ne quis sacerdos ad tabernam eat uel tabernam teneat uel scotale.
      An instruction on the Seven Sins .   .   .   .   .   6 *b*
      Dicatur omnibus parochianis omnibus dominicis diebus uel aliis festis a sacerdotibus que sunt vij; criminalia peccata
      ending on Gula: quia ubi plus regnat ebrietas plus accidit (8 *a*).
      Alex. de Stavenby was bishop 1224–38. He introduced the Franciscans into his diocese.
      On 8 *b*, in a small hand, are glossed verses on the Articles of Faith, Sacraments, Commandments, Works of Mercy.

II. The main volume.

His vision of delivery from devils when sick.
—uidit se liberari.

(11) Pilgrim in the Sea. Erat nauis in medio maris   .   .   103 *b*
—protegere uiderit misericorditer.
Ward, 626.

(12) Stephen saved from shipwreck. Fuit clericus quidam
Stephanus nomine gallus genere (on the way to
Jerusalem)—semper applicare uolenti paratus   .   .   104
Ward, 640.

(13) Child granted to a barren mother dies and is raised   .   104 *b*
In gallie partibus—infans reuixit.

(14) Revelation of Feast of the Nativity of the Virgin .   .   104 *b*
Dulcia christi magnalia (angel revealed to hermit).

(15) Institution of Hours and Mass of the Virgin   .   .   104 *b*
Constantinus augustus cum in aliis—omnesque horas
eius ex ordine iuuante filio eius d. n. I. C. etc. per omn.
sec. sec. amen. Ward, 638.

(16) Compline of the Virgin. Plura sunt sancte dei genitricis
miracula .   .   .   .   105 *b*

(17) Lily in mouth of dead clerk (cf. Ward, 605) .   .   .   106
Fuit in rotomagensi ecclesia—ut dignum erat sepeliunt.

(18) De quodam clerico submerso in cuius ore pendebat
cedula continens Aue maria   106
Set et hoc non uidetur omittendum—ad honorem omnip.
dei.

(19) De S. Maria Egyptiaca. Gloriosum exemplum uere
penitentie—intrare in regnum celorum. amen   .   .   106 *b*

(20) Unchaste Abbess delivered. Non uidetur loquendum
cum fuco (Ward, 626) .   .   .   .   .   .   107 *b*

(21) Mead multiplied. In britannia maiore .   .   .   108
—tanto magis habundabat. Ward, 614.

(22) de duobus monachis. Bina in fine huius libelli miracula
de duobus monachis   108
Monk of Jumieges, drunk : thrown to a distance from altar.
Monk of Evesham in extremis visited by St John, sent
by the Virgin   —mereamur esse consortes. Amen.
Expl. lib. primus mirac. b. v. m.
Inc. prol. libri sequentis   .   .   .   .   .   108 *b*
Ad omnip. dei laudem—recitare studeamus.
This is the prol. of Lib. II. of the Cleop. collection.
Ward, 604.
The Miracles, but for an insertion, correspond.

(1) Hildefonsus. Fuit in tholothana urbe. Ward, 604   .   108 *b*

(2) Drowned Sacristan. In quodam cenobio. Ward, 604 .   109
Inserted : (*a*) Clerk at York, ill, could not confess. Virgin
shows him his sins in a cedula : he confesses, recovers,
becomes a monk in abatia de funteines   .   .   .   109 *b*

(5) St Bonetus and his vestment. Ciuitas in Aruerno. Cf. Ward, 622 . . . . 117 *b*

(6) St Dunstan and the Virgin's choir. Britannia maior que nunc anglia. Cf. Ward, 631 118

(7) St Fulbert and the milk of the Virgin. Transactis temporibus. Cf. Ward, 637 119

(8) Monk cured by Virgin's milk. Similem lactationis pietatem. Cf. Ward, 613 (not the same) . . . 119

(9) Abbot Elsin and Feast of Conception (called Eglesius). Guillelmus ex comite normannie. Cf. Ward, 614 . . 120

(10) De Wimundo regis capellano. De similitudine miraculi adducor. Guimundus and Brogo voyaging to Jerusalem: becalmed: various saints invoked. Guimund says: Leave your Greek saints and call on the Virgin: this is successful 120

(11) Devil in three Beast-shapes appears to drunken Sacristan. Non parui momenti. Cf. Ward, 612 . . 120 *b*

(12) De Vectino monacho. Settinus (Vettinus) erat aput alemannos. His vision 121

(13) Monk in Burgundy dies suddenly: is he to be buried with honour? His ghost appears and tells how the Virgin saved him.
Res est acta in burgundie. Cf. Ward, 620 . . . 121 *b*

(14) Dying monk sings. Gaude maria. Illud quoque non est omittendum 122

(15) Clerk does homage to the devil to gain a girl's love. Refuses to deny the Virgin: her appearance to him: his repentance. Similar stories, Ward, 629.
Clericus erat quidam transacta tempestate . . . 122

(16) Clerk of evil life: confesses and dies: his companion sees the Virgin at mass a year after and hears of his salvation.
Admiranda est Christi misericordia 123

(17) Merchant Theodore and Jew: Virgin's image as surety . 123 *b*
In constantinopolitana urbe. Ward, 638.

(18) In terra s. edmundi erat campestris ecclesia modico situ ab antiquo posita. Rustic rides by at night, hears voices: summoned in by St Margaret. Virgin and choir of virgins within. She tells him to tell the priest the church must be enlarged: measures the ground and marks it with stones: gives him a sign about money hidden by the priest in maioris arche angulo: adds threats. Priest's concubine protests: falls and breaks her leg. Priest says he will obey if the Virgin cures her: applies earth from the places marked by the Virgin as internal and external remedies. Immediate cure: the whole population combine to enlarge the church . 124

(19) Rerum (Verum) quod multa pietatis documenta　.　.　124 b
　　Knight takes refuge at Virgin's altar. His enemies
　　attacked with 'sacer ignis' : healed by Virgin.

(20) Fallen nun confesses to Abbess and dies. Abbess's inter-
　　cessions answered by ghost of nun, who reports her
　　deliverance.
　　Quoniam uero sufficienter...in principali sexu facta
　　texuimus　.　.　.　.　.　.　.　.　124 b

(20) Mead multiplied (again). Rex athelstanus. Cf. Ward, 614　125

(21) Woman jealous of rival (wife and mistress). Cf. Ward, 621　125
　　Coniunx cuiusdam cum maximo odio

(22) Two images of the Virgin at Constantinople. 'in agia
　　sophia and in eccl. balcherne
　　Sunt in constantinopoli. Cf. Ward, 616　.　.　.　125 b

(23) Saracens unable to deface image of Virgin at Ramula.
　　Pauci admodum anni sunt (Ward, 687, *Spec. Hist.* vii. 110).

(24) Victory of Christians. Archadii imp. tempore cum roilas
　　dux scitarum

(25) Feast of Purification instituted after plague　.　.　.　125 b
　　Justini)anus imp. rempublicam regebat Ward, 638.
　　—et perducas ad celestia regna. amen.
　　Expl. lib. III^us mirac. b. v. m.
The collection is apparently not identical with any described by
　　Ward, but has much in common with Cleop.

Sermo de natiuitate sancte semper uirginis Marie　.　.　.　126
　　Natiuitas gloriose uirginis marie precelsa sollempnitas
　　—ad celestis palatia regni. Quod beatissima d. n. etc.
　　—gloriatur deus per om. sec. sec. Amen.

Sermo uen. Fulberti ep. in natiuitate b. marie　.　.　.　130
　　(A)ppropriate (Approbate) consuetudinis aput christianos
　　(*P.L.* cxli. 320)—gloriam filii tui d. n. I. C. qui etc.

Inc. miraculum sancte dei genitricis Marie editum a d. Willelmo
　　quondam abbate de binetona (Bindon in Dorset, Cisterc.)　.　132

Diu est quod quedam miracula b. genitr. dei marie...scribere
　　disposueram (has omitted this one from motives of timidity)...
　　Monachus quidam cisternensis.(!) ord. Walterus nomine
　　uolente d. henrico Winton. ep....ad eorundem monachorum
　　habitum et uitam se transtulit. vnde in abbatem staichothie
　　assumptus quod est monasterium in episcopatu oxoniensi
　　(! exon-) led a loose life : had an illness for years. Vision of
　　judgment : long supplications : delivered by intercession of
　　the Virgin : died three days after.

Illum enim repellere non nouit qui de ipsa nasci uoluit. Expl.
　　mirac. per genitr. dei factum.

This miracle may be regarded as an appendix to the larger
　　collection.

5. Inquisitio facienda a sacerdotibus ad confitentes .   .   .   135
   Hunc modum et cura (in) huius modi habent.
  Directions for examination and penances.
  Ending 142 *a*: ut ad satisfactionem moueatur Ignorantia pro-
  babilis non supina (unfinished?).

6. Three Lessons for the Invention of the Cross .   .   .   .   142 *b*
   Regnante uen. cultore dei constantino
  Six Lessons for the Exaltation. Postquam a b. helena .   .   143
  Nine Lessons for the Decollation of St John Bap. .   .   .   144
   Adest uobis kariss. die sollempnis quem consecrauit

7. Runic alphabet (27 letters) with equivalents, a–u, then
  egh. eth. ge. huz. ea. ene. and.   .   .   .   .   .   144 *b*
  Hebrew alphabet fairly well written, with equivalents.

8. The Fifteen Signs .   .   .   .   144 *b*
  Jeronimus inuenit in annalibus hebreorum—et mane erit
  iudicium. Often printed, e.g. in *Legenda Aurea*.
  Verses (8): Cur homo qui cinis es per auaritiam sepelis es?
         Eri cur heres cuius cras non eris heres?
         Quando sepultus eris quicumque sepultor es eris
         Dici nosse putes cum iam sub marmore putes
         Mox hodie quod heri nouus heres imperat eri
         Lingua breuis breuitate leuis etc.   145

9. De amore dei. Inter amorem huius mundi et amorem dei hec
  est differentia   145
  May continue till 148 *a*, ending: Ecce frater petitionem non
  qualiter debui sed qualiter potui interim adimpleui.

10. Dixit petrus alfunsus seruus Christi Ihesu compositor huius
  libri   148
  An abridgment of the *Disciplina Clericalis*, on which see Ward,
  Cat. of Rom. II. 235 sqq. It ends: quam cum bonis operibus
  superba gloriatio.

11. Vision of St Paul: shortened form   150
   Dies dominicus dies letus in quo gaudent angeli
   —et tu paule dilectissime dei intercede pro nobis ad dominum.
  Several forms printed by H. Brandes, Halle, 1885, *Visio S.
  Pauli*. For the full text see my *Apocr. N. T.* and reff.

12. A series of excerpts, beginning   151
   In paradiso VII peccata adam perpetrauit
  The matter is such as might come from the Numerale of
  W. de Montibus.
  On 154 *b* is a story from the *Disciplina Clericalis*, no. 15.
  Ward, p. 239.
   Quidam filium habuit cui post mortem,
  followed by a series of moral sayings, and extracts, and defi-
  nitions, ending 156 *b*:
  Matrimonium est legitima coniunctio—uite consuetudinem
  retinens.

138. UBERTINO DE CASALI.

$\left\{\begin{array}{l}\text{Old marks} \\ \text{C}^2. \ 4. \ 80 \\ \text{C. } 5. \ 21 \\ \text{II. } 5. \ 4\end{array}\right.$

Vellum and paper, $8\frac{1}{2} \times 5\frac{1}{2}$, ff. 205, 32 lines to page. Cent. xv in a clear rounded Gothic hand, Italian.

Binding, old red leather.

Collation: 1^{10} 2^8–4^8 5^{10} 6^{10} 7^{12}–14^{12} (wants 12) 15^{10} 16^{12}–19^{12}.

Liber Acad. Marischallanae.

From Dr Guise?

> Nel nome de yhesu et de la gloriosa madre maria Incomenca el quarto libro de frate Vbertino de la passione Resurrectione et ascensione del nostro signore yhesu christo . . . f. 1
>
> Multiplicati i rami de la perfectione de la uita et doctrina de yhesu
>
> ...Hora mai e tempo che in questo quarto libro questo felice arbore se perduca al sommo.
>
> There is a gap (of one leaf?) after f. 147, and changes of hand occur near the end of the book, e.g. at f. 199. Rubrics are in Latin: the last is Yhesus dilectam eleuans. Yhesus dux laureatus (dealing with the Assumption).
>
> The book ends imperfect:
>
> Secondo fo elleuata in premio de eleuatione gloriosa a la sublimita
>
> An initial in gold with white branchwork on f. 1 has been pretty.

The author died 1338. His book, *Arbor vitae Crucifixi I. C.,* was printed at Venice in 1485.

139. BIBLIA.

$\left\{\begin{array}{l}\text{Old marks} \\ \text{H. } 3. \ 27 \\ \text{O. } 4. \ 21 \\ \text{C}^2. \ 4. \ 86\end{array}\right.$

Vellum, ff. 375, double columns of 48 lines. Cent. xiii late or xiv early, in a good small English hand.

Binding, old calf.

Collation not practicable.

On flyleaf: Liber Acad. Marischallanae Aberdonensis. Ex dono Moderatorum Paedotrophii Gordonii Aᵒ 1738.

Contents :

The greater part of the Bible, beginning imperfectly in 2 Reg.
(2 Sam.) xiii. 14, Noluit adquiescere.

Continues to 2 Par. No prayer of Manasses.

Esdr., Neem., Judith, Esther, Tobit, Job.

Prov.—Ecclus.

Isa.—Mal. A leaf gone at end of Jer. and beginning of Lam.

1, 2 Macc.

Evv., Paul. Epp. (Col. follows 2 Thess.) Act. (ending: totus
mundus iudicari, amen.), Cath. Epp., Apoc.

Epitome of the Gospels in verse (Alex. de Villa Dei).

A. generat. b. magos uocat. egiptum petit. exit.

Followed by

List of the Canons of the Gospels,

and, in other hands, notes including lists of the Miracles,
Parables, sufferings of Christ.

Some liturgical lessons are noted in margins. There is no
attempt at decoration, save the simplest.

148. CATO. BOETHIUS.

{ Old marks
C². 6. 71
II. 5. 14
H. 3. 26
O. 4. 18

Vellum, 6½ × 4½, ff. 2 + 46 + 2, 23 lines to page. Cent. xvi early,
in a very clear good Gothic hand, probably Flemish.

Binding, original stamped leather over boards : each cover has
a panel much obliterated. That on the first cover shows a half-
figure in air, inscribed scroll below, figures kneeling at bottom : the
other has inscribed bands at top and bottom, but the subject is
indecipherable : two clasps.

Collation: a² | 1⁸ (wants 7, 8 blank) 2⁸–6⁸ b² (2 pasted down).

Names of owners : A. Warmyngton (p. ii) in red (xvi): Nich.
Charles, 1607 ; R. Gordon, 1697.

Liber Acad. Mariscallanae Abredon. Ex dono Moderatorum
Paedotrophii Gordonii A° 1738.

On i b entry of birth of Robert, Sunday, 1 Nov. 1500.

No. 25, folio 9, verso

No. 25, folio 6, verso

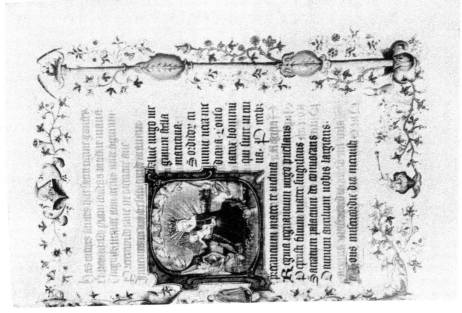

No. 25, folio 69, recto

No. 25, folio 17, verso

On i and ii are moral sayings.

At the end a copy of a letter of indulgence, no names inserted. Cupientes igitur ut altare SC. infra ecclesiam parroch. N. per bone memorie N. anglorum regem fundat.' in qua quedam laudabilis confraternitas christi fidelium etc.

1. Catonis disticha . . . . f. 1
    Cum ego Catho animaduerterem quamplurimos homines grauiter
      errare—non intelligere est negligere.
    Itaque deo supplica.
    Ama parentes et—Libenter ferto amorem.
    Si deus est animus nobis ut carmina dicunt
      ......
    Hos breuitas sensus fecit coniungere binos.
        Finit liber moralis Cathonis.

2. A table of the Kings of England from William I to Henry VIII
    in red and black, giving the following particulars . . 6 b

Inceptio	Tempus	Obitus	Tempus (place of
Regnacionis	coro.	regn'	regn. regum burial)
W. Con.:			a. m. d.
14 Oc. 1066	25 De. 1066	9 Sep. 1087	20 11 22 Cane.
Ends: H. 8us:			
21 Ap. 1409 (1509)	24 Ju. 1509		rest blank.

3. Boethius de Consolatione Philosophiae (no title) . . . 7
    Carmina qui quondam studio florente peregi
    Lib. I. ends 22 b. Heading in red to Lib. II 23
    Postquam philosophia in primo libro inuestigauit causas
      radicales infirmitatis B. in hoc secundo procedit ad eius
      curacionem primo adhibendo sibi remedia lenia secundo
      remedia validiora in libris sequentibus.
    Ends 44 : quo celum regitur regat.
      Finit liber secundus boecii in Consolacionem Philosofie.
    On 44 b, 45 are moral sayings.

Decoration: in the Cato the initials of lines are in gold on a continuous band of blue or red. There is ornament of naturalistic flowers on ff. 1 and 7: initials are of fluid gold on blue or red patches. All foreign work, French or Flemish.

152. MARTIALIS EPIGRAMMATA.

{ Old marks
  C². 6. 78
  H. 3. 15
  O. 4. 30

Vellum, 5⅝ × 3⅜, ff. 81, 37 lines to page. Cent. xiii early (al. xii late), in a rather pointed hand, which might be French.

Binding, paper boards and calf back (xviii).

Collation: 1⁸–3⁸ | gap | 4⁸ (wants 4, 5) 5⁸ 6⁸ (wants 1, ? 8 canc.) 7⁸ (wants 7?) 8⁸–10⁸ (wants 5) | 11⁸ (wants 8).

On f. 2 the inscription: Liber Acad. Marischallanae Abredon. (xvii).

Contents. Martialis Epigrammata,
    beginning imperfectly in Lib. III, 72, l. 3,
        Os tibi percussum (*sic*)
Lib. III, f. 2 *a.*
  ,,   IV, 10.
  ,,   V, 18 *b.*
  ,,   VI, 27.
  ,,   VII, 33, ending mando deo (vii. 99).
  ,,   VIII, with Preface to Domitian, 41 *b,*
        ending imperfect with 69. 2 mortuos poetas, 48 *b.*
  ,,   IX, 49, beginning imperfect with 4. 3,
            grandis in ethereo
  ,,   X, 59.
  ,,   XI, 68 *b,* ending imperfect in 71. 7,
            mediceque recedunt
  ,,   XII, 75, beginning with 60. 9,
            Turbida sollicito,
        ending with 99. 8, ferre potest.
  ,,   XIII, 78.
  ,,   XIV, 81 *b,* ending imperfect with 12,
            ligna ferant.
In IV, after f. 27, two leaves are wanting, from 10. 6 preces
    to 37. 3, Et prurit.
In VII, after f. 38, a leaf gone, from 58. 8 trucem to 69. 2
    cuius cecropia.

154. SERMONES.

⎧ Old marks
⎪ C². 6. 80
⎨ II. 5. 15
⎩ O. 4. 45

Vellum, 6½ × 5, ff. 155, 29 lines to page. Cent. xiv, in two main hands, the second of charter type.

Original binding, skin over boards, a clasp gone.

Collation: a paste-down | 1¹² 2¹⁴ 3¹²–12¹² | 13¹⁰ (wants 6): 1 paste-down.

Foliated in red from 211 to 368 : 364 gone.

Acad. Marischall. Abredon.

From the Carthusians of Hinton, Somerset : at foot of f. 2 is

(xiv) Paruus liber de sermonibus · xx · primus in H. Hentone. ordinis Cartusie.

At top of 235 is: J. Winterbottom, June 3, 1756, Nottingham. On 366: Georgius Woodall. William hereford (xvi).

A collection of Sermons, beginning .   .   .   .   .   f. 211

> *Precinxisti me uirtute ad bellum.* Mos istorum nobilium est sicut regum et principum quia quando filios suos de nouo milites faciunt

Ponite corda uestra in uirtute eius   214

> Hystriones illi quos ysandos nominamus quando uiderint aliquem in armorum exercicio uiriliter et strenue laborantem clamare solent et dicere ki nad quer ici le pregne.

French tags are usual at the beginnings of the sermons.

Hardly any have titles, but on 340 *b* is one: Sermo in dedicacione templi on Vere deus est in loco etc.

The last (356) is on Resplenduit facies eius sicut sol.

It ends unfinished with a quire on 358 *b*.

359–363 blank, 364 cut out: on 365 *b* lines (xiv) on the order of the Books of the Bible: 366, 367 blank but for scribbles.

On 368 *a* note on superbia.

On 368 *b* some English. At top, the line:

> Yore was a londe. Wrathe and hate an honde.

A note from Greg. *Dial.* iv. 19.

Three stanzas of English verse:

> (*a*) Wane þe niþi(n)g his deyd me buriieth him cove
> comez þe yunge strupling and wocth is loue
> he drinket of his god ale an het of his lowe
> an singez for his soule giuele goue.

Carleton Brown, *Register of M. E. Religious Verse*, no. 2578.
Only one copy cited, B.M. Add. 33956.

> (*b*) Waylaway nu his me vo nou rot y richt hunder mold etc.
> C.B. 2490 (Harl. 2316).

> (*c*) Hwo so him bi þohte ynwardliche an hofte etc.
> C.B. 2626: there are many similar forms.

Evidently the collection of sermons had a first part, comprising ff. 1–210. I do not recognize this portion.

155. SUMMA RAYMUNDI ETC.

{ Old marks
{ C². 6. 81

Vellum, 6¼ × 4¾, ff. "173" (169), 34 lines to page. Cent. xiii, in several clear small hands, English.   2 fo. officio suo.

Binding, stiff vellum.

Collation: 1^8 (+ 2 slips) 2^6 3^{10} 4^8 (+ 2 − 1) 5^6 6^{10}–17^{10} (wants 9–10) 18^{10}. Soiled and crumpled.

Liber Coll. Regii Abredon.

1. Summa Raymundi (no title) . . . . . . f. 1
   Quoniam ut ait ieronimus secunda post naufragium
   Part II, f. 66. III, 98 *b*, ending imperfect 163 *b*.
   An old (xiv) note at bottom: Expl. notabilitas reymundi breuiter
      in tribus libris collecta.
   So the loss (of two leaves?) is old.
2. Inc. summa mag. Tancredi bononie 164
   Cum in omnibus fere causis quilibet uiri,
   ending imperfect on 173 *b*.

Both treatises are very common.

156. BERNARDUS.
$\left\{\begin{array}{l}\text{Old marks} \\ \text{C}^2.\ 6.\ 82 \\ \text{O. 4. 46}\end{array}\right.$

Vellum, $6\frac{1}{8} \times 3\frac{3}{4}$, ff. 28, 34 lines to page. Cent. xii, in a clear small pointed hand, French: with variations of script.

Binding, calf (xviii).

Collation: 1^8 2^8 (1, 2 canc. + 1) 3^8 4^6 (1 canc.).

Acad. Marischall. Given by Dr Guise.

At the end, at the bottom of the page, original inscription:

liber s͞c͞e marie ursi campi.

This was a Cistercian abbey founded 1129 at Orcamp or Ourscamp, S.W. of Noyon (Chiry-Ourscamp).

1. Bernardus de gratia et libero arbitrio (*P.L.* clxxxii. 1001) . f. 1
   Title neatly cut off at top.
   Prol. sequentis operis. Domino W. abbati s. theoderici
      bernardus—uitam eternam habebunt.
   Inc. liber b. abbatis de lib. arb.
      Loquente me coram fratribus aliquando
   At bottom is the quire number xxv, and traces of like numbers
      are in the other quires, so this is just a piece of a larger book.
   —et magnificauit. Expl. lib. domini b. de gratia et lib. arb.
2. Sermons xviii–xxiii of St Bernard : another hand . . . 16
   xviii. Accedit medicus 16
   xix. Angelica creatura . . . . 16 *b*
   xx. A magistro uerbis 19
   xxi. Trahe me 22
   xxii. Si ita preciosa 25
   xxiii. Introduxit . . . . 28 *b*
   ending imperfect in 33 sequentia ex his que

161. De Sacramento.

$$\left\{\begin{array}{l}\text{Old marks}\\ \text{C}^2.\ 6.\ 87\\ \text{O.}\ 4.\ 48\end{array}\right.$$

Vellum, $5\frac{1}{8} \times 3\frac{7}{8}$, ff. 102, 15 lines to page. Cent. xii, in several good hands, one admirable.

Binding, old brown leather.   2 fo. quid est sacramentum.

Collation: 1^{10} (10? canc.) 2^8–7^8 8^{10} (6 canc.) 9^8–11^8 12 (four) | 13^8: old foliation incorrect, used here.

Acad. Marischal.

From Dr Guise.

I see no trace of provenance.

    I.   In nomine domini inc. libellus de corpore et sanguine domini
         ex dictis SS. patrum collectus .   .   .   .   .   . f. 1
              Tria esse in ecclesia principalia sacramenta
        The first authors named are Augustine, Paschasius; on p. 8 Ivo,
            10 *b* sqq. Magister Hugo, who figures much, 22 *b* Sergius
            papa, Hildebertus, 33 Aug., ad hireneum etc., 38 Hilarius
            ep., 42 Am(brosius), 43 Jeronimus, 44 *b* Basilius, 45 Ful-
            gentius, 46 Eusebius, 46 *b* Cirillus, 47 *b* Hylarius, 48 Eus.
            Emisenus, 48 Ex decretis Iulii, 49 *b* Rufinus, 51 *b* Beda,
            52 sqq. Lanfrancus
        ending 59 *b* : officio subinde contigerint.
        Contra eos qui dicunt naturam non pati ut panis in corpus
            christi et uinum uertatur in sanguinem.
        Ex libro Wimundi monachi discipuli Lanfranci archiep. .   .   60
              Cotidie natura panis
        The extracts from Wimundus are interrupted at 69 by Confessio
            berengarii...sub presentia pape nicholai coram omni sinodo
            turonis habita.
        Ego berengarius
        —de reuerso atque conuerso.
        Alia confessio berengarii in presentia domini pape gregorii septimi   70 *b*
        Anno ab incarn. sempiterni principis mill. septuag. nono
        —ab ea recesserant.
        Wimundus continues to 80 *b*
        Contra eos qui corpus domini asserunt secessum pati...Johannes
            Scottus[1] in libro de corpore domini dicit   81
              Nunc inquit respondendum est
        with other excerpts, ending 86 *b*: contactuque illius unum fieri.
        Tract. Mag. Hugonis. De quinque quibus mens humana agenda
            constat   87

---

[1] Not by Erigena: examined by Dom Morin. Printed in *P.L.* cxxxix ("anonyme de Cellot").

Quinque modi sunt

—pro quo commutatio nulla dari possit.

92 *b*, 93 blank.

II. In a larger and very fine rounded script.

Decrees of a Council   94

Sanctorum patrum uestigiis inherentes nouis morbis noua remedia procuramus

Statuimus igitur ut si quis possessiones ecclesiasticas inuaserit (dealing with excommunicated persons)

—Sciat itaque unusquisque quia quod quis dicit ueritati debet et quod promittere fideli.

On 98 *b* in a different and more pointed hand

Letter of Hildebert to Honorius (Epp. II. 41. *P.L.* clxxi. 265).

Honorio etc....I. humilis turonorum minister...Philosophus ait, Colere officiis

—suscipiet ubertas delictorum.

The last page or so is in the hand of the previous article.

163. CICERO DE ORATORE.   { Old marks
                                   C². 7. 61
                                   Z. 12

Vellum and paper, ff. 144, 29 and 24 etc. lines to page. Cent. xv, in two scratchy pointed hands.

Binding: black leather with incised lines over wooden boards: clasp gone.

Collation: 1¹⁴ (outer sheet vellum): rest not practicable.

Ex Bibl. Coll. Regal. Aberdon.

At top of f. 1:

Liber Willelmi laurencii Archidiaconi brechinensis.

Contents. Inc. tullius de oratore .   .   .   .   .   . f.   1

Lib. I. Cogitanti michi sepe numero

—confessus est.

Expl. lib. primus magistri (*corr. to* marci) tullii Cyceronis de oratore Inc. 2ᵘˢ ad quintum fratrem. sequitur prohemium.

,, II. Magna nobis pueris .   .   .   .   42 *b*

At f. 45 *b* (half blank) is a gap in the text from the end of IV (18) coacti sumus. Tum catulus

to end of XI (49) in arte tradere. Nichil sane inquit Catulus, f. 46.

On 82 *b* another gap is noted in the margin by a recent hand, but no indication in text

—velle dixerunt. Expl. lib. 2ˢ.

,, III. Inc. lib. tercius .   .   .   .   99 *b*

Instituenti michi

Little is written on 144 *b*, which is torn and mended, but the
  text ended complete: cursuque laxemus,
after which is:

> Expl.   liber   Tercius
> Inc.   Quartus.

It is a very roughly written book. There are not a few marginalia. Passages are often crossed out.

164. POMPONIUS MELA.

> ⎧ Old marks
> ⎪ C². 7. 62
> ⎨ II. 5. 3
> ⎩ O. 4. 16

Vellum, $8\frac{1}{4} \times 6\frac{1}{8}$, ff. 48 + 1, 24 lines to page. Cent. xv, in a pretty hand of Roman type: Italian.

Binding, rough sheep (xvii).

Collation: 1^8–6^8 1 flyleaf: many margins cut off.

Lib. Acad. Marisch. Aberd.

I give this book to the Library of the Marischal College of Aberdeen. Witness my hand John Gordon: like entries on f. 1, one with date 1761.

At end: Liber Joannis Gordon Iurisconsulti qui natus Abredoniae $\frac{2^o}{13}$. die Maii 1715.

Also   Samoth. llab (Thomas Ball?).

The flyleaf at end of cent. xv has some entries of payments, beginning apparently:

A horse price	vj^s viij^d
A Jacke of fence pr . .	xx^s
bowe and aroe pr . . .	iiij^s
A sadyll a payr of botis . .	iij^s iiij^d
A scole (?) pr . . .	xiiij^d
A swyrde and buckler . .	iij^s iiij^d
A bytt pr	xij^d

etc.

In red capitals: Pomponii Melae de cosmografia liber primus
  inc. .   .   .   . f.   1
Orbis situm dicere aggredior
Names of places, etc., written by the original hand in the
  margin.

Lib. II. 17 *b*. Here is an entry: Edinburgi 16° die Maii 1761:
Liber Jo. Gordon de Buthlay advocati: a quo scripta disser-
tatio de nuptiis Roberti Senescalli Scotiae atque Elizabethae
Morae anno 1749.

Lib. III. 34 *b*: Ioannis Gordonii Buthlaei 1761 nat. $\frac{2^{o}}{13}$ Maii 1715,

ending 48 *b*: operis huius atque athlantici littoris terminus.
There follows without break in red capitals the name of the
scribe

     Andreae Scorti de $\overline{\text{Sco}}$ Miniate. v. m.

The Books have decent initials of white or yellow branch-work
on grounds of red, blue and green.

165. OVIDII METAMORPHOSES. $\left\{\begin{array}{l}\text{Old marks}\\ \text{C}^2.\, 7.\, 63\end{array}\right.$

Vellum, $9\frac{7}{8} \times 4\frac{1}{2}$, ff. 1 + 116, 48 lines to page. Cent. xiii early,
in small good hand, pale ink. Many marginalia in charter-like
hand.

Binding, rough sheep (xvii).

Collation : 1 flyleaf 1^8–12^8 (wants one) 13^8 14^8 (wants 7, 8) 15^8
(wants 8).

Last leaves much damaged.   2 fo. Mollia.
On the flyleaf (xv–xvi)

     Liber m$\overline{\text{g}}$ri dauid guthre vtriusque Juris doctoris.

Ovidii Metamorphoses—no title   .   .   .   .   .   f.   1
Lib. I. In noua fert animus
Lib. II. 9, III. 18, IV. 25, V. 33, VI. 40, VII. 47, VIII. 56 *b*,
     IX. 64 *b*, X. 72 *b*, XI. 80, XII. 87, XIII. 94 *b*, XIV. 104.
     After 109 (l. 579) two leaves are gone to xv. 25 Post ea dis-
     cedunt.
ending imperfect with xv. 724: numinis usus

The tall narrow format of the book is common in copies of
Latin poets, intended, as I think, for the use of students, since they
could be conveniently carried.

It is a rough production, evidently much used. I am not sure
whether the writing is French or English; probably French.

184. Henr. Bohic.   { Old marks
                              D². 3. 31

Vellum and paper, 11 3/10 × 8, ff. 282, double columns of 50 and 37 lines: two main volumes. Cent. xv late, in several ugly hands.
Binding, old leather over wooden boards: hatched lines.
Collation: 1¹⁴–8¹⁴ 9¹⁴ (one gone) 10¹⁶ 11¹⁴ (one gone) 12¹⁴ ‖ a¹²–i¹² k⁶. In Vol. I outer and sometimes middle sheets of vellum.
Liber Coll. Regii Aberdon.
At each end: Liber magistri Willelmi de Elphinstoune.

I. Distinctiones Henrici Bohic super decretales Gregorii   .   . f.   1
       Venerabilibus et discretis uiris doctoribus licenciatis bachalariis
          et aliis scolaribus auditorium lecturi (!) decretalium de mane
          par' instantibus henricus bohic leonensis dioc' in britanea.
       Lib. I ends 164 a: si prelatus.
       Expl. primus liber mag. Henrici boychic.
       Inc. tabula distinctionum mag. henr. boyhic super libro
          decretalium   164
       —Et sic finiuntur Rubricelle primi libri.

II. In a worse hand: all paper
       Quartus liber de boyc   169
       De materia istius quarti libri quid sit,
       ending 282 b: male fidei li° vj°, etc.
       Expl. liber quartus secundum henr. boyc.
       Laus tibi christe quoniam liber explicit iste.

A most unattractive book. Works of Bohic are entered in the Cathedral Inventory (no. 249) under nos. 108, 109, 123.

205. Seneca etc.   ⎧ Old marks
                           ⎪ D². 4. 83
                           ⎨ II. 3. 16
                           ⎪ O. 4. 13
                           ⎩ 1. 1. 16

Vellum, 10 × 6¾, ff. 161; three volumes.
I. Single and double columns, 41 lines to page. Cent. xiv early, fine hand.
II. 39 lines. Cent. xiv, two decent hands, Italian.
III. Double columns of 41 lines. Cent. xiii, good English hand.

Binding, stamped leather over wooden boards: A $\overline{\text{B D}}$ on sides: two clasps gone.   2 fo. sed eciam.

Collation: (I) 1¹²–4¹² 5¹⁰ (wants 9, 10) | (II) 6⁸–10⁸ | (III) 11⁸–17⁸ 18¹⁰ (wants 10).

Liber Acad. Marischall. Abredon.

It is no. 23 in the list of T. Reid's books. From St Paul's, London.

I. 1. Seneca de clementia .   .   .   . f. 1
   Inc. primus liber de clementia completus.
   Scribere de clementia
   Double columns begin on 1 *b*.
   —praua flectantur. Expl.

  2. Extract from Jerome: liber de illustribus uiris de seneca . 10 *b*
   Lucius anneus—interfectus est.
   Hic. inc. epistole senece philosophi ad b. paulum et pauli ad
    senecam.
   Seneca suo p. salutem. Credo tibi paule
   The 14 letters, ending: lucone (!) et sauino consulibus.
   See Lightfoot's *Philippians* and my *Apocr.* N.T., p. 480.
   Epitaph of Seneca. Cura labor meriturus
   —ossa tibi (*Anth. Lat.*, no. 667).

  3. In single lines
   Annei lucii senece de naturalibus questionibus ad lucilium
    iuniorem. liber primus. inc. prohemium .   .   .   .   12 *b*
     Quantum inter philosophiam
   Lib. II. 19 *b*, III. 27 *b*, IV. 34 *b*, V. 39 *b*, VI. 43 *b*, VII. 50 *b*.
   Ending 56 *b*: et leui manu querimus.

II. 4. Marci tulii ciceronis nouus liber rethoricorum inc. Rubrica
    (Rhet. ad Herennium)   57
   Et familiaribus si negociis (*sic* for Etsi famil.)
   The hand seems to change on 58 *b*.
    Lib. II. 62, III. 72, IV. 79 *b*,
   ending 96 *b*: consequamur exercitacionis. Amen.
   Expl. nouus lib. rethor. marchi tulii ciceronis.
   A piece of very characteristic Italian ornament is on 57 *a*. On
    96 *b* was an inscription in English hand mostly erased: Iste
    liber est... *ending* scriptoris.

III. 5. Epistole Petri Blesensis Bathon. Archidiaconi .   .   .   97
   (See *P.L.* ccvii. and J. A. Giles's edition, 1847, vol. 1.)
   (Prol. ad Henricum.) Henrico etc. Rogatus a uobis
   There are 100 Epistles in this collection, numbered, but not
    completely or correctly, in the rubrics.
   They appear to correspond to the first 100 letters in Giles
    (and *P.L.*). The last is
   Amico R.... Innocentem—malignitates effudit = Giles 100.

On 161 *b* is a scribble (xiv):
contra lolard' epistola xiii et lij in (?) principio.
The entry in the St Paul's catalogue of 1458 under letter C is:
Item Seneca de clementia ad Neronem 2 fo. *sed etiam inter illos.*
Epistole Senece ad Paulum et e contra in eodem vol.
Seneca de naturalibus questionibus ad Lucillum ⎫
Tullius in Rethoricis   ⎬ in eodem
Virgilius in Bucolicis   ⎭ vol.
Epistole Petri Blesensis

The Bucolics are now missing.

214. OROSIUS ETC.   ⎧ Old marks
                                          ⎨ Θ. 1. 19
                                          ⎩ D². 6. 33

Paper, 11⅜ × 7½, ff. 11 + 218, 29 lines to page. Cent. xv, in a rather current hand not unlike lettre bâtarde, and possibly French.

Binding, brown leather, blind tooling (xviii).

Liber Coll. Regal. Aberdon.

On f. 1 of text:
    Collegii aberdonens. do. magistri hectoris boetii primi
                    primarii eiusdem.

On f. i: Alex^i gallouai.

At end in pencil: Liber M^ri Michaelis ffrasser.

On 202 (212) *b* neatly written: liber archibaldi quhitelaw archidiaconi scī andree infra partes laudonie quem fecit scribi.

The same on 147 *b*, ending: Archibaldus quhitelaw propria manu.

Collation: 11 leaves prefixed contain table. *a*¹⁰–*p*¹⁰ *q*⁸ | *r*¹⁰ (1 canc.) *s*¹⁰–*x*¹⁰ *y*¹⁶ (one canc.) *z* (six).

Registrum pro capitulis tocius libri inquirendis   .   .   . f. ii
    Capitula to Orosius only.
    ff. x, xi blank.
    In a different hand from the rest.

1. Pauli Orosii viri doctissimi historiarum inicium ad Aurelium
    Augustinum   1
    Preceptis tuis
    Lib. II. 19, III. 33, IV. 52 *b*, V. 74, VI. 87, VII. 112,
    ending 147 *b* : si deleas.

In a neater hand, of Italian character   148

       Bartholomeus paiellus eques vicentinus in P. orosium

           Ut ipse titulus margine in primo docet

              Orosio nomen michi est

          Librariorum quicquid erroris fuit

             Exemit eneas michi

          Meque imprimendum tradidit non alteri

             Hermanne quam soli tibi

          Hermanne nomen huius artis et decus

             Tueque laus Colonie

          Quod si situm orbis: si que nostra ad tempora

             Ab orbis ipsa origine

          Quisquam tumultus bellaque et cedes uelit

             Cladesque nosse me legat.

     148 *b* blank.

2. Lucii Amnei Flori Romane historie liber primus .   .   .   149

       Populus Romanus a rege Romulo

     Lib. II. 160, III. 174, IV. 190,

     ending 202 *b*: et titulo consecraretur

       Finis libri quarti et ultimi Lucii Amnei Flori.

3. Historia de origine Troianorum 203 (213)

       Origo Troianorum dardanus fuit

       —qui eneam filium procreauit.

     Epistola Cornelii Nepotis ad Salustium Crispum

          Cornelius nepos...Cum multa athenis

          —ad pollicitum reuertamur.

     Inc. historia Daretis Frigii de excidio Troie .   .   .   203 *b*

       Pelias rex in peloponense Nesonem fratrem habuit,

     ending 218 *a*: palamonem. Epistropum. Scedium

       De bello Troiano liber expl.

     218 *b* blank.

Very likely all copied from printed texts.

215. AUGUSTINUS ETC.

> Old marks
> D². 6. 35
> H. 1. 11
> II. 3. 11

Vellum, $11\frac{1}{4} \times 9\frac{1}{4}$, ff. 81, double columns of 40, 38 etc. lines. Cent. xii late–xiii early, in several good hands.

Binding, old wooden boards covered with stamped leather. On each cover is A $\overline{\text{B D}}$: clasps gone.

Collation: 1^8–6^8 (wants 5) 7^8–9^8 (+ 1) | 10^8 | gap | 11^2 (wants 2).

Liber Acad. Marischallanae.   2 fo. ut habitaret.

It is no. 20 in the list of Thomas Reid's books.

1. Aurelii Augustini egregii doctoris liber primus inc. de concordia
　　euangelistarum　.　.　.　.　.　.　.　.　.　.　f.　1
Inter omnes diuinas auctoritates
Lib. II. with capitula 11.
Lib. III. 44 *b*, a leaf gone after 44.
Ends 72 *a* : apud eum discipulis pedes lauat.
72 *b* blank.

2. Begins in a hand rather like the preceding, but after a few lines
　　changes to one of earlier type, with many variations.
Petrus Blesensis super Iob (ed. Giles II. 19)　.　.　.　.　73
Henrico d. g. illustrissimo...suus Petrus Blesensis...Gratias ago
　　gratie largitori—me recolo uel legisse.
Uir erat...Tria hic ponuntur
Ends imperfect : iam non moritur non crucifi(gitur)
　　Giles, opp. II. 59 *sub fin.*
A gap of uncertain length follows: a leaf would contain the end
　　of the tract, but on f. 1 a list of contents (xvii ?) adds
　　　　Idem de transfiguratione domini
　　　　Idem de conuersione S. Pauli
(for which see Giles II, 1–19).
f. 81 in a similar, if not the same, hand, contains two extracts
　　from the Policraticus of John of Salisbury :
　　(*a*) Dubitabilia sapienti sunt hec
　　　　—ut tamen dubitatio ipsa uulgum pretereat (Lib.
　　　　VII. 2, ed. Webb II. 98, 99).
　　(*b*) Item in Polycratico Iohannis.
　　　　Quomodo diuicie et honores—qui in hyrcum [s]trans-
　　　　formatur aut suem (VIII. 11, Webb II. 304 *sub fin.*—
　　　　305, with omissions).

The coloured initials do not seem to agree completely with the
style of the writing.

The provenance is not clear. The probability of its being
à St Paul's book is considerable, but it does not appear, any more
than T. Graunt's books do, in the catalogue of 1458.

216. BEDA ET HIERONYMUS IN APOCALYPSIM.
$\left\{\begin{array}{l}\text{Old marks}\\ \text{II. 3. 13}\\ \text{O. 4. 42}\\ \text{D}^2\text{. 6. 36}\end{array}\right.$

Vellum, $11\frac{1}{2} \times 7\frac{1}{2}$, ff. 2 + 37, 41 etc. lines to page. Cent. xii early,
in perhaps two excellent hands, rather irregular. English, probably.
Binding, old wooden boards with mark of clasp. At end is a

pencil copy of an inscription: Hunc librum in antiquis eius oper-
culis ligavit Joh. Jackson Londini A.D. 1780.

Collation: a² | 1⁸ (wants 1, 8) 2⁸–5⁸ (wants 8): quires 3, 4 with
original mark iii, iiii at end.   2 fo. in preceptis.

Liber Acad. Marischal.

From Dr Guise.

The flyleaves give no information as to provenance.

1. Beda super Apocalypsim (*P.L.* xciii. 129) . . . . f. 1
   Beginning imperfect in the preface:
   In preceptis habemus ut percepta talenta—Bedanque tui
   semper memor esse digneris.
   Inc. expositionis Apocalipsis S. Iohannis ap. liber primus.
   (Small capitals.)
   Apocalipsis ihesu christi et....Fundata per apostolos ecclesia.
   A leaf gone after 6.
   Lib. II. 7 b, III. 16,
   ending 28a: faciant uisu fructuque potiri. Amen.
   Expl. domino iuuante expositionis in Apocalipsin S. Ioh.
   Libri III Bede famuli Christi. Amen.

2. Prologus Beatiss. Ierónimi ad Anatolium de explanatione Apocalipsis S. Johannis Evangeliste   28
   Diuersos marina discrimina transuadentes—sudabit ingenium
   an(a)tholi carissime. Expl. prol.
   Principio libri beatitudinem legenti audienti et seruanti
   promittit 28b
   —qui cum cherintho heretico sentiunt. Expl. explanatio Apocal.
   b. Ioh. secundum Ieronimum ad Anatholium. 36b blank.
   On flyleaf, pen trials 'quicquid delirant reges plect(untur
   achiui)' and 'probatio penne et incausti.'

This form of Victorinus' Commentary is printed in Galland
Bibl. Patr. Tom. IV and *P.L.* V: and see Bardenhewer, *Patrol.* II.
593.

218. BERNARDI QUAEDAM.

{ Old marks
D². 6. 39
II. 3. 7
H. I. 15

Vellum, 11⅜ × 8½, ff. 4 + 180 + 5, double columns of 49 and 52
lines. Cent. xiii, in several fine hands, one particularly good,
narrow and tall.

Binding, old stamped leather over wooden boards, lettered A B̄D̄
on sides: clasps gone.

Collation: a^4 | 1^8–3^8 (wants 8) 4^8–11^8 12 (two) | 13^8–23^8 (wants 8) | 24^4 | b^4 1 flyleaf.

Lib. Acad. Marischall. Abredon.

From T. Reid, no. 12 in his list.

On the flyleaf at end (xiv): liber M. J. Mawnshull de Oryell Oxon. quondam socii.

> The leaves at beginning and end are in single lines, in charter hand. The first set contains letters of 1297-8.
>
> 1. Edward I. dated a ffiues sanct Bauon sur le lis le ior de la feste seint Dinis (? Denis) en lan de grace m^c. cc. iiij^{xx}. xvij.
> This and most, if not all, the other documents will be found in Rymer, *Foedera* II. 795 *et seq.*
>
> 2. William Abp. of Dublin, Antony Bp. of Durham, etc., reciting their commission in Latin, dated Ghent, 23 Nov. 1297. Dated a Croylingis labbeye pres de Courtray en fflandre. le xxiij^e ior de Nouembre lan de grace (1297).
>
> 3. The same as plenipotentiaries at Tournai.
> Done a Tornay a labbeye saint martin le mardi de la purif' notre dame. 1297.
>
> 4. Arbitration of Boniface VIII. Dudum inter karissimos
>
> 5. The like, dated 14 June 1298. 4th year
> reciting the letter of Edward from Ghent, 18 Feb. 1297.
>
> 6. Boniface to Edward. Inter te ex parte una
> Lateran 8 kal. mai. 5th year.
> Those at the end, in somewhat larger hand, contain:
>
> 1. The King of France: terms of peace.
> Ceo fu fait en labbaille de Laumosne de Cisteaux Lundi le iour de feste del Inuencion seint Estiefne. En lan de grace mil. deux centz Quatrevintz et dis et neuf en le mois daoust.
>
> 2. Informacio de uiribus que Rex anglie debet habere in Petragoric' Caturc' et Lemouic' ciuitatibus et dioc.' et de supprisis per Regem ffrancie factis de illis.
> Speciali suo et amico suo d^{no} Reymundo de fferrar scī Seurin' dur' decano suus Bern' fabri canonicus,
> occupying about two leaves. On the last page we pass from Latin to French:
> Au primer article du mariage le fiz nostre seigneur le Roi et de la fille le Roi de ffrance nostre seigneur le Roi si acorde sur les seurtes etc.
> The last lines cut off.
> I have not found this document in Rymer.
> The last flyleaf is from a roughly written MS. dealing with Canon Law (xiii-xiv).
> On iv$b$ is a table of contents (xv) headed
> In hoc vol. continentur

I. 1. (Bernardus de consideratione) . . . . . . f. 1

Inc. prefacio exortacionum bernardi abb. clareualensis ad Eugenium papam.

Subit animum—non sentit amoris. Expl. prol.

Inc. lib. 1....Unde iam ergo incipiam

Lib. II. 4, III. 8, IV. 11, V. 15.

—non finis querendi.

2. Epistola d. Bernardi abb. ad Mag. Hugonem de S. Victore (super hoc: Nisi quis renatus fuerit ex aqua etc.) . . 19*b*

Si tibi tardius uideor—de persone quoque electione.

Most of 23*b* blank. Up to this point a variety of hands.

II. The finest hand now begins.

3. (Sermones S. Bernardi) 24

Inc. sermones per anni circulum tam in dominicis sollempnitatibus et quorundam festis sanctorum quam aliorum temporum diebus priuatis. pro diuersis rerum euentibus et causis negotiorum titulo nominis uen. patris nostri bernardi deo dilecti abbatis de clara ualle presignati. Sensus enim eius in his est sed non stilus (they were taken down by his hearers) —ut uberiorem faciat fructum.

Inc. sermones Bernardi de Claraualle. Sermo de aduentu domini. quibus modis ad nos uenerit.

Hodie fratres celebramus aduentus initium.

The entry in the list of contents is

Item 88 sermones eiusdem quorum inicia notantur in folio 178 et incipiunt fo. 24⁰ et perdurant usque fo. 89.

The last complete one is on All Saints:

Quia sanctorum omnium festiuam

On 89*b* another is begun: (Ad)vertistis nisi fallor, but only 3½ lines are written: a column blank.

III. 4. Item quedam exposicio ut suppono eiusdem Bernardi super 8 primos psalmos psalterii 90

Deus canticum nouum cantabo tibi etc.

Liber psalmorum canticum dicitur spiritualiter

Only two quires remain, ending with f. 105,

on Confitebor tibi domine....

IV. 5. In a fine small hand. Flores Bernardi.

Item plures textus sumpti de libris biblie quos idem **Bernardus** in diuersis suis operibus multum fructuose exposuit . . 106

Rubric. quod carnalis cogitatio cohercenda sit ut spiritualis amplius augmentetur.

A list of 28 texts from Genesis. 1 Terra autem erat inanis xxviii. Ruben primogenitus meus

Similar lists are given for the several Books.

Ending on Apoc.: sponsata per fidem.

Expl. flores Bernardi.

No. 25, folio 266, verso

No. 25, folio 110, recto

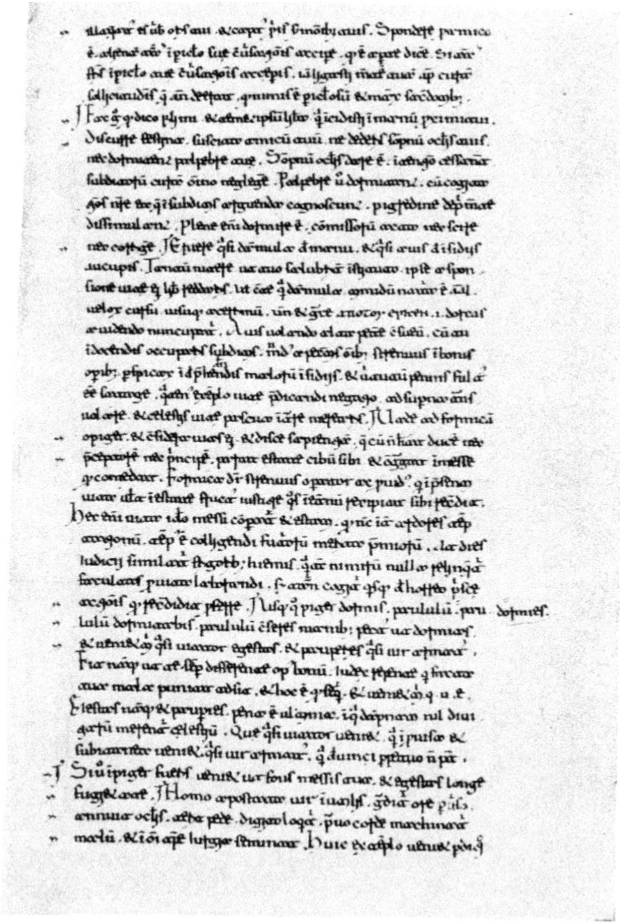

No. 106, folio 91, recto

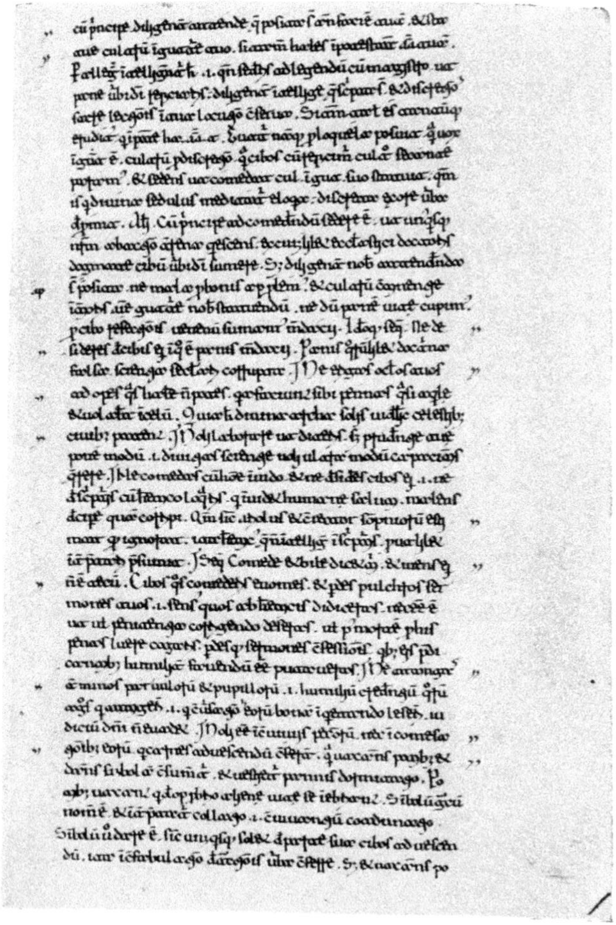

No. 106, folio 99, recto

The lower r. corner of the leaf cut off: doubtless it had an
inscription of ownership; and I feel sure the book belonged
to a Cistercian house and was pledged or sold to an Oxford
stationer. It may well have made its way to St Paul's, and
is quite likely to have been one of T. Graunt's books; see
no. **10**.

180*a* blank: on 180*b* initia of the sermons.

219. Augustinus super Iohannem.

$\left\{\begin{array}{l}\text{Old marks}\\\text{D}^2.6.40\\\text{II. 2. 6}\\\text{4. B. xv}^8\\\text{H. 1. 10}\end{array}\right.$

Vellum, $12\frac{1}{4} \times 9\frac{1}{4}$, ff. $3 + 282$, double columns of 35 lines.
Cent. xii late, in more than one hand, the first curious and narrow.

Binding, stamped leather, xvi, over wooden boards, clasps gone,
lettered on each cover $A\overline{BD}$.   2 fo. (table) quia uenturi
(text) ut hec uel

Collation: *a* (three) 1^8–34^8 35^2 | 36^{12} (wants 9–12).

Lib. Acad. Marischal.

It is no. 8 in the list of T. Reid's books. Like others it
belonged in cent. xv to Thomas Graunt (see below) and therefore
is from St. Paul's.

f. i *a* blank: on i*b*–iii*a* an original table of the Homilies, on iii*b*
a xv^th-cent. list of days for which the Homilies may be used: at
the end

Supplico oretis pro Thoma Graunt.

D. Augustini Homiliae super Johannem .   .   .   .   . f.   1
(The name Graunt in the upper corner.)
Intuentes quod modo audiuimus (xxxv. 1379)
ending 275 (274)*a*: terminare sermonem.
Colophon (xv). Expl. cxxiiii omelie beatissimi Augustini super
Euangelium Johannis.
274*b* blank.
A xv^th-cent. Table by Graunt   275
Abrahe—Zelum.
Expl. tabula super omelias Aug. in euangelio Johannis quod
Graunt.   283 (282)*b* blank.

Initials, mainly in red and blue, seem to have been added.

222. LAUR. VALLAE ELEGANTIAE.

$\left\{\begin{array}{l}\text{Old marks}\\ \text{D}^2.\ 6.\ 61\\ \Theta.\ 1.\ 12\\ \text{O.}\ 1.\ 17\\ \&.\ 3.\ 50\end{array}\right.$

Paper, $11\frac{1}{2} \times 8$, ff. 147, 42 lines to page.
Cent. xv in current hand.
Binding, old paper boards.
Collation: 1^{12}–12^{12} 13 (three).
Liber Coll. Regii Abredon.
At each end is (xv–xvi) Liber Willelmi de Elphinstoune.

> Elegantiae Laurentii Vallae . . . . . . f. 1
>> Cum saepe nostrorum maiorum Res gestas aliorumque vel
>> populorum (vel) Regum considero.
> Ends 147*b*: vt tallio stellio curcullio.

This famous book was first printed in 1471.

223. SUPER ORGANON.

$\left\{\begin{array}{l}\text{Old marks}\\ \text{D}^2.\ 6.\ 62\\ \text{WPB.}\ 3.\ 11\\ \text{O.}\ 1.\ 12\end{array}\right.$

Paper, $11\frac{3}{4} \times 8\frac{1}{4}$, ff. 206, double columns of 53 lines.
Cent. xv, in a small and much abbreviated script.
Has suffered much from damp: many leaves are loose.
Binding, paper boards.
Collation: impossible.
Liber Coll. Regii Aberdon.

> 1. Super Porphyrii isagogen. Begins imperfectly . . . f. 1
>> Queritur utrum tantum (?) sunt predicabilia—vero talia (un-
>> finished?) 23
>> 23*b* blank.
> 2. Super predicamenta 24
>> First words written large round a square: cf. **261.**
>>> Equiuoca dicuntur quorum solum nomen etc.
>> Iste est liber predicamentorum Aristotelis in quo—magis usitati.
>> Sic sit (? sic) est finis libri predic. Arist. 61
>> On 61*b*, faint, liber andree ? lesley studentis alme uniuersitatis
>> Aberdonensis
>>> ex dono (illegible to me)
>> Some English verses and other scribbles.

3. First words written as in Art. 2
   (Super periarmenias)
   Primum ergo oportet scire quid sit nomen etc.   .   .   .   62
       Iste est liber peryarmenias Aristotelis in quo determinatur
       End illegible.

4. First words as before:
       Super Analytica Priora.
   Primum oportet dicere quid etc.   84
   Iste est liber priorum analeticorum Aristotelis etc.
   —et habet de 2° priorum.

5. Super Analytica Posteriora 110*b*
       Omnis doctrina et omnis disciplina etc.
   Iste est liber posteriorum Aristotelis
   Lib. II. 154.
   Et hec de 1° posteriorum scripta sub honorabili uiro arcium
       magistro uituo iusticie regenti mᵣᵒ Johanne gilelmo forcifille
       pictaido
   The name of Mag. Gawinus (illegible) as owner added.

6. Super Topica.
   Propositum quidem negocii etc.   164
   Iste est liber thopicorum Arist. in quo determinatur
   170*b* mostly blank.
   A fresh beginning on 171 (Lib. II ?).
   Iste est liber thopicorum Arist. in quo Arist. docet
   Lib. III. 176, IV. 178*b*.

7. Super Sophisticos Elenchos   181
       De sophisticis autem etc.
   Iste est liber elenchorum arist.
   Lib. II. 190.
   At 195 the headline changes to
       primus liber priorum Arist.
   and continues to 206*a* where text ends unfinished (?).
   On 206*b* are scribbles.

The book is ugly and in bad condition.

239. GUL. HAY QUAESTIONES. $\left\{ \begin{array}{l} \text{Old marks} \\ \text{D}^2. 7. 31 \\ \Theta. 2. 20 \end{array} \right.$

Paper (and vellum), $10\frac{3}{4} \times 7\frac{1}{2}$, ff. 124, double columns of 49 etc. lines.

Cent. xvi (1535), in a small current hand: for date and scribe see later.

Binding, old panelled calf (1721).

Collation: a vellum flyleaf at each end and 2 old paper flyleaves, a^{12} (+ 1) b^{12}–e^{12} f^{14} g^{14} h^{12} i^{14} k^{12} (wants 9–12 blank).

On a tattered flyleaf at the beginning is Liber M. Alex...
Anderson No....Subprincipalis (xvi).

At the bottom of f. 1: Liber mag. W. Haye primarii.

And: Iterum compactus Anno 1721 impensis Joannis Ker. Graec.
Lit. Prof. in Acad. Regia Aberdon.

It is from King's College.

The vellum flyleaves are from a finely written MS. of cent. xiii
on iusticia and peccatum.

On a second tattered flyleaf are xvith-cent. copies of

> (*a*) The letter of Lentulus about the personal appearance of
> Christ.
>
> Apparuit temporibus—maxime filius.
>
> (*b*) Pilate to Claudius.
>
> Nuper accidit—omne malum mentiuntur.

See my *Apocr. N.T.*, pp. 477 and 146.

Will. Hay Quaestiones.

A long rubric precedes the text:

Hoc collectarium est in supplimentum preclarissimi doctoris
Marcilii Inguen. in quartum sententiarum quoad tria sacramenta viz. Extreme Unctionis ordinis et matrimonii ex
variis authoribus collectum per M. Vill^m Haye primum
subprimarium Regalis Coll. Aberdonen. rogatu uen. et
egregii viri M. Dauid Dischenton Cantoris eccl. cathedralis
eiusd. Vniuersitatis Rectoris dignissimi cum absolutum fuerat
hoc opus. Regnante Illustriss. Jacobo Quinto ex vtroque rege
Albanie prognato.

Text begins: Cum magister sentenciarum in vigesima tercia and
ends 122 *a*: et per consequens ad totum dubium. Finis.

Absolutum utquunque est hoc opus super sacramentum matrimonii et impedimentis eiusd. in alma Vniuersitate Aberdenen.
Collectum promulgatum et publice lectum in magnis scolis
regalis coll. aberdenen. coram theologorum ibidem conuenien-
cium solenni auditorio. Per ven. virum Mag. guilermum
hay prefati coll. pro tempore subprincipalem Eiusdemque
impensis et sumptibus in hanc publicam lucem redactum Per
manum sui proprii scribe viz. fratris guilermi scenan carmelite
Cuius labore et industria In ethicis atque plerisque aliis codicibus per eum collectis vsus est prefatus subprincipalis Anno
dⁿⁱ milles. quingentes. trices. quinto mensis Julii 23. Regnante
Jacobo quinto scotorum principe inuictissimo. Venerandoque
patre et d^{no} D^{no} Vilelmo stewart sedem episcopalem aberdenen. dexterrime moderante.

A table of the questions   123

240. Legenda Aurea.

$$\left\{ \begin{array}{l} \text{Old marks} \\ \text{D}^2.\ 7.\ 32 \\ \text{II.}\ 3.\ 15 \\ \text{H. II.}\ 3 \end{array} \right.$$

Vellum, 10½ × 7, ff. 209, double columns of 50 lines. Cent. xiv early, in a beautiful even script (English).

Binding, stamped leather (xvi) over wooden boards, two clasps gone. Stamped A $\overline{\text{B D}}$.   2 fo. Aduentus *or* scindentur.

Collation: 1¹²–16¹² 17⁴ 18⁸ (wants 5–8 blank?) | 19¹⁰ (wants 10 blank).

Lib. Acad. Marischall. Abredon.

It is no. 22 in the list of T. Reid's books, and belonged to T. Graunt, of St Paul's.

1. Legenda Aurea Iacobi de Uoragine.
   Prol. Uniuersum tempus--ad aduentum .   .   .   .   f   1
   Capitula. (179)   1
   Text. Aduentus domini per IIII᷒ septimanas .   .   .   2
   The numbering of the capitula is incomplete in the table, but
      the headlines carry it on to 179, that being the Legend de
      dedicacione ecclesie, ending 194 *b*:
         cohabitare dignetur per gloriam. Amen.
            Suffocet infestum completum murmuris estum
            Hoc opus ad festum penthecostes fit (*or* sit) honestum.

2. In another hand, narrow and pointed.
   Tractatus de vij sacramentis ecclesie   .   .   .   .   .   194 *b*
   Septem sunt sacramenta ecclesiastica que notantur hoc uersu.
      Bos · ut · erat · petulans · cernentibus · obice · cursum,
   which words stand respectively for
      baptismus · unctio · eucaristia · penitencia · confirmacio · con-
         iugium,
   ending 198 *a* (unfinished):
      Secunda est fornicacionis remedium
   Most of 199, 200 blank. There may have been an inscription
      on 200 *b*.

3. In a third hand : Inc. tabula super legendam sanctorum .   201
   Prol. Ad conuersionem fidelium
      —indiuisa manet.
   Inc. prima pars huius tabule
   Aduentus domini—Dedicacio ecclesie.
   List of chapters with incipits of text and lectiones.
   Expl. prima pars tabule in qua ad modum capitulorum diui-
      duntur singule historie sanctorum.

Inc. 2ª pars in quo omnia notabilia colligi possunt per modum
alphabeti . . . . *202 b*
Abscondita—Zelotipiam.

The name Graunt in red, which shows the St Paul's provenance.

Expl. tabula super legend. sanct.

209 b blank.

The first leaf or two crumpled. There may have been an
inscription at foot of 1 *a.*

Initials in blue and red, not remarkable.

Compared with Graesse's ed., 1890, I find these differences
(apart from some variations in order):

> Graesse cap. 52 de S. Timotheo ⎫
> ,, ,, 64 ,, Fabiano ⎪
> ,, ,, 66 ,, Apollonia ⎬ omitted.
> ,, ,, 118 ,, Hippolyto et soc. ⎪
> ,, ,, 151 ,, Margarita ⎭

Instead of Margaret (whose absence is curious) we have
St Justina of Padua, and after All Souls (c. 164) we have
St Prosdocimus, also of Padua.

That is to say, their names occur in the table at the end, not in
that at the beginning: but neither Justina nor Prosdocimus
appears in the text: but Hippolytus does. In short, the
second table disagrees with the first, and with the text.
There are no added local legends.

241. RIC. DE S. VICTORE ETC.

> Old marks
> D². 7. 33
> II. 3. 17
> O. 17. 2
> H. 4. 5

Vellum, 10 × 6⅗, ff. 1 + 181, double columns of 40, etc. lines.
Cent. xiii in several hands: also single lines, 56 to page, of
cent. xiv. 2 fo. Rursum crucifigentes.

Binding, old stamped leather over wooden boards: lettered A B̅D̅
on sides: clasps gone.

Collation: 1 flyleaf *a*⁴ 1¹² 2¹⁰ 3¹²–6¹² (wants 8) 7¹²–9¹² 10⁶ 11¹⁰
12¹² 13¹² (+ 1) 14¹² | 15⁸ (wants 1) 16¹².

Liber Acad. Marischall. Abredon.

From T. Reid, no. 21 in his list.

From St Paul's Cathedral: on iv *b* is an inscription in several
lines, of which 2½ are scribbled over, but in part legible.

Iste liber est datus......librarie ecclesie sci pauli apostoli lond/londonie

et omnis spiritus laudet domnum pro sc̄o pauli apostolo et doctore orbis et amico/dei omnipotentis ceraphico. i. ardente in dei amore.

Another line erased

...sus istius libri est.

It is entered in the old catalogue : see below.

At top of the page a list of contents.

In hoc vol. continentur tract. mag. Ricardi et qui uero desiderat ocupari honestis et sanctis meditacionibus legat uel audiat meditaciones de xii patriarchis (similar remarks about each tract).

Vtilis est vobis liber iste. non recedat a camera vestra. ne putrescat quod absit (erasure of some words : then a further list of items).

On the last page a later list of contents: and notes partly erased. One which is intact is noteworthy : In die s. basilii magni ego m. thomas gascoigne incepi oxonie in sacra theologia in die lune anno christi ihesu 1434

Gascoigne is the author of the *Liber Veritatum,* of which large portions were edited by Thorold Rogers (*Loci e Lib. Verit.*).

Other notes on these pages are his (e.g. at top of last page): nota Ivonem Carnotensem in sermonibus suis in loco Bradnestok (i.e. Bradenstoke Priory). Gascoigne had a considerable knowledge of monastic libraries.

    The four first leaves of the volume are in single lines in a charter-like hand. They contain

        De Sacramento Altaris .   .   .   . f. i

  Cautels of the Mass, beginning

    Quia summo opere cauendum est ne quis ad hoc sacramentum

  f. ii. Sequitur de quibusdam casibus que possunt contingere.

  iii *b.* Story of a madman in Apulia who continually said Kyrie eleison etc.

    Beatus Oswaldus regni culmine sublimatus

    Bede's story of the preservation of the hand which Aidan blessed.

  iv *a.* Magister Alanus, his saying to knights who inquired of him that the greatest courtesy was to give, and the greatest vulgarity to take away.

Deliverance of the soul of an imperator Alemannie by St Laurence.

On iv *b*, besides the lists, etc., a note on the sapphire in Ezekiel.

I. 1. Inc. tract. Mag. Ricarde canonici de S. Victore de patriarchis .   1
Audiant adolescentuli
—humana ratio applaudat. Amen.

2. De horilogio achaz . . . .   24 *b*
Denotatio quindecim graduum
—in dictis uanitas.

3. Inc. prefacio Mag. Hugonis de arra anime . . .   25 *b*
Dilectissimo fr. G.—exopto. Valete.
Inc. liber Hugonis de arra anime.
Loquar secreto—concupisco
(unfinished).

4. Inc. liber de consideracione Bernardi abb. Clarev: ad papam
Eugenium 33 (37)
Subit animum—finis querendi.

5. Hic est sermo beatiss. presbiteri (Ieronimi) de omnipotentia et
inuisibilitate et inmensitate atque eternitate dei et de menbris
dei uariisque affectibus more prophetico figuraliter ei assig-
natis 57 (61)
Omnipotens deus—hostibus fortis appareret.

6. Sermo de assumptione 59 (63)
Assumpta est maria...Non solum fratres
—in te tronum meum. Amen.

7. Inc. pref. S. Gregorii pape in exposicione libri Ezechielis
prophete. Dilectissimo etc. 61 (65)
Omelias que—auidius redeatur. Expl. pref.
Inc. omelia prima S. Gregorii pape in prima parte Ezech. proph.
Dei omnipotentis aspiratione
—roborare I. C. d. n. qui uiuit etc. per omn. sec. sec. Amen.

8. Exposicio Anselmi Cantuariensis archiep. supra euuangelium.
Intrauit ihesus in quoddam castellum 110 (114)
Intrauit—Quid ad gloriosam...meritis et precibus eius per I.C.
etc. per omn. sec. sec. Amen.

9. Another hand (on Confession).
Sequitur quomodo sacerdos debet procedere . . .   111 *b* (115)
De xii abusionibus claustri (Hugo de Folieto).

10. The former hand.
Inc. omelia prima S. Gregorii pape urbis Rome in extrema
parte Ezechielis 112 (116)
Quoniam multis curis prementibus
—ad perpetuam hereditatem erudit. Sit itaque gloria omnip.
d. n. I. C. etc. per omn. sec. sec. Amen.

The page is partly filled by notes of Gascoigne's: from Bede on the five loaves, ending with a note on Bede and date of his death in monasterio S. Ap. pauli quod iam dicitur 3arho vulgariter (cf. notes by him in MS. Lambeth. 202).

II. 11. In single lines: thick xivth-cent. script.

Didascalicon Hugonis de studio legendi. Inc. liber primus de origine arcium 159 (163)

Omnium expetendorum prima est sapientia

On the next leaf the script becomes much closer. f. 175 interrupts the text: it had notes on the recto, some by Gascoigne: some erased: verso blank.

Ends: et torpere ocio.

Didasc. Hug de studio legendi hic expl.

179 *b*, 180 *a* blank: on 180 *b* notes by Gascoigne.

Memorandum quod aº gracie Christi 1434º hec que sequuntur dixit michi Johannes de Dene de comitatu Glocestrie qui fuit inter saracenos cum soldano babilonie qui moratur in ciuitate vocata kar (Cairo) iuxta aquam (uel riuum) currentem vocatam nylle

primo dixit michi in octauis pentecostes quod in quodam libro legis machometi habetur et legitur omni vj feria in lingua hebraica et arabica ista uerba que sic sonant in nostra lingua ego machometus nuncius dei precipio vobis ut cum mortuus fuero sepiliatis me in lapide marmoreo incluso que est in ciuitate meke : et si ascendero post mortem : custodiatis fidem meam et cum descendero scitote quod non erit pax in toto mundo quousque una sit fides omnium. et tunc veniet rex henricus de norhtwest et rex johannes et isti facient vnam esse fidem omnium. hoc in quodam libro machometi et legitur omni vj feria inter saracenos. et vocatur liber ille alkorayn et continet legem ipsorum saracenorum traditum eis per maledictum machometum.

Item dixit michi quod predicta capella tegitur in parte inferiori tecti. cum adamantibus qui post mortem eius quando corpus eius fuit positum in predicta capsa ferrea extraxerunt illam capsam ita quod uirtute lapidum capsa illa pendebat in aere et populus estimabat quod corpus ascendebat ad tectum uirtute propria miraculose et non uirtute lapidum. et cecidit ad terram anno gracie 1428. quod ferrum corumpitur per rubiginem. et ideo quod iam cecidit capsa ad terram credunt saraceni finem mundi appropinquare. et sunt iam mille nonginta anni et 30 ex quo moriebatur et amplius. sed predictus iohannes dene nescit certum numerum.

Item dixit quod vocant saluatorem nostrum ihesum magnum prophetam et machometum nuncium dei et dominam nostram uirginem mariam perpetuam matrem magni prophete.

Item uocant sanctam katerinam consanguineam magni prophete
s · Ihesu Christi. et nota monasterium alborum monachorum
grecorum quod fuit ad tumbam s. Katerine uirginis iam
destructum est per arabicos pessimos qui non reguntur per
aliquem soldanum licet sint saraceni.

Item in ciuitate que uocatur dra que distat a ciuitate jerusalem
per xx miliaria est sancta crux noster saluatoris in bassa domo
sub terra per xiii passus. et predictus iohannes dene fuit cum
soldano et uidit soldanum intrantem ad sanctam crucem
(erasure) et sunt 7 ostia. antequam qui(s) potest intrare ad
illam sanctam crucem. et dixerunt sibi quod illa sancta crux
est integra et indiuisa et nullus potest intrare nisi soldanus.

Two lines partly erased.

......homo qui fuit. In next line mention of s. helena.

Next page: ipsum hominem ad ostium primum quando intrauit
soldanus

On the verso list of contents. Note by Gascoigne on Virginity,
with a reference to Jerome on Isaiah, which vidi in originali
Aᵒ Chr. 1433 quando fui opponens in sacra theologia oxonie.'
T. Gascoigne.

The other notes, except one already given, are erased.

The entry in the old catalogue of St Paul's, of 1458, *ap.* Dugdale,
Hist. p. 392, is:

Gregorius super Ezechielem. *rursum crucifigentes.*

Tract. de sacramenta Eukaristie.

Tract. Ricardi de S. Victore de patriarchis.

Tract. de arra anime incomplete, etc., ending with this:

Hugo in Didascalicon idest de studio legendi, and the note *In
uno vol.*

242. IN PSALMOS LXXI–CL.

Old marks
D². 7. 34
II. 3. 18
O. 4. 41

Vellum, 10½ × 6½, ff. 110, 39 lines to page. Cent. xii late, in a
rather irregular pointed hand, Italian apparently.

Binding, old green leather: thick coarse vellum.

Collation: 1⁸ (2⁶ misplaced: should be the last) 3⁸–14⁸.

From Dr Guise. Acad. Marischal. Abredon.

On f. 1 a late number (foreign). No. 12 (cf. no. **106**).

On 14*b*, the original last leaf, in two hands of cent. xv and
xvi (?):

Statio huius libri est in quinta sede.

Iste liber est monasterii caritatis sce marie et inscribitur hieronimo sed non uidetur hieronimi ex eo quod in ps. 58. eripe me de inimicis meis deus meus dicitur predicatores sicut canes arcere lupos a gregibus sicut fecit Ambrosius Augustinus hieronimus.

> The comment begins on Ps. 72.
>> Quam bonus Israel
>> Quasi dicat quam incomparabiliter est bonus deus.
>> israel. i. uidentium deum.
> It ends on the present f. 14*b*: on ps. 150.
> Nos quoque quia operis ac laboris magnitudinem terminauimus
>> IN spiritu dominum laudemus.
> At bottom is added a note on Pascha.

The script alters and also the quality of vellum: but I doubt whether the scribe changes. I think the book is North Italian.

The title of S. Maria de Caritate was not uncommon, especially for Cistercian houses: this may be the house at Milan or at Venice.

244. HISTORIA ECCLESIASTICA RUFINI.

Old marks
D². 7. 36
II. 3. 12
S. B. XVI. 8
O. 4. 1
H. 2 (or 4). 1

Vellum, 11⅛ × 8¼, ff. 99, double columns of 46 etc. lines.

Cent. xii late, in several good hands.

Binding, stamped leather, xvi, over wooden boards: remains of one of the clasps: lettered on each cover A̅B̅D̅.

2 fo. Incipit *or* si qua uero.

Collation: 1⁸–12⁸ (wants 1) 13 (four: the last a supply).

Liber Acad. Marischall. Abredon.

It is no. 17 in the list of T. Reid's books. Like others it belonged in cent. xv to T. Graunt who writes the colophon. It is therefore a St Paul's book: see on no. **10.**

> Inc. prol. Ruphini presbiteri ad cromatium ep. in ecclesiastica
>> historia (XXI. 461) . . . . f. 1
> Peritorum dicunt esse medicorum
>> —ad obitum theodosii augusti.
> Inc. capitula libri primi. Expl. cap.

Inc. prefatio b. Eusebii cesariensis ep. . . . . . 1 *b*
  Successiones—temptabimus. Expl. pref.
Inc. liber primus historiarum 2
  Incipiet igitur michi sermo
Lib. II. with capitula 9*b*, III. 17, IV. 26*b*, V. 35*b*, VI. 46*b*,
  VII. 58, VIII. 66*b*, IX. 74, X. 80*b* (a gap after 88), XI. 91.
f. 99 is a supply of cent. xv : ending
  percepturus premia meritorum.
Expl. lib. vndecimus eccl. hist. et sic totum opus. deo gratias.
  T. Graunt.
99*b* blank.

The initials to Books are handsome: that on f. 2, an I almost the length of the page, has its stalk panelled with gold.

248. ABERDEEN CATHEDRAL REGISTER.   { Old marks
                                                     { D². 7. 48

Vellum, 10½ × 7½, ff. 2 + 26 + 87, 30 lines to page (usually). Cent. xvi, partly in a good Gothic hand: with later additions by many scribes.

Binding, old stamped leather over wooden boards. The stamps are two decorative foliage panels: four metal bosses and corners to each cover: clasp.

Collation: A⁸ (1 flyleaf) B⁸–D⁸ (wants 4) E⁸–K⁸ (wants 1) L⁸ (wants 1) M⁸ (1 canc.) N⁸ O⁸ P⁶ Q (two).

The Kalendar not foliated originally: the text foliated in red at top from I to LXXXXI, with errors.

On the flyleaf: Necrologia Ecclesiae Cathedralis Aberdonensis Bibliothecae Coll. Regii Aberdonensis. Hunc librum MS. e libris D. Patricii Leslaei de Edden, Equitis, Consulis Abredeensis Georgius Leslaeus de Edden ejusdem ex filio Nepos et successor, auctoribus Archibaldo Setonio A M et Mᵈ Joanne Ker Graecarum Literarum Professore in dicto Collegio dono dedit mense Novembri A. AE. C. M. dcc. xxvii.

Contents.

  1. ff. 1–26 are in Kalendar form, with four lines to a day, largely
       blank: in red and black. Headline: Anniuersaria fundata in
       ecclesia Cathedrali Abridonen.
    Of the original entries the latest is of 1544: that of Alex.
       Galloway, of 1552, is added.
    The last leaf is gone (after f. 26).

2. A Register of deeds, beginning with one of Bp. William
   (Elphinstone) of 1537, blank shield in initial: apparently
   written by Alex. Galloway (rector of Kynkell).

There is some occasional decoration: on iii*b* initial with dove,
   v *a* two faces etc., xvi *b* initials AG and *az* a lion rampant *arg*
   xix a small picture of S. Michael and the dragon under a
   cusped arch.

On liii *b* a list of Misse quotidiane followed by particulars of
   the same.

On lvii *b* sqq.

> Repertorium in hoc regestro Cartarum contentarum per
> ven. virum mag. Alex. Gallouai rectorem a Kinkell
> fact'.

covering ff. i–xlix.

On lix *b*–lxv particulars of the anniversaries.

On lxv *b* to lxxvi (wrongly written lxxix) a further series of
   deeds beginning with

> Carta obitus d. Jacobi Kyncragg decani abirdonen. (of
> 1543).

The Gothic hand of Galloway's period continues to lxxvi *a*.

After this the deeds are in various hands of more modern type,
   the latest being of 1557. The two last have the notarial marks
   of John Chalmer and John Kalman.

249. REGISTRUM CAPELLANORUM CHORI   { Old mark
      ECCLESIE CATHEDRALIS ABERDONENSIS.   { D². 7. 40

Vellum, 10⅛ × 7, ff. 1 + 213 + 1, varying numbers of lines to page.
Cent. xv late to xvi (1552), in many hands.

Binding, old wooden boards covered with vellum: rebacked:
clasp.

The collation (eights) is hardly worth making.

On ff. 1–5 late charters have been added:

   (1) of 1547, (2) of 1546, (3) of 1552.

We then have hands of cent. xv writing charters of 1484, 1489,
1487 (f. 12), 1493 (13 *b*), 1450? (14 *b*).

At f. 15 another series: 1493, 1492, 1493 (f. 17 in Scots) etc.
Charters continue to f. 80, with later additions.

On 81–83 Inventories.

Charters resumed.

On 98 *b* letter of James V, 28th year 23 dec.

Copies of deeds resumed, continuing to the end.   There are

occasionally heraldic or decorative initials of a rude kind, e.g. 167, 176, 177 (two), 182 *b*, 184 *b*, 185 *b*, 187, 188 *b*: also a variety of notarial marks.

The Inventories are of more than local interest, and are given in full here. They are rather careless copies of rolls, perhaps, and some entries are unintelligible. But the list of nearly 140 books is a substantial addition to our stock of medieval catalogues.

f. 81. Iocalia.

In primis decem calices argentii deaurat'. Et decem patene deaurat'. Et una patena mutuat' in Rane per mag. thomam tynnyngam

Item una patena de numero illarum dict' perdita per eundem archidiaconum

Mem. quod unus de supradictis calicibus cum patena per mag. Joh. Clat deperdita pro quo ipse contulit nouum

It. mag. Henricus Rynde thesaur' contulit unum calicem argenteum partim deaurat'

It. unum calicem arg. per d. Ingerannum episc. portu de Capella de Rane

It. unum calicem deaurat' ex dono d. Walteri ogilby pro altari S. Iohannis

It. unus calex arg. pro altari b. Machorii dat' per d. Ricard. fortess decan. aberdon. Et sic in toto sunt quindecem calices et tredecem patene

It. unum crucifixum argent. deaurat' cum magno pede

It. una crux in qua est pars ligni dominici de arg.

It. una crux in qua est pars ligni s. andree de arg. deaurat' ex dono d. Gilberti ep.

It. una crux cum paruo pede et crucifixo de arg. deaurat' cum quatuor ymaginibus deaurat' situat' super curillo

It. una crux de arg. deaurat' cum tribus lapidibus ligno coopert'

It. crucem de auricalco

It. ex dono mag. henrici heruy cantoris Aberdon. unus annulus aureus cum a gren stan

It. ex dono eiusd. unum monile aureum cum tribus Rubeis et tribus peirl'.

It. ex dono eiusdem unus annellus argenteus cum magno capite in quo continetur crucifixus marie et Johannes

It. brachium argent's. fergusii cum ossibus eiusdem

It. una pixis de cristallo cum pede arg' deaurat' cum diuersis rel(i)quiis

It. le culp pro eukarist' de argent' deaurat'

It. due thece de auricalco pro reliquiis conseruand' quarum una habet sex ymagines ex parte claus' et unum altare cum calice depicto super altare depictum in qua continentur ossa s. elene katerine et s. margarete et ysaac patriarcharum et s. duthaci

It. in alia theca viz. de vestimentis b. uirginis marie et de pluribus aliis
viz. ossa petri et pauli et b. brigide de crinibus b. edmundi archiep.

It. unum Jocale eukaristie de arg. deaurat' ad modum castri cum le
bazillo dat.' per d. henric' de ly^tton ep. aberdon. In cuius summitate
ponitur Jocale aureum cum ymagine pietatis dat' per d. Joh. Frostar
de cyrstorfyn

It. unus annulus argenteus cum lapide de columpna dat' per Nicholaum
lesur

It. unus annulus aureus cum lapide de columpna dat' per elenam
de ly^tton

It. lapis cristalli de argent' coopert'

It. una pixis eburnea dat' per mag. Henricum Rynde

It. due corone de arg. deaurat' pro Christo et nostra domina cum
lapidibus quarum sex pecie fra(c)t' a coronis et seruantur in una
bursa per custod' thesaur'

It. quinque burse auree

It. quinque phiole argente(e)

It. tres ampulle argent' coopert' cuius una ampulla deperdit' ex missione
ad brechyn pro crismate per d. Willm donald capellanum d. episcopi

It. unus annulus argenteus cum lapide de cristallo quadrato dat' per
quendam scotum existentem in francia et per ipsum in scocia trans-
missum

It. unum lwche argenti deaurat' in qua continetur ymago s. olaui

It. duo cristall'

It. a pax brede de argent' deaurat' cum ymaginibus b. Crucis b. Marie
et S. Joh. Euvang. ex dono Reuerendi patris Thome ep. Aberdon.

It. ex dono eiusdem ep. duo candelabra deaurat'

81 b. It. peluis cum lotorio de arg. ex dono d. gilberti ep.

It. due pelues argent' pro lauacro in circumferenciis deaurat' dat' per
henricum ep. aberdon. cum circumscripcione utriusque peluis sic
incipiente. Henricus dei gratia ep. aberdon. fecit nos fieri ad magnum
altare ecclesie cathedralis eiusdem Anno d^ni etc. xxxiii et quicunque
nos ab isto altare alienauerit sit a deo et a nostra domina maledictus
et imperpetuum condempnatus amen

It. una casula serata pro duobus pelluis (*sic*).

It. unum turibulum argent'

It. unum magnum thuribulum argent. dat. per. d. Henricum Ly^tton ep.
aberdon.

It. custos thesaurarie habet iiij^or ?ferres de eodem thuribulo de arg'

It. due mitre una preciosa de peirlis et lapidibus preciosis. Et a parte
ante tresdecem lapides deficientes et a parte post xi lapides de quibus
restant sex lapides in cista communi et iiij^or pauones in dicta mitra
remanen' in dicta cista. Et tria pendilia aurea de dicta mitra in
predicta cista et quartum pendile absens

It. altera mitra de serico deaurat' cum lapidibus. Restant in toto cum
custode thesaurarie de lapidibus preciosis xi lapides

It. de dicta mitra in cista communi una pecia valde preciosa ad modum unius floris cum magno lapide Rubeo in medio et sex lapidibus in circumferenciis

It. unum par cerothecarum pro episcopo cum duobus Jocalibus ymaginibus sanctorum Jacobi et Johannis inclusis et in circumferenciis deaurat' unde unum perdetur (!) per d. nostrum Henricum ep. morauiensem

It. unus magnus annulus aureus et notabilis tantum (?) pro episcopo conueniens cum magno saphiro et lapidibus preciosis inclusis dat' per Alexandrum ep.

It. duo textus euangeliorum unus de arg. deaurat' et ailius de auricalco deaurat'.

It. duo baculi pastorales de arg. quorum unus est deauratus et caput alterius baculi deaurat' et melior baculus dat. per Alex. ep.

It. duo textus euangeliorum unus de arg. deaurat' et alius de auricalco deaurat' quorum unum caret ymagine b. virginis

It. quinque strenia (? scrinia) magna pro libris etc.

It. iiij^{or} ciste rotunde de pcia serat'

It. sex tagete magna quarum una fuit destructa tempore tynnyngham archidiaconi

It. a gret lettron cum quatuor candelabris ereis magnis de donacione d. Alex^{ri}. ep.

It. duo ornamenta pro pedibus sancte crucis cum duobus cristallis

It. iiij^{or} alia candelabra antiqua

It. duo candelabra pro magno altare de donacione mag. Henrici Rynde thesaur'

It. mem. quod henricus de lython ep. aberdon. contulit incudem magnum ecclesie et canonicis primo die Januarii dⁿⁱ M° cccc° xxxvij°.

It. una cathedra ferrea

It. a cressent etc.

———

Hic incipit inuentarium et registrum (librorum ?) ecclesie aberdonensis quos recepit mag. Duncanus de lython cancellarius ecclesie aberdon. xij° die mensis marcii anno dⁿⁱ M° cccc° sexagesimo iiij^{to}.
Et primo librorum theologie

1. Una parua minuta biblia in parua litera in secundo folio textus
    prolonge figur'

2. Una cum quaterno ante incept' biblie in secundo folio
    extensio ecclesie (?)
    et cum uno quaterno de interpretacionibus hebraicorum nominum in fine biblie incipien' *A. B.* et in fine *posim* (zuzim) *consilium*

3. Una biblia in asseribus in 2° folio incip.   *Et sub ne ste*
    non completus

4. Una biblia in asseribus noncomplet' in 2° fo. [f. 82]   *pene sillabice*

5. Una biblia non complet' in 2° fo.   *vixit*

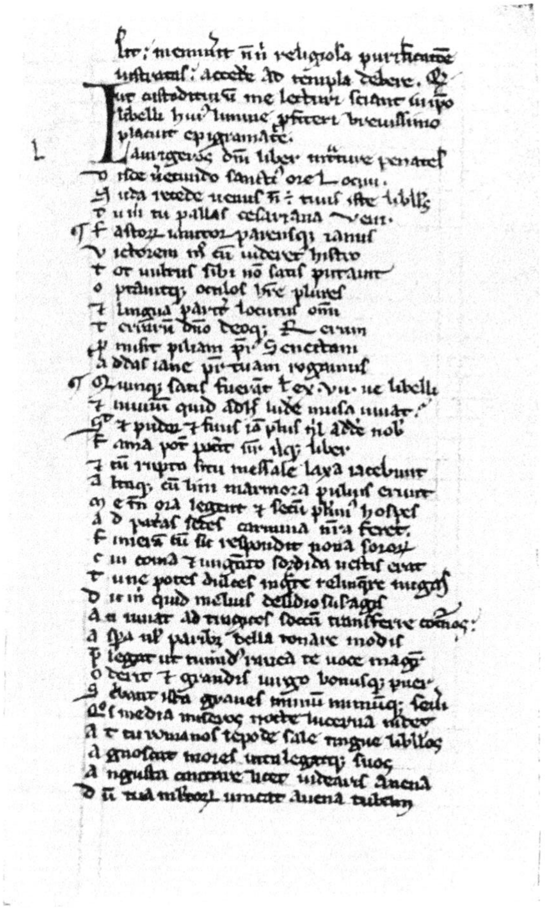

No. 152, folio 42, recto

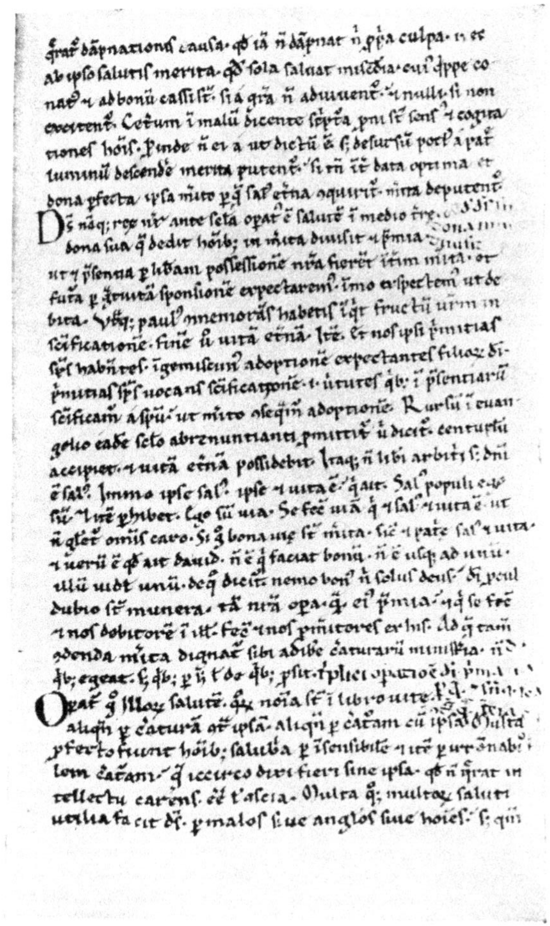

No. 156, folio 13, recto

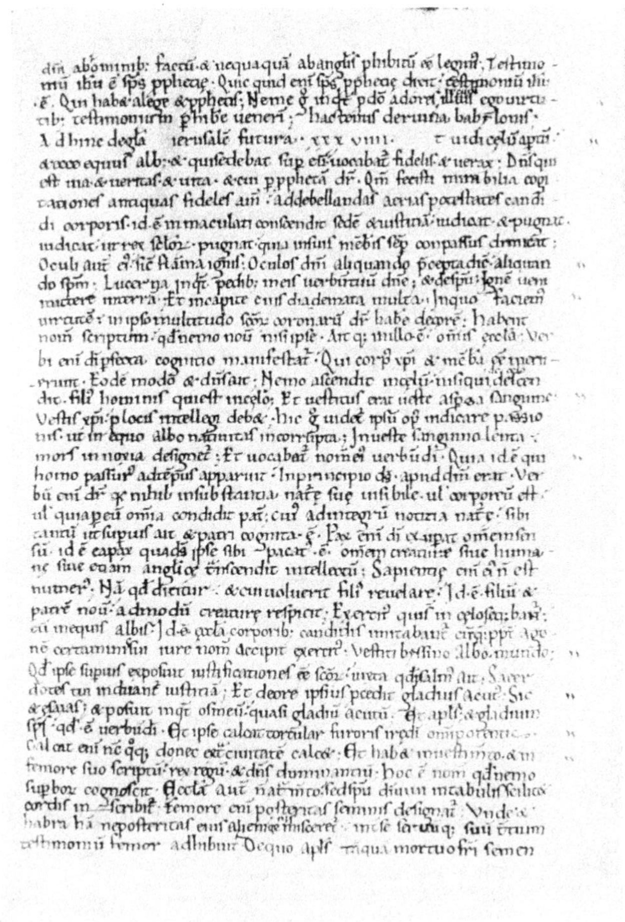

No. 216, folio 21, recto

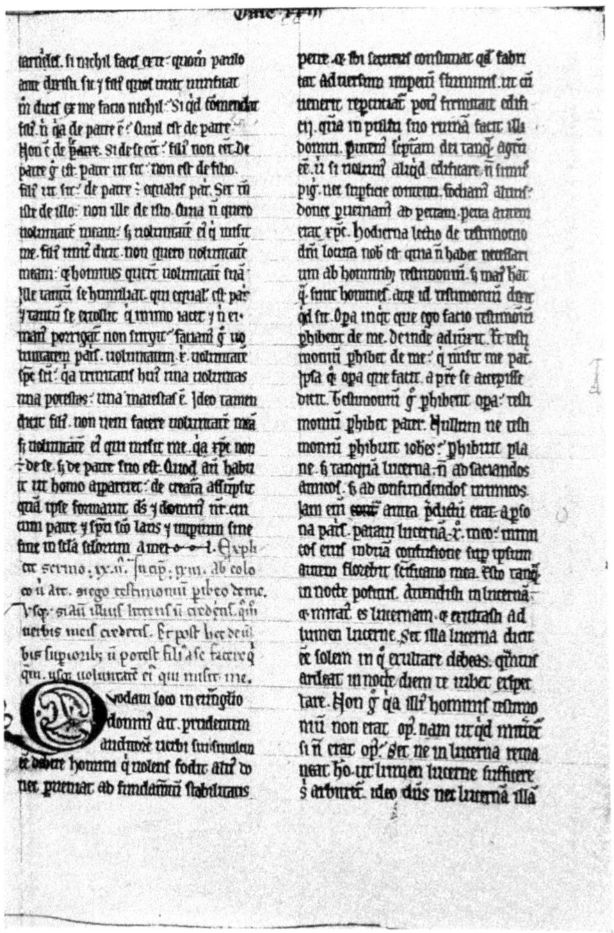

No. 219, folio 93, recto

6. Unus textus sentenciarum petri comestoris (!) incip. in 2° fo.
　　　　　　　　　　　　　　　　　　　　　　　uterum semel

7. Unus textus sentenciarum in 2° fo.　　　　　　*quare spiritus*

8. Libri leuitici numeri deutronomii in uno vol. in 2° fo.　　*de bobus*

9. Libri Josue Judicum Ruth Thobie Judith Hester in sec° fo.
　　　　　　　　　　　　　　　　　　　　　　in inferioribus
　　in uno vol.

10. Libri ezechiel et ysaias in (uno) vol. in 2° fo.　*ori imposuit*

11. iiij°ʳ libri Regum duo paralipomenon et duo libri machabeorum in uno
　　vol. in 2° fo.　　　　　　　　　　　　　　　*prophetarum*

12. Summa confessorum in 2° fo.　　　　　　　　*de usu pallii*

13. Sermones dominicales Jacobi Januensis in sec° fo.　　*an*

14. et sermones Jacobi Januensis de sanctis in 2° fo.　*vit singulariter*

15. Lectura super lib. sentenciarum in asseribus coopert. coreo albo in 2° fo.
　　　　　　　　　　　　　　　　　　　　　　quod angelus

16. Isydorus de summo bono et quidem (quedam) concordancie super libro
　　senicie (!) in 2° fo.　　　　　　　　　　　　*cuis est*

17. Secunda secunde fo. thome de aquino in (2°) fo.
　　　　　　　　　　　　　　　　quorum est intellectus

18. Aug'. de ciuitate dei in asseribus in 2° fo.　　*sententia*

19. Lectura sentenciarum in asseribus in primo fo. *spiritus eius ornauit celos*
　　et in 2° fo.　　　　　　　　　　　　　　　*inquantum*

20. Lectura sentenc. et inc. *Vtrum frui* et in 2° fo.　　*anime*

21. Tabula subtilis Scoti et inc. *Abstraccio* et in 2° fo.　*utrum habitus*

22. De proprietatibus rerum in uno vol. in 2° fo.　*Et spiritus sancti*

23. Alius liber de proprietatibus rerum in 2° fo.　　*nec ibid*

24. Manipulus [rerum] florum inc. in 2° fo.　　　*ad celeuciam*

25. Liber de naturis animalium inc. in 2° fo.　　*aquatilium*

26. Epistole senece ad paulum et lucillum cum xiiij tractatibus in 2° fo.
　　　　　　　　　　　　　　　　　　　　　in tua persona

27. Manipulus florum in 2° fo.　　*Aug*ᵘˢ *in libro de questionibus*

28. Questiones siue lectura sentenciarum que inc. in primo fo. *exemplo veri*
　　et in 2° fo.　　　　　　　　　　　　　　　*angelorum*

29. Exposicio b. ambrosii super beati immaculati 2° fo.　*Rīmus*

30. Liber confessionum b. Augustini in 2° fo.　*cedam (or cedaui)*

31. Tabule super Valerianum et inc. *ut de infrascripta* et in 2° fo.
　　　　　　　　　　　　　　　　　　　　　　Inferre

32. Liber ancelmi et inc. *Tres tractatus* et in 2° fo.　*veritatem*

33. Summa de sanctis et inc. *In baculo meo* et in 2° fo.　*B. (?) ut ad fidem*

34. Barnardus super genesim *Terra autem erat* et in 2° fo.　*addidit*

35. Summa Cantoris Parisiensis in 2° fo.　　　　*vias*
　　cum aliis diuersis tractatibus

36. Exposiciones epistolarum Pauli et in 2° fo.　*explicit*

37. Quolibita octam (occam) et inc. *Prima questio* et in 2° fo.   *in aliquo*

38. Questiones Joh. Scoti super primo sentenciarum et inc. *circa prologum* et in 2° fo.   *methafe*cam

39. In uno vol. Pastorale b. Gregorii b. Ambrosii de officiis et misterio ecclesie

40. Liber b. Barnardi ad Eugenium papam in 2° fo.   *mundi sunt*

41. Concordancie librorum sentenciarum et inc. *lybsolide* (?) et in 2° fo.

        ginui

42. Pastorale Ambrosii in 2° fo.   *episcopum non alitā*

43. Isydorus super vetus testamentum in 2° fo.   *quare autem primo*

44. Tituli sermonum quinti (!) partis collect' in 2° fo.   *contra adam*

45. Epilogacio tocius biblie in papiro in 2° fo.   *Audiens Jacob*

46. Barnardus ad Eugenium coopertus in parchameno in 2° fo.

        neque enim

47. Legenda aurea in 2° fo.   *de sancta maria magdalena*

48. Epistole pauli ad romanos in 2° fo.   *consecutos*

49. Psalterium glosatum in 2° fo.   *in via*

50. Legenda aurea in 2° fo. in textu   *de s. geruasio*

51. Psalterium pulcrum in 2° fo.   *qui habitat caput meum* in stallo de elon.

52. Unus liber qui dicitur Aurora editus mitrite (metrice) super biblia in 2° fo.   *ut zacharia*

53. Catho glosata in 2° fo.   *spectacle*

54. Hystoria troiana in 2° fo.   *In troianorum*

55. Magister de hystorie super biblia dat' per mag. henricum cantorem inc. in 2° fo.   *cro disposicionem*

56. Liber de ecclesiastica potestate ex donacione dat' (dicti) magri henrici in 2° fo.   *Est spiritualis*

57. Liber de confessionibus ex donac' Willmi Calabr*um* qui inc. *Misericors* et in 2° fo.   *in quo dotemur*

58. It. quinque libri in uno vol. ‖ 82 *b* ‖ primus de bellis assiriorum secundo de bellis francorum Tercius de bellis britonum Quartus de passagio ad terram sanctam Quintus de mirabilibus mundi inc. in 2° fo.

        dico autem presidem

    ex donacione magri henrici hervy cantoris

59. Scotus in libro sentenc. inc. *Samaritanus* et in 2° fo.   *nec creare*

60. Questiones magri Joh. Scoti super tres sentenc. in 2° fo.   *cludañt*

61. Unum pontificale solempne ex dono Jngerami ep. aberdon. inc. in 2° fo.

        seruos tuos

62. Unum aliud pontificale in 2° fo.   *ordo septem graduum*

63. It. unum aliud pontificale in 2° fo.   *luisti*

64. Bestiale et liber de ecclesiasticis officiis inc. in 2° fo.   *tendit finitis*

65. Sermones de quibusdam sanctis inc. de 2° fo.   *textus et asper*

66. Unum manuale in percamino inc. in 2° fo.   *ma queque*
    ex dono mag[ri] henrici Rynde

67. Unum pontificale inc. *Ad casulam* et in 2° fo. inc.   *benedictio*

Incipiunt libri Iuris

68. Unus liber decretalium inc. in 2° fo.   *ad salutem*

69. Alius liber decretalium in 2° fo.   *vidimus*

70. Alius liber decretalium in 2° fo.   *ex maria*

71. Decretales parue in asseribus et in 2° fo. in textu
           uariam esse fatetur inc. ℞ (Rubrica)

72. Alius liber decretalium in 2° fo.   *episcopus s̄c̄s̄ abbāt*
    per mag. Robertum stewart prebe[us] de turreff.

73. Decretum incipiens in 2° fo.   *quod est corrigat*

74. Decretum inc. in 2° fo. in textu   *prouincie* ℞

75. Decretum modice valoris tal' ablat' per mag. Joh. barber cantorem

76. Sextus glosatus per cardinalem in 2° fo in textu   *bus*
    coopertus nigro

77. Summa de casibus Astensis in 2° fo.   *noue legis*

78. Nouella Joh[is] andree super decretal' in duobus voluminibus prima pars
    in 2° fo.   *usque*

79. Et secunda pars in 2° fo.   *excepcionem*

80. Nouella Joh[es] andre super sextum in 2° fo.   *certa*

81. Et in mercurialibus in alio vol. coopertus pellibus viridibus in 2° fo.
                                          (blank)

82. Dinus de regulis Juris in pellibus veridibus in 2° fo.   *ciat*

83. Lectura super decretales in 2° fo.   *credit ecclesiam* (?)

84. Lectura Innocencij in asseribus in 2° fo.   *sedis*

85. Speculum iudiciale in 2° fo.   *singulis*

86. Aliud speculum iudiciale in 2° fo.   *mittere*

87. Roffredus de ordine iudiciorum in 2° fo.   *Rius*

88. Extrauagantes Joh. pape xxij glosatum per Gesselinum cum operatu
    (app-) Will[i] de monte landuno super clementinas in 2° fo.   *ac si*

89. Lectura Will[i] Tarleth super sextum in papiro in 2° fo.   *solum bene*

90. Rosarium archidiaconi super decretum in duobus voluminibus primum
    vol. in 2° fo.   *Jus naturale*

91. Secundum vol. in 2° fo.   *mathee*

92. Repertorium mag. Will[i] Durandi in 2° fo.   *non veni*

93. Summa Monaldi in 2° fo.   *Item abbas*

94. Martiniande (*sic*) decretorum et decretalium cum sacramentali Will[i] de
    monte hauduno in uno vol. in 2° fo.   *prelati*

95. Sextus et clementine cum lectura Joh. Andree in 2° fo.   *laboribus*

96. Apparatus archidiaconi in 2° fo.   *sponsare*

97. Cronica martini de papis et imperatoribus in 2° fo.   *te fili*

98. Sextus in 2° fo.   *incommutabilis*

99. Sextus et clementine in uno vol. cum apparatu Will[i] de monte landuno in 2° fo.   *fragranti diuina*

100. Lectura prima (?) Joh. Andr. super sexto in 2° fo.   *Jubemus*

101. Archidiaconus super sextum in 2° fo.   *hereticum*

102. Martiniana decreti et decretalium in 2° fo.   *quod abbas*

103. Willelmus de Mandagota super electionibus in 2° fo.   *post consensum*

104. Speculum iudiciale modici valoris in 2° fo.   *tradita*

105. Tancretus de iudiciis in 2° fo.   *pertractato*

106. Lectura Innocencii quarti super decretal' in 2° fo.   *con. i.*

107. Clementino(-e) cum constitucionibus Joh[is] pape XXII in uno vol. ‖83‖ in 2° fo. in textu   *manifestatis*

108. Prima pars henrici boyk et in 2° fo.   *i. q. septima*

109. Secunda pars henrici boyk in 2° fo.   *loquitur*

110. Distinctionis decretalium mag[ri] Petri sumne in 2° fo.   *Ria sabbati*

111. Summa Goffridi de Trano in 2° fo.   *getur*

112. Ordo iudiciarius in 2° fo.   *uti vel*

113. Summa Raymundi de matrimonio in 2° fo.   *permutacionis*

114. Decretales et inc. in textu *Filii hominum* et in 2° fo.   *dignitatis*

115. Apparatus Will[i] de monte lauduno super clementinis in 2° fo.   *hibens*

116. Receptorium (!) Will[i] durandi in 2° fo.   *ignoranciam*

117. Una glosa decret' sine asseribus *Hec* in textu

118. Liber de extrauagantibus Joh[is] pape XXII cum apparatu Gesselini et cronica bruti ex dono d. Alexandri Kynnyndrunde ep. et inc. in 2° fo.   *iudicium*
in textu et in glosa   *nulli*

119. Tractatus Will[i] de monte handuno et inc. *Karissimo filio suo* et in 2° fo.   *effectus uerborum*

120. Una rotula de cronicis ex utroque latere script' et inc. in primo latere   *quinque plagas*
et in 2° latere   *principio mundi*

121. Decret' cuius textus inc. in 2° fo.   *penitus officio*
ex donacione venerabilis viri mag[ri] thome edname quondam canonici aberdon.

122. Alius liber decretalium in 2° fo.   *ad illam communem*
ex donac' eiusdem mag[ri] thome

123. Receptorium henrici buyk in 2° fo.   *utrum in eleccionibus*
ex donac' eiusdem

124. Unum temporale notatum ad stallum de Clat donat' per eundem in 2° fo.   *te spiritus*

125. Unum breuiarium ad altare s. andree in 2° fo.   *Presta quesumus*
ex donac' eiusdem

126. Unum psalterium in 2° fo.   *ipsi in deo eius*
     ligand' ad altare antedictum s. andree ad beneplacitum filii sui mag^{ri}
     duncani scherar prebend^{us} de Clat

Libri Juris ciuilis

127. Digestum vetus in 2° fo.   *nostrorum ordinacione*
     in textu   *premunirent*

128. Lectura super codice incipiens *Cum post* et in 2° fo.
                                           quandoque (?) *ponitur*

129. Apparatus super codice et inc. *Juris operam* et in 2° fo.   *quod constare*

130. Digestum vetus inc. in 2° fo.   *quod communicare non possit*

131. Digestum nouum de dono mag^{ri} Thome forstar in 2° fo. in textu
                                                  prohibetur

132. Codex in 2° fo. in textu   *cum nue aduersantur*

133. Casus longi digesti noui et inforciati in 2° fo.   *non habeo*

134. Summa Roffredi Juris ciuilis in 2° fo.   *non sit*

135. Cinus super codicem in litera *multum curvent* in 2° fo.   *via*

136. Codex ex dono mag^{ri} thome frostar in 28 (*sic !*)
     in Rubro de sacrosanctis ecclesiis non reperitur

137. Liber codicis ex dono eiusdem in 2° fo.
     in Rubro de sacrosanctis episcopis in nigro inc.   *hec est*

138. Digestum in 2° fo.   *opus fiat etc.*

---

250. INVENTORY OF PLATE, VESTMENTS ETC.   { Old mark
                                              { D². 7. 50

Vellum, 8⅜ × 6, ff. 47, 15 lines to page. Cent. xvi (1549), in
large Gothic script, by more than one scribe. Binding original,
stamped leather over wooden boards, metal corners, clasp, and
small central bosses.

Collation: hardly practicable.

Liber Coll. Regii Aberdon.

In pencil: 'from the Scougals.'

f. 1. A blank.
     On 1 *b* within a painted circle a shield *az* a lion rampant *arg*
         crowned *or* langued *gu.* At top the initial M in gold: on *L.*
         and *R.* H G.
     Motto on scroll: Memorare.
     Inc. Inuentarium Iocalium...eccl. cathedralis Aberdonensis   . f.   2
     —per ven. vir. mag. Alexandrum Gallouay eiusd. ecclesie
         canonicum ac prebendarium a Kynkel in eadem actum ap.
         Canoniam Aberdonen. Idibus ianuarii (1549)...post redemp-
         tionem eorundem de manibus quondam Jacobi forbes a

corsinda suorumque satellitum raptorum. Et per Reu. in Chr. patr. ac dom. dom. Gul. Steuart aberdonen. Ep. nuper defunctum non absque ingenti pecunie summa redempta. Before their recovery many of the Jocalia had been damaged or alienated, to the great loss of the Church and in contravention of the law.

List of chalices f. 3.

Sequuntur Jocalia ex antiquo per diuersos pontifices et alios
    Christifideles oblata ut infra   6

Description follows. A note of 1587 on 11 *b*.

Item per reu. in Chr. patr. ac dom. Thomam Spens quondam
    Ep. Aberdon.   12

Item per...Vilhelm. Steuart quondam Ep. Aberd. . . .   12 *b*

Late note on 13 *b*.

Vasa et iocalia...per Gauinum...Aberd. Ep. donata eccl. Aberd.
    comperta post reductionem eorund. ad eccl. per supradictos
    ablatores sequuntur   14

Note of weight 18 *b*. 19 *a* blank.

Pro pontificali d. Episcopi Aberdonie . . . . .   19 *b*

Note of weight 22 *b*.

Sequuntur vasa enea per...Gauinum et suos executores empta .   23

24 *b* blank.

Inuentarium ornamentorum...altaris eccl. cathedr....fact. per
    supradict. mag. Alex. Gallouay 1549   25

Vestments. Gifts of Bp. Elphinston   29

Ornamenta summi altaris huius templi per...Gauinum...Ep. .   31 *b*

Account of the seizing of the Jocalia in 1544 by Jac. Forbes of
    Corsinda, when they were being carried off to be hidden (by
    order of Bp. Steuard) from the English and their redemption
    for 600 marks . . . .   38 *b*

          Demum huius ecclesie calamitatem

Marginal note that the document was produced in Court 15 Jan.
    1556 by Jo. Leslie.

Description in Scots of certain pieces not recovered . .   40

Ornaments of the altar of the Virgin . . . . .   42 *b*

   ,,   ,,   ,,   St Michael   43

   ,,   ,,   ,,   St Katherine   44

   ,,   ,,   the Virgin of the hospital   45

   ,,   ,,   the altar of St Maurice . . . . .   45 *b*

46 *b* and 47 blank.

At top of i *a* is a distich:

          O sacral seat wherein Astrea still
          With æquitie the sword & ballance beares.

Most of the initials have a blank shield surmounted by a mitre, on coloured ground.

253. Ricardus de Media Villa.

$\left\{\begin{array}{l}\text{Old marks}\\ \text{d. 3. 14}\\ \text{O. 4. 7}\\ \text{II. 3. 40}\end{array}\right.$

Vellum, $11\frac{1}{2} \times 8\frac{1}{2}$, ff. 209, double columns of 55 lines. Cent. xv, in a fine small hand, doubtless Italian.

Binding, red morocco of cent. xviii.

Collation: 1^{10}–20^{10} 21^4 22^6 (wants 6).

At top of f. 1 in a modern hand: Liber Academ: Marischallanae.

Contents.

Ricardi de Media Villa quaestiones super librum IV Sententiarum .   .   .   .   f. 1

Innoua signa et immuta mirabilia

—A quo calore et frigore nos defendat et ad gloriam electorum
perducat d. I. C. qui cum etc.—per omn. sec. sec. amen.

Distinctio prima. *Samaritanus.* In primo libro determinat

Dist. L. ends 193 *b*: paratus essem humiliter retractare.

Expl. quartus lib. super sent. edditus a fr. Richardo de media
uilla de ordine fr. minorum.

A table of the questions .   .   .   .   .   .   193 *b*

ending 209 *a*: Expl. tituli questionum quarti lib. super sent.
editi a fr. Richardo etc. (ut supra). 209 *b* blank.

There is a handsome initial containing a fish on f. 1: other initials in red and blue. The book is very clean and little used.

This work was printed at Paris 1504 and at Venice without date.

254. Aristotelis Politica.

$\left\{\begin{array}{l}\text{Old marks}\\ \text{O. 4. 8}\\ \text{H. 2. 2}\\ \text{II. 4. 3}\\ \text{D}^2. \text{7. 46}\end{array}\right.$

Vellum, $11\frac{3}{8} \times 8$, ff. 2 + 125, 28 lines to page.

Cent. xv, in an exquisite Roman hand: written by Johannes Andreae.

Binding, old brown leather.

Liber. Acad. Marischall. Aberdon.

Collation: 2 flyleaves 1^{10}–12^{10} 13 (five).

On flyleaf. Volumen m^{ri} richardi iruying (xvi) and, later, M. R. Irving. At end, in neat Roman hand, Volumen Magistri Richardi Iruing 1603 13 Maii.

Titles etc. throughout are in faint red capitals widely spaced.

Contents.

Leonardi Arretini prefatio in libros Politicorum Aristotelis   f. 1
Inter moralis disciplinae praecepta
—ad uitam suscepturos. Finis proemii in lib. polit. Aristotelis.
Po. liber primus inc. Leonardus arretinus traduxit lege feliciter   2
Quoniam videmus omnem ciuitatem
Lib. II. 13 b; III. 31 b; IV. 50; V. 67 b; VI. 89; VII. 98; VIII.
116 b,
ending 124 a : possibile ac decens.
Politicorum aristotelis liber octauus et ultimus quam/124 b/
Leonardus Arretinus e Greco in Latinum interpretatus est.
Ioannes Andree de Colonia hunc librum scripsit quem tandem
gratia divina absolvisse letatur Deo gratias referens infinitas.

The version was made 18 years after that of the Ethics, and was dedicated to Eugenius IV (1431–47): the translator died in 1444.

The decoration is of the familiar Florentine sort: initials in gold on fields of blue, green and pink, filled with white branchwork.

Each Book has one, and on f. 1 is a full border of the same with *putti* and birds, but no heraldic adjunct. The work is excellent.

255. Bernardus de Gordonio.

Old marks
D². 7. 61
Θ or O. 2. 19

Paper, 11 × 8¼, ff. 202, double columns of 50 lines. Cent. xv late 1462), in a very ugly current hand.

Binding, stiff vellum.

Collation: not worth making.

Lib. Coll. Reg. Aberdon.

At top of f. 1 a name, possibly M^rcoll.

1. Inc. Lilium medicine magistri Bernardi de Gordonio   .   . f. 1
A band of rude ornament down the page on *l*.
Interrog(at)us a quid (quodam)
—a. d. M.CCC. tercio mense Julii.
Capitula.
Febris est calor   .   .   .   . 1 b
Pars II. 39; III. 70 b; IV. 92; V. 115; VI. 142 b; VII. 159 b.
—abolere uetustas.

2. De pulsibus (change of hand) 178
   Pulsus est numerus
   —paribus. Et sic est finis.
   186 *b* (half leaf) blank.
3. De urinis: with comment 187
   Dicitur urina. Iste liber diuiditur in duas partes
   Ends 202 *a*: non dicitur illud nisi (illegible).
   In hoc expl. tract. de pulsibus (!) editus a mag. bernardo de
   guordonio in studio montis pursullani et scriptus per me
   Jacobum fodr*i*ngam scotum primo die mens. marcii a.d.
   m°cccc° sexages. secundo.
   Receipts added. 202 *b* blank.

260. ALEXANDER DE VILLA DEI ETC. { Old marks
                                        { ϴ. 2. 15

Paper, 11⅜ × 8¼, ff. 241, double columns of 46 etc. lines. Cent. xv,
in two very ugly hands.

Binding, old stamped leather over wooden boards, clasp gone.
The stamps are of two kinds, a circular motto and lozenges with a
fleur de lys, and a beast with branching tail.

Collation: 1²⁰ (wants 1) 2²⁰–12²⁰ (wants 13, and 16–20 blank) 13⁸.
Liber Coll. Regii Aberdon.

1. Alexandri de Villa Doctrinale cum commento . . . . f. 1
   Domine labia etc.
   O deus triclinium unitatis trine
   Ortus et exordium tocius doctrine
   Tu meum principium guberna diuine
   Cui tres persone tria nomina sunt sine fine.
   The preface proceeds for a time in rhyme, and then in prose.
      The text of the Doctrinale begins to be written large on 18 *b*.
   Scribere clericulis paro doctrinale nouellis pluraque doctorum
      hic ostendit modum.
   The end of the verse-text may have gone with a leaf removed
      after 232. The whole ends 233 *a*.
         ut panthus etc.
               Expl. regule versuum etc.
   233 *b* blank.
2. In single lines (except 239 *b*). 234 *a* blank.
   A tract on Dictamen by Laurence of Aquileia . . . 234 *b*
   Ad doctrinam dictaminis intendere cupientes
   The prologue ends with memorial verses.
   Uniuersis tabellionibus ciuitatis Bononie dominis et amicis
      carissimis Laurencius Aquilagius salutem. The formulae are
      arranged in eight Tabulae,
   ending on 241 with forms of salutation in verse, ending
   Quot sunt virtutes tot vobis mando salutes. The rest gone.

261. Super Organon.

$$\left\{ \begin{array}{l} \text{Old marks} \\ \text{O. 1. 21} \\ \text{D}^2. \text{ 7. 67} \end{array} \right.$$

Paper, $11\frac{1}{2} \times 8\frac{1}{4}$, ff. 281, 48 lines to a full page. Cent. xv late, in a hideous and much abbreviated hand.

Binding, brown calf over wooden boards, with hatched lines. There have been five metal bosses on each cover.

Liber Coll. Regis Aberdonensis (f. 1).

Collation: not worth making.

Contents.

Questions on the Liber predicabilium . . . . . . f.	1
Round the initial C in large letters	
(C)irca inicium libri Predicabilium Porphirii quidam incipiunt copii.	
Queritur primo quot sunt habitus intellectuales.	
Cum sit necessarium grisarori et ad eam que est apud Aristotilem (Isagoge of Porphyry)	7 b
Queritur quomodo intitulatur liber predicabilium porphirii.	
f. 30 inserted: another hand.	
Ends 42 a: verso blank.	
Super librum Predicamentorum	43
Queritur utrum de decem principiis sit sciencia	
Ends 102 a: verso blank.	
Circa inicium Primi libri Periarmenias Aristotilis . . .	103
Queritur utrum de enunciacione sit sciencia	
Lib. 1 ends 131 a: verso blank.	
Quoniam autem est aliquando affirmacio significans . .	132
At 144 a Finitur vetus ars. 144 b, 145 blank.	
Super libros Priorum	146
179 b blank. Lib. 11. begins f. 214: 216 b blank.	
221 in another hand.	
Super Topica	222
Circa inicium libri thopicorum Aristotilis.	
Queritur primo utrum noticia	
On this page are scribbled names: ego Andreas Blake manu propria. Alexander (Iru)yng manu propria	
Lib. 1. ends 250. Verso blank. Lib. 11. 251.	
Super librum elenchorum	264
ending 281 a.	
On the verso are scribbles, xv and xvi, e.g.:	
Mag. Andreas Gallaway	
Paulus seruus seruorum dei,	
and a longer one in French:	
la sus a J. voq'...que demande (part of a draft of a letter).	

It resembles 223.

262. Petrus de Ancharano.
$$\left\{ \begin{array}{l} \text{Old mark} \\ \text{O. 1. 16} \end{array} \right.$$

Paper, $11\frac{1}{2} \times 8\frac{3}{4}$, ff. 145 +6, double columns of 45 lines. Cent. xv (1484), in a very ugly hand.

Binding, old stamped leather over wooden boards: circular stamps of six-petalled flower, bird, and deer. Clasp gone.

Liber Coll. **Regii** Aberdonensis.

Collation: 1^6 (wants 5) 2^8 3^{12}–13^{12} ‖ 5 paper flyleaves and 1 vellum.

On the first and last leaves (xv late): liber mag^{ri} Willelmi de Elphinston.

Contents.
Petri de **Ancharano** Repetitiones . . . . . . f. 1
1. (Possessor). Solent iurisconsulti cum materia utilis et quotidiana
—in secula benedicamus.
Repetitum per me petrum de ancharano mag. utriusque...in
magistra arg. alma Ciuitatis Bononie studiorum matre ibi
regentem cathedram, 1398, An. xxi mens. febr.
(Sexti Clementinarium), followed by a summary of the topics . 46
2. Peccatum. Quia sequens regula 48
ending 71: postea Bononie redegi 1412 die tercia Iunii Ego
petrus de ancharano etc.
Summary 71.
3. Peccati venia. Super...et proxima 72
ending 89 *b*: m°. cccc°., xij. per me petrum de ancharano etc.
Summary 89 *b*.
4. Ea que 91
ending 117 *b*, no year mentioned.
Summary 117 *b*.
5. Accessorium 119
ending 145 *a*.
On 145 *a* verses by the scribe. He seems to have been ordered
to write the book by Villelmus sapidus. The date is thus
given:
Nam maris et celi primordia quadruplicati (i.e. m. cccc.)
L semel x ter et i quater hec finem tibi scripti (= l. xxx. iiii.)
Monstrant. atque veram dant counita datam.
The verses are as bad as the hand.

The author died 1416. On him see Tiraboschi, *Hor. Lett. Ital.* V. II. 370.

263. BOETHIUS.
ARISTOTELIS ETHICA.

$\left\{\begin{array}{l}\text{Old marks}\\ \text{D}^2.\ 7.\ 69\\ \Theta.\ 2.\ 16\end{array}\right.$

Paper, $11\frac{3}{4} \times 8\frac{1}{4}$, ff. 108 and 160, two volumes, double columns of 50, 44, 43 etc. lines. Cent. xv, in several hands; those of the scribes Wallace and Morris neat, others abominable.

Binding, wooden boards covered with parchment. Clasps gone.
Collation: not practicable. The book has suffered from damp, and the binding is tight.

Liber Coll. Regii Abredon.

On f. 1: Iste liber pertinet Iohanni Vaus: studenti alme uniuersitatis (Aberdon.). Another inscription cut off the bottom of the leaf.

At the end: Ex libris collegii Aberdonensis ex dono magistri Joannis Vaus regentis gramaticorum.

> I. Boethius de Consolatione Philosophie cum commento.
>   Prol. Tempore quo Gothorum rex—et iusticiam *Carmina qui quondam,* hunc librum de consolacione philozofie in quo per dyalogum
>   Lib. II. 22, III. 40, IV. 63 *b*, v. 79 *b*,
>   ending 92 *a* ab ipso recipiatis. Expl. finis etc.
>   92 *b* blank.
>
> | | |
> |---|---:|
> | Table to the five Books . . . . . . | 93 |
> | Sententiae from them in alphabetical order . . . . | 96 *b* |
> | Agrorum pulcritudo | |
> | Sententiae from (Ps.-)Boethius de disciplina scolarium . . | 103 |
>
>   ending 104 *b*: Expl. sentenciarii ven. boecii super de cons. phil. et disc. scol. compendiose et artificialiter collecti sec. ord. alphabeti.
>   Jam scripsit totum pro cristo da sibi potum
>   Qui scripsit scriptum caput eius sit benedictum.
>   Wil^{us} Walace.
> 105–108 blank.
>
> II. Aristotelis Ethica cum commento   I
>   Iste est liber ethicorum Aristotelis qui principali diuisione diuiditur in 10 libros.
>   After Lib. I the hand is abominable. After Lib. VIII it becomes neat again.
>   Ends 160 *a*: leges, etc.
>   Expl. exposicio libri ethicorum aristotilis noue translacionis finita colonie per manum morris etc.

271. PSALTER AND HORAE.

$$\left\{ \begin{array}{l} \text{Old marks} \\ \text{II. 5. 5} \\ \text{C}^2. 4. 81 \\ \text{MSS. 4. 22} \\ \text{O. 4. 14} \\ \text{H. III. 1} \end{array} \right.$$

Vellum, $8\frac{1}{2}$ × 6, ff. 230, double columns of 23 lines. Cent. xv, in good rounded French hand.

Binding, trim leather (xix) with stamp of Marischal College.

The collation is not practicable: the quires have been largely misbound.

There is some faint writing in English (xvi) on f. 1 a.

On the last page is this record (an erased one above is illegible): Edwardus Conwey the sonne of John Conwey knyght was borne at Arrowe the ffowertene day of August in the ffyfth yere of the reign of Quene Elyzabeth A° d^ni 1563 vnder the signe of Cancer. And at his Christenyng Humfrey Asshfold of heythropp Esquier Edward Morgan of lytell Comberton gent. were Godfathers And Anne Grey of Enfyld widow was Godmother.

Little Comberton is in Worc^s.

On f. 11 in the border is a shield of six parts 1, 3, 5 *az* a greyhound's head erased *arg* collared *gu* and *or*, 2, 4, 6 *arg*.

Probably no. 24 or 25 of T. Reid's books.

Contents. Kalendar in red and black, not full   .   .   . f.   1
Sequences of the Gospels. Mark only   7
Memoriae, much mutilated: End of Anne (8), Magd. 8*b*,
    Katherine 9, end of Margaret 10, 10*b* blank, John Bapt. 11,
    Thomas Cant. 11*b* (beginning).
Hours of the Virgin. Use of Sarum, beginning imperfect
    in the hymn at Matins.
f. 16 has parts of two Prayers. O Ihesu uitis uera and D. d.
    omnip....da michi famulo tuo N. uictoriam
f. 17 continues with Lauds.
f. 21 end of Office of the Dead and beginning of Commendations.
f. 22 continues the Hours (sext).
None 25*b*.
f. 30. Memoria of St Erasmus and beginning of Fifteen Oos of
    St Bridget.
f. 31. Five Joys   Gaude virgo mater christi

f. 31 *b*. Gaude flore virginali

f. 32. Salve regina farced, beginning imperfect.

f. 33. End of O intemerata. 33 *b* Obsecro te, imperfect.

f. 35. Seven Joys, imperfect.

f. 37. Prayers to the Five Wounds, imperfect.

f. 38. Prayer of Bede (of the Seven Words).

f. 39. Continuation of Fifteen Oos.
Libera me 43 *b*.

f. 44, 45 prayers at the sacrament, imperfect.

f. 46. Seven Psalms and Litany, beginning imperfect.

f. 56. Office of the Dead, beginning imperfect, also Commen
dations, with gaps.

86 *b*. Rubric to Psalter of St Jerome, gap, followed by rest of
psalter 87–95 *a*. 95 *b* blank.

At f. 96 begins the Psalter, at
qui iudicatis terram (ii. 10),
and continues to the end, with Cantica (213 *b*) and Litany.
The beginnings of the Nocturnes have been removed and
there may be other small gaps.

The Kalendar is Sarum without SS. Osmund, Chad or Winifred.
The hand is foreign: we have S. Augustini primi angelorum
apostoli (!). The first Litany (f. 52) has no English Martyrs
but Thomas. *Conf.* Cedda...Suichine Burine; ends Prisca
Tecla Edita Affra. And the second Litany at the end is
precisely the same.

Decoration. Line and leaf borders with insertions in colour.
Pictures of not more than decent execution: foreign. Most
have been removed. The survivors are:

f. 7 in text. Mark writing in a room, winged lion by him.

f. 8 *b* in text. Mary Magd. long hair and gold casket, in room.
Katherine, crowned, with sword, standing on Maxentius
(turbaned, with scimitar).

f. 25 *b*. Nones of Virgin. Presentation: several attendants,
Simeon in cope and mitre.

f. 37. Initials with pictures of the Wounds in *L.* hand, side
and both feet.

f. 38. Initial. Crucifixion with Mary and John.

272. HORAE.

$\left\{ \begin{array}{l} \text{Old marks} \\ \text{II. 5. 6} \\ \text{C}^2\text{. 4. 82} \\ \text{H. 3. 33} \\ \text{O. 4. 17} \end{array} \right.$

Vellum, $7\frac{1}{4} \times 5$, ff. 131, 18 lines to a page. Cent. xv early, in good English hand.

Binding, calf (xviii).

Collation: a^2 (1 pastedown) 1^6 2^8–7^8 8^2 9^8 10^2 11^8–14^8 (wants one) 15^8 16^4 17^{10} 18^{10} (wants 10).

Marischal Coll.

On f. 127 is an entry in English, erased and revived, of the birth of Nicholas Cra-ford, 1 June 1537, 29 Hen. 8: names of godparents difficult.

Probably no. 24 or 25 of T. Reid's books.

Contents. Kalendar in red and black . . . . . f. 1
Hours of the Virgin : sec. usum Sarum.
Memoriae in Lauds include : John Bapt., Laurence, John Ev.,
    Peter, Thomas of Cant., Andrew, Stephen, George,
    Nicholas, Magd., Katherine, Margaret.
Hours of the Cross are intercalated.
After Compline and Salve regina are
Five Joys (Gaude virgo mater christi) 46
with collects.
O intemerata, 47 *b*; O domine glorie, 49; Prayer of Bede, 49 *b*;
    Aue I. C., 51 *b*; D. d. omnip....da michi famule tue
    uictoriam, 52; Salue sancta facies, 53 *b*; and other prayers,
    incl. Veni creator, 55, and Memoria of St Christopher, 56.
Seven Psalms and Litany 57
After Fidelium deus is Pietate tua quesumus and Hec or.
    dicatur ad placitum. Per horum omnium et aliorum sanct-
    orum, 74 *b*.
Office of the Dead 75
Commendationes animarum, 1st leaf gone 105
Psalms of the Passion 117
Psalter of St Jerome 128
ending imperfect in a prayer. Liberator animarum
The Kalendar, in a delicate script often seen in Kalendars of
    this period, has at foot of each page a prognostic in English
    of thunder, e.g.:
Feb. And yf it thono^r in ffeuer it betokyneth deth of many people
    and most of riche men.

Mar. 1. Albane (for Albine) ep. c.

,, 2. Cedde ep. c.

Ap. 21 added. Hoc die incepit J. T. sacerdos celebrare pro anima Elizabeth hames.

June 11 added. Obitus henr. ducis Warr'.

July 2 added. Visitacio S. m. virg. duplex fest. cum Oct. cum regimine chori.

,, 10 added in red. Apud villam northam' fui...

Oct. 17 added. S. Etheldrede v. ix. lect.

Nov. 3 ,,   S. Wynefride v. et m. ix. lect.

,, 14 ,,   S. Herkenwaldi ep. c.

Dec. 4 ,,   S. Osmundi c. ix. lect.

Edith is omitted.

In the Litany: *Martyrs* end Albane Thoma Edwarde. *Conf.* include Cuthberte, Dunstane. *Virgins* Columbina...Petronilla, Radegundis, ending with Spes Karitas Castitas.

There are no pictures, but each principal division has a very fine initial of the regular English type, in which the letter is quartered in blue and pink, and green is used. There is no little gold, and the execution is admirable. Smaller initials are also well done.

273. HORAE (AMIENS).   { Old marks C². 4. 83

Vellum, 7 × 5, ff. 126, 16 lines to page. Cent. xv late, in a poor French hand (two hands at least).

Binding, black leather with oval stamp of Crucifixion (xvii ?).

Collation : 1⁶ 2⁶ 3⁸ (7, 8 canc.) 4⁸ (one canc.) 5⁸–8⁸ 9¹² (two canc. ?) 10⁸ 11⁸ (+ 3) 12⁸ 13⁸ 14¹⁰ 15⁸ (one canc.) 16⁸ (wants 8).

Two late engravings pasted on flyleaf.

Stamp: Ex bibl. Univ. et Coll. Regal. Aberdon.

Contents:

Kalendar in blue red and black, in French .	.	. f.	1
Sequences of the Gospels (John and Luke only) .	.	.	13
Obsecrate 15 *b.*			
Oraison de saint Fremin le confes. *added* .	.	.	18*b*
Hours of the Virgin (use of Amiens) .	.	.	19
De sainct Fremin le martir, *added* .	.	.	59
Seven Psalms and Litany . . .	.	.	60
Hours of the Cross 74, of the Holy Ghost .	.	.	76*b*
Office of the Dead . . .	.	.	79

No. 686, folio 43, verso

No. 274, folio 157, recto

tare non oportere·

HILARII PICTAVENSIS EPI
DE FIDE CATHOLICA CONTRA
ARRIANOS ET PREVARICATO
RES ARRIANIS ACQVIESCEN
TES LIBER INCIPIT FELICITER

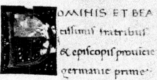
DOMINIS ET BEA
tissimis fratribus
& episcopis prouicie
germanie prime·
& germanie secunde : & lug
dunensi prime· & lugdunensi
secunde : & prouincie aquita
nice· & prouincie nonempopu
lane : & ex narbonensi plebis :

No. 687, folio 77, recto

Auete omnes anime 118

D. I. C. salus et liberatio 118*b*

Memoriae: Michael, John Bapt., John Ev., Peter and Paul,
    Anthony, Nicholas, Katherine, Margaret, Barbara . .   119*b*

Added Deuote contemplacion etc.: Stabat mater .   .   .   124
    (Memoria of S. Apollonia 126. Prayer at the sacrament.
    O sacrum conuiuium 126*b*).

The characteristic entries in the Kalendar are

    Jan. 13 Fremin   in red

    May 16 Honnoure   ,,

    Sept. 1 Fremin. Leu. ,,

       25 Fremin   ,,

    Dec. 11 Fussien   ,,

Of these feasts 13 Jan. is the Finding and Translation of
St Firmin M., 25 his martyrdom, Sept. 1 is of St Firmin II.
Conf.

The Litany is poor and has not St Firmin.

Decoration. The pictures are of decent execution: borders
ordinary: one divided into geometrical fields. Fluid gold is
used.

The pictures are by two hands, one very poor. 1. *Matins of
Virgin.* Annunciation in a room with red bed: both figures
kneel.

2. *Lauds*, in text. Visitation in landscape.

3. *Prime.* Nativity. Virgin, Joseph and the angels adore the
    Child lying in the Virgin's robe, in stable.

4. *Tierce.* Angel and Shepherds, in landscape: shepherd on *L*
    plays bagpipe.

5. *Sext*, in text. Adoration of the Magi: one king is black.

6. *None.* Presentation. Virgin and maid before the altar, Simeon
    and another behind it.

7. *Vespers.* Flight to *R*. Idol on pillar on *L*. falls.

8. *Compline.* Coronation. The Virgin attended by three angels
    kneels to God throned on *R*.

9. *Seven Psalms.* David kneels in landscape, harp by him, God
    above.

10. *Hours of the Cross.* Crucifixion with Mary and John.

12. *Hours of the Holy Ghost.* Group of Virgin and Apostles kneeling
    in room. Dove above.

13. *Office of the Dead.* A skeleton with a gravecloth on *L*. brandishes
    a dart at a robed man and woman on *R*.
    Of these nos. 3, 4, 5 are quite inferior.

274. Horae, Flemish.   { Old mark
                                     { C². 4. 84

Vellum, 6⅜ × 4½, ff. 210, 18 lines to page. Cent. xv (1st half), finely written and ornamented.

Binding, old red morocco: gold tooling.

Collation: 1⁶ 2⁶ | 3⁸ (wants 1) 4⁸ 5⁸ (one canc.) 6⁸–12⁸ (wants 8) 13⁸–19⁸ (wants 3) 20⁸–27⁸ | 28 (two).

Stamp of Bibl. Univers. et Coll. Regal. Aberdon.

On flyleaf: Liber Coll. Reg. Aberdonen., ex dono Mʳⁱ Jac. Fraser a Chelsea 1725.

On f. 209 (xv): helena vander schagen.

Contents:

Kalendar in red and black	f. 1
Hours of the Virgin in Flemish: first leaf gone . . .	13
Hours of the Eternal Wisdom	47
Hours of the Cross (die langhe cruus getide in duutsche) .	68
Hours of the Holy Ghost	90
Hours of the ? Name of Jesus	115
Seven Psalms and Litany: first leaf gone	140
Office of the Dead	157
Mass of the Virgin	193 *b*
Prayer at the Sacrament	201 *b*
Prayer after the Sacrament	205
Prayers with indulgence of 400 days	206 *b*

On f. 210, in a late current hand,
    Dit sijn de xlij gregoriensche messen etc.

The Kalendar has in red: *Jan.* Ponciaen; *Feb.* Gheertruut; *Ap.* Pancraes, Seruaes; *June*, Bonifaes, Odulf, Lebuin en radbodi; *Sept.* Lambert, Mauricius; *Oct.* Remigius, Bauo (10 Vechter m.); *Nov.* Willebroort, Lebuijn.

Litany: *MM.* Cornelius...Adriaen Nicasius; *CC.* Dominicus Franciscus Barnardinus Hubert Willibroert Thomas van Aquinen; *VV.* Walburch...Brigida.

The decoration is of very good quality, consisting of full borders and historiated initials. I note the following:

f. 19. Lauds, Angels, and monkey. 26 *b*. Angel with shield of three nails.

29 *b*. Angel: half-length figure with scroll: Rubum quem viderat moyses incombus(tum); 32, Angels, one with scroll: diffusa est gracia in labiis; 34 *b*, Angel and prophet; 37 *b*, Angels; 42 *b*, Angel.

47 (Eternal Wisdom). Initial. The Father in crown and pink robe, with blank scroll; 54 *b*, Bear; 57, Angel and Prophet; 58, Angels and monkey; 59 *b*, the same; 61, Angel with lute; 63, Angel scr: Annuncio vobis; 65, Angel scr: Benedicimus te.

68 (Cross). Initial. The Man of Sorrows: Angel with crown of thorns, another with cross; 74, Angel with lance; 77, with pillar; 79, with Veronica; 81, with scr: Ecce mulier filius tuus; 83 *b*, Initial, John with gold cup: angel with cord?; 86 *b*, Initial, man with small cross, Angel, scr: clama ne cesses quasi tuba exalta.

90 (Holy Ghost). Initial, Moses kneeling receives the Law; in border, Elisha, the widow and two sons: pots before them: Angel; 97, Angel; 100, Angel scr: Veni sancte spiritus imple tuorum; 102, Angel with trumpet; 104, birds; 106, Angel, butterfly, Peter in initial; 108, Initial, Thomas (?) with square: border, Prophet scr. damaged, ...eius...capite; 111, Paul in initial: Prophet scr? infiniti eius locuplet....

115 (Name of Jesus). Initial. The Transfiguration: border of vines with fruit and fine gold leaves; 122 *b*, James with club in initial: angel scr.: salige siin si die den he; 125 *b*, Angel with skull on shield; 127 *b*, Paul with sword in initial: Angel; 129 *b*, Andrew in initial: Angel scr.: dat heilige choer; 131, Angels; 133, Bartholomew with knife in initial, Angel, moth; 136, James the Great in initial, Prophet, scr.: et perdes omnes qui loquuntur, Angel.

(Seven Psalms, 1st leaf gone).

157 (Office of the dead). Initial. Souls in flames of purgatory: rocks above. In border: *R*. the Harrowing of Hell; at top, Angel carrying soul; below, the ostrich applying the worm schamir to the vessel in which her young is imprisoned—a type of the Harrowing of Hell from the Speculum Humanae Saluationis.

193 *b* (Mass of the Virgin). Angels, scr.: veritas de terra orta est.

————————

275. Biblia Sacra.
{ Old marks
C². 4. 85
II. 5. 16
O. 4. 44

Vellum (uterine), 6 × 3¾, double columns of 49 lines. Cent. xiii, late, in fine small hand: French.

Calf binding (xviii) with gold tooling.

Collation: not practicable.

On flyleaf: Acad. Marischal. Abredon. Beautiful Latin Bible compleat from Dr Guise.

Contents: Proll. of Jerome. Frater Ambrosius
                      Desiderii mei
        Genesis—2 Paral. Prayer of Manasses follows with-
            out break.
        Esdr. I (Ezra), Neem., Esdr. II (Et fecit), Tob.,
            Jud., Hest., Job.
        Psalter Gallican.
        Prov.—Ecclus.
        Isa.—Malachi.
        1, 2 Macc. Prol. of Rabanus.
        Evv.
        Paul. Epp.
        Act.
        Cath. Epp.
        Apoc. Prol. of Gilbert.
        Interpretationes nominum. Aaz—Zuzim.
It seems a perfectly normal copy, of the Parisian type. The decoration is good average work. Few initials are historiated.
Prol. Jerome writing. *Gen.* The six days of Creation and the Sabbath rest. *Psalter.* David harping. *Prov.* Solomon birching Rehoboam. *Matt.* Matthew writing. *Rom.* Paul with sword.

276. HORAE.

$$\left\{\begin{array}{l} \text{Old marks} \\ \text{II. 5. 22} \\ \text{C}^2. \text{ 4. 87} \end{array}\right.$$

Vellum, 3 × 2, ff. 276, 10 lines to page. Cent. xv, in narrow upright English hand.

Binding, red morocco (xviii or xix).

Collation: partly at least in eights, but difficult.

On flyleaf. Acad. Marischall. Abredon. from Dr Guise (xix). At bottom of f. 1: Claude Crespigny (xvii–xviii). On last page: Edward Sheffeld's book in anno 1552. In the Kalendar are obits (xv) of Bredons and Beltons.

Contents: Kalendar in red and black, not full . . . f. 1
        Memoriae: St John Baptist, George (Apollonia
            added). Katherine (Sebastian *added*) . . 19
        Hours of the Virgin (use of Sarum) . . . 29 b
        Memoriae in Lauds: Cross, Michael, John Bapt.,
            Peter and Paul, Andrew, John Ev., James,
            Thomas, Philip and James, Bartholomew,

Barnabas, Matthias, Simon and Jude, Matthew,
Mark, Luke, Laurence, Stephen, Thomas of
Canterbury, Christopher, Nicholas, Katherine,
Margaret, Mary Magd.

Verses of St Bernard *added* 124
Seven Psalms, Gradual Psalms and Litany . . 124*b*
Gaude flore virginali *added* 164*b*
Office of the Dead 167
Psalms of the Passion 232
Prayers for Pope, Emperor, and King (none named:
   added xvi) 245*b*
Commendaciones animarum 247

In the Kalendar.

Jan. 6. Illegible entry of birth of a Bredon (?).
Feb. 21. Nat' John̄e Bredon a. d. 1461.
    Nat' Ric. Bredon a. d. 1474.
Mar. 14. Ob. Johanna filia M. Rob. Bredon de Ely a. d.
    M° CCCC° lxxx° quinto in sua virginitate cuius
    anime etc.
Mar. 21. Ob. Ric. Bredon 1462.
Ap. 12. Ob. Jo. Belton 1481.
   26. Nat. Alicie Bredon.
June 13. Nat. Joh. Bredon 1463.
July 8. Nat. Christina Belton 1474.
   20. Agnes Bredon.
   27. Nat. Eliz. Br.
Oct. 15. Ob. Alic' Br.
Nov. 12. Nat. Edw. Br. 1472.
   13. Nat. Isab. Br. 1476.

The Kalendar is Sarum with a few additions.

Feb. ult. Oswalde ep.
Mar. 1. David ep. (not Chad).
May 7. Joh. beuerlac.
   23. Helene regine *added*.
Oct. 17. Transl. S. Etheldrede *added*.

The Litany is pure Sarum, but to the invocations of Virgins
are added in upper margin a mutilated name and S. Etheldreda, S. Withburga.

The indications agree with the mention of Ely as the home of
the Bredons.

On 19 *a* an added prayer.

Hec or. dicatur tempore euuangelii In principio Virtute istius
euuangelii a morbo febrium et dolore dencium libera me
domine qui natus es de virgine cum patre et sancto spiritu
in sempiterna secula.

Decoration. Some full-page pictures of poor and rough execution, viz. in Memoriae, St John Baptist with book in landscape: lamb by him.

St George on horse piercing dragon.

St Katherine crowned, with wheel.

Matins of Virgin. Virgin and child seated on a grass seat.
Initial Virgin (in pink) and child.

Seven Psalms. Last Judgment. Judge on rainbow, trumpet-
angels (blue) on *R.* and *L.* Virgin and John Ev. on earth.

Office of the Dead. Coffin with blue pall; two mourners; three
clerks sing from book.

Psalms of the Passion. The Man of Sorrows, half length,
on cloud, above the sepulchre; the Cross behind Him, the
instruments of the Passion on *R.* and *L.* and in front.

Commendations. Two angels in air bear up a soul in a linen
cloth, two graves below, God above.

These pages and those facing them are bordered.

686. HIERONYMUS IN MATTHAEUM.

Vellum, $9\frac{1}{8} \times 6\frac{1}{4}$, ff. 170, 24 lines to a page. Cent. xii early, very
finely written by a scribe Bertolfus.

Binding, red morocco with gold tooling by R. de Coverley.

Collation: 1^8 (wants 1) 2^8–21^8 22^4 (wants 4).

Purchased with the Carnegie Grant in 1924 (pr. £50) from
Messrs Maggs, whose description, with two earlier ones, one from a
Sotheby sale catalogue, the other a good deal older, are in the book.
From Bamberg (?): see later.

Contents: Hieronymus in Matthaeum (*P.L.* xxvi. 15)

Inc. prol. S. Hieronimi Presbiteri (red capitals) .   .   . f.   1
     Plures fuisse—concludat. Expl. prol.

Inc. tract. S. Hieronimi Presb. In Matheum.

Inc. liber primus   4
     Liber generationis I. C. In esaia legimus

Inc. lib. secundus   .   .   .   .   .   . 43^b

Inc. lib. Tertius   82

Inc. lib. Quartus   .   .   .   .   .   . 125^b

A change of ink on 144 sqq.

—futurum (*corr. to* uenturum) cum apostolis.

Expl. Tract. S. Hieron. Presb. in Matheum.

Smaller script: Indignus alumnus sancte marie nomine Bertolfus
mo(nachus) scripsit hunc codicem optans a domino pro hoc
ueniam peccaminum suorum.

In another small hand the beginning of Jerome's letter to
Sunnia and Fretela   170

   Dilectissimus fr. sunnie etc....Uere in uobis—breuiter
admoneo ut sciatis

In a large script resembling that of the book 170*b*

   E. dei gratia babbgensis eccl. humilis minister Venerabili et
in christo plurimum dilecto fr. G. geng'. abbati salutem et
fraterne caritatis dilectionem. Nouit prudentia tua quod filii
huius seculi prudentiores filiis lucis in generatione sua sunt.
ideoque simplicioribus quibuscunque ab eis timendum et
cauendum est. ubicunque fieri potest. Verbum quod nobis
significasti de monte commutando non sedit animo nostro.
quia plus mali quam boni inde prouenturum esse prospicimus.
ideoque modis omnibus id fieri prohibemus. De seruitio
autem nostro nullam te uolumus habere sollicitudinem. sed
utinam nos tuam subleuare possemus inopiam. pro seruitio
uero tua nobis et tuorum non desit oratio. Bene ualeas tu et
omnes qui tecum sunt. et dextera (unfinished)

Geng' seems likely to be Gegenbach or Gengenbach where
was an abbey founded in 712: but that is in Strasbourg
diocese. An exchange of property has been suggested to them
by some child of this world and the abbot has asked the
bishop of Bamberg's advice—who may have been a personal
friend, but does seem to speak as his diocesan. Seruitium
nostrum, I think, merely means that the abbot has asked if
he can do anything for the bishop, who says he cannot; let
him have their prayers instead. Two bishops of Bamberg
were named Eberhard, (1) E. of Magdeburg 1007-41, (2)
Eberhard II 1146-72. This letter may be from the earlier
one, copied into this book to preserve it.

The volume is a fine piece of writing. Of the few ornamental
initials, the first is perhaps in purple with some convolutions, the
others are in plain red.

There are a number of marginalia, seemingly of cent. xvi.

687. HILARIUS PICTAVENSIS.

Vellum, 6¾ × 4, ff. 114, 16 lines to a page. Cent. xv, in a pretty
Roman hand with a slight backward slope.

Binding, modern vellum.

Collation: 1¹⁰–4¹⁰ 5⁸ 6¹⁰–9¹⁰ 10⁸ 11¹⁰ 12¹⁰ (wants 11, 12).

Formerly Phillipps MS. 6241. Purchased with the Carnegie
Grant 1924.

Contents:

The first page has a fine border of Italian 'line and leaf' work with many small gold studs rayed in black. A blank shield in an elaborate frame in the lower border. Initial in gold.

The set-off of a large circular device is on this page. The other treatises have titles in red capitals and gold initials on fields of pink and blue, dotted with white.

688. Historia Scholastica Petri Comestoris.

Vellum, 12 × 8½, ff. 7 + 178 + 2, double columns of 48 lines. Cent. xiii, fairly early, in a fine regular hand.

2 fo. text. Angelos.

Binding, parchment over wooden boards.

Collation: 1 flyleaf *a*⁶ 1¹² 2¹² (one canc.) 3¹²–15¹² (wants 12) *b*².

Presented by Francis Edmond, LL.D., of Kingswells, as an addition to the Library of Dr James Melvin, 1884.

On the flyleaf, in a later hand, notes on Scripture, verses on the Books of the Bible, note on the Herods.

Table in a current hand of cent. xiv occupying a quire of six leaves.

> Inc. scolastica historia. prefatio   .   .   .   .   .   . f. 1
> > Imperatorie maiestatis est—et principium.
>
> In principio erat uerbum
> ending 176: s. in Cathacumbis.
> Added in a charter-like hand (xiii–xiv) the epitaph
> > Petrus eram quem petra tegit etc. and this note:
>
> Hoc epithalamium (!) composuit apud S. victorem vbi totam
> > pecuniam quam habuit feria 6. et sabato distribuit manibus
> > propriis indigentibus erogandam sed (?) et munitus (?)
> > christiane fidei sacramentis nocte dominica migrauit a seculo
> > a. d^{nice} incarn. M. C. lxx. vii. vi kal. nouembres.
>
> On the flyleaves at end are notes as at the beginning by the
> > same hand. The most important is about the husbands of
> > Anne, beginning with the verses
> > > Ex Joachim. theopha (cleopha). Saloma. tres anna marias etc.

The decoration is neat: initials alternately in red and blue.

SUPPLEMENT.

17. DOMINICUS DE S. GEMINIANO.

Old marks
D². 5. 67
Θ. 1. 6
& 2. 39

Paper, 14¾ × 11, ff. 219, double columns of 58 lines. Cent. xv (1469): written at Paris by R. de S.: in a regular but scratchy and abbreviated hand.

Paper boards.

Liber Coll. Regii.

At each end : Liber mag. Will. de Elphinstoun.

Collation: A¹²–S¹² T (only 5 and another left + flyleaf).

 1. Dominicus de S. Geminiano. Recollecta super Sexto . . f. 1
  Rubrica de vita et honestate clericorum. Opponitur quod
  Rubrica non fuerit bene formata.
  Lib. II. ? III. ? IV. 126, V. 132 ; no others marked.
  A gap after f. 216 (S. 12). The next leaf is T. 5. One other leaf
  from the second half of the quire remains : the text ends on
  it (218 *b*): quoniam vinculum est dissolutum sec. paulum.
  Expl. Recollecta super vjᵒ composita per ven. mag. et dominum
  Dominicum de S. Geminiano decretorum doctorem finita
  parisius A. d. mᵐᵒ. ccccᵒ lxᵒ ixᵒ die xi mens. maii per R. de S.
  Deo gr. Amen.

 2. The last leaf, in another hand, has (219) a bull of Innocent VIII (?)
  ad reformand' ecclesiarum mores et actus. Recites acts of
  Boniface VIII, Alex. V, etc., and ends: dat. rome. anno
  14·4·5· anno primo publiᶜᵃ in scotia per Jac. Ymolens. ep.

The book much resembles nos. **12–16**, and has been very little used.

21. POLYCHRONICON IN ENGLISH.

Old marks
D². 5. 73
Θ. 3. 1
AA 3. 3

Vellum, 15¾ × 11, ff. 171, double columns of 45 lines. Cent. xv early (near 1400), finely written and with good ornaments.

Modern binding and clasps.

At bottom of f. 1, rather rubbed : This book was gifted/to the Kings Colledge of Aberdeen/by Mr Charles Gordon Son/to the laird of Strath'...h/5ᵗ(?) Aprill(?) 1683(?).

Collation: 1⁸ (wants 1) 2 (four) (gap) 3⁸ (wants 3?) 4⁸–15⁸ (wants 1) 16⁸ 17¹⁰ 18⁸–20⁸ 21 (three) 22⁸ 23 (five). Quires 10 and 11 are transposed: after 10 is a gap of a quire: again after 13 a quire gone: after 14 1 leaf: after 20 further losses, and the end is gone.

Other names of owners occur : on 13 *b*

Liber O. Johannis hay de ȝestir 1554.

On 171 *b*: Mr Allexander Fraser of fraserbrughe knicht (xvii).

On the flyleaf (xix) the initials W. P. B. and some modern notes on Trevisa.

> The Polychronicon of R. Higden in the English version of John Trevisa.
> Tables. Latin 1. English 8, imperfect, ending in L.
> Prologue . . . . f. 12
>   Affter solempne & wise writers of art—
> A leaf is gone after f. 12 (Rolls ed., i. 18, l. 12 to 371 *b*).
> A large blank piece of 13 is cut out. The text ends in col. 2 :
>   þe ȝere of grace of þe prince þᵗ regneþ.
> A note follows : hic nichil deficit quia scribitur in prima pagina reuolucionis alterius folii.
> Accordingly, 13 *b*, 14 *a* are blank. Text continues 14 *b*. Cap. 5ᵐ
>   De orbis dimensione etc. Iulius cesar by counsail (*l.c.* i. 41).
> Lib. II. 52 : two quires transposed ; ff. 67–74 should follow 75–82.
> Lib. III. 71 *b*: after c. 5, lese þerefore (*l.c.* III. 155, l. 16), is a gap to 'the whiche þe lif of man' in c. 18 (f. 83) : *l.c.* III. 291, l. 2.
> In c. 33 : after 'porta collina þe consuls' (IV. 69, l. 3) a gap to c. 41 (40) 'hit after his owne name ludgate' (f. 99) (*l.c.* IV. 187, l. 2).
> Lib. IV. 103 : in cc. 3, 4 a gap of a leaf 'Cesar louȝ'—'drynke' (IV. 309, l. 2–325, l. 8).
> Lib. V. 130 *b*: defective after c. 33 'Etheldredus kyng' (*l.c.* VI. 351, l. 6).
> Lib. VI. 156 begins imperfect in c. 10 'eyȝteþe leo was pope' (*l.c.* VII. 13, l. 12).
> A leaf gone in cc. 14, 15 : another in 25, 26.
> Lib. VII. begins 171 *b*, ending with the page 'Aȝenst wynter kyng William cum yn to (VII. 251, l. 22).

The decoration, consisting of borders to the principal divisions (Table and beginnings of Books) and small initials to chapters, is of admirable English work of the time : gold, blue, scarlet, and other shades of red are employed. The Prologue, f. 12, has a small and excellent pictured initial of Higden, a black monk seated writing on a desk fixed across the arms of his chair: an open book on a table on *R*. The initial of Lib. II. is cut out. There is a neat drawing of the Ark on f. 56 *b*. The greater part of the book, if not all, is the work of two scribes.

This copy was not used for the text of Trevisa in the Rolls Series edition by Babington, Lumby, etc. It superficially resembles the fine MS. at St John's College, Cambridge (no. 204), which was so used.

John Lord Hay of Yester, whose name is in the book, was also owner of two MSS. in the Pepysian Library at Magdalene College, Cambridge. See my Catalogue of the Medieval MSS., p. 19 (nos. 1576 and 1584).

Some not uninteresting annotations occur: on 48 *a* (xvi) is: (Cretton) called Crediton or kirktown near fullfoord Mr Justice ? Perysun his place here I preached many tymes. J. d.

22. Epistolare in usum Ecclesiae Cathedralis Aberdonensis.

Vellum, 13 × 9⅛, ff. 179, 20 lines to page.

Written at Antwerp in 1527 to the order of Bishop Gavin Dunbar (1518–1531).

Printed in full as no. 93 of Aberdeen University Studies, 1924. Edited by the late Rev. Bruce McEwen, with Preface by the Rev. Professor W. A. Curtis and Introduction by F. C. Eeles, F.S.A. Scot.

Facsimiles in *Registrum Episcopatus Aberdon.* (Spalding Club, 1845: ed. Cosmo Innes.) In the list of the Registers I. lxii. it is entered as H.

105. Albertus Magnus.   { Old marks
                                            { C². 3. 62

Paper and vellum, 8 × 5⅞, ff. 138, 36 etc. lines to page. Cent. xv, in a number of hands; the first respectable, some of the others very rough. Written in Germany. Many leaves are crumpled and defective at the edges.

Old calf binding over wooden boards.

Liber Coll. Regii Aberdon.

Collation : in twenties and sixteens, hardly practicable from tenderness of paper: outer and middle sheets of quires are normally vellum.

f. 1 has on each side diagrams in red : those on recto faint ; f. 2 has Themata and a note from Bernard on septem misericordiae.

1. Table . . . . f. 3
2. Albertus Magnus de Muliere forti 6
    Laudes ecclesie describit salomon in forma mulieris fortis
    ending 123 : quod vobis paratum est ab origine mundi. Ad quod nos...in sec. sec. Amen. deo gr. quod Wus ll.
    Supplico cordintime oretis pro illuminatore LL.
    Expl. tract. super epistolam mulierem fortem quis inueniet. editus a fr. Alberto Magno de ordine predicatorum.
3. Sermo S. Augustini ep. de c(elo etc.) et de penis impiorum.
    (*P.L.* XL. 1341) . . . . 123 *b*
    Apostolica leccio fr. k. hunc sonitum
4. Breuis historia de vita et doctrina Alberti magni quondam Ratisponensis Ep. in omnibus expertissimi etc. . . . 125
    Gloriosus Albertus Magnus ordinis fr. pred. doctor egregius
    —librum de lanificio. de armatura librum. lib. de agricultura. lib. de venacione. lib. de nauigacione. et lib. de arte theatrica etc. quod p. de handlueh.
    Expl. hist. Alberti m. quondam Ratispon. Ep.
    It is the life by Ludov. Vallesoletensis entered in BHL. 224.
    The words after lanificio were wanting in their source.
    On 131 *b*-136 are miscellaneous notes.
    137 *a* blank. On 137 *b* a list of books:
    libri Ricardi crultere quos reliquit in abba*ti*a de Abb24 .
    Primo postilla super lucam Alberti
    They are largely postils, of Albert and Lyra.
    17 is this MS. : Item sentencia Alberti super epistolam aa que vocatur mulierem fortem.
    There are 31 entries and the beginning of another.
    f. 138 blank.

108. G. DE CAYOTO.

Old marks
C². 3. 65
II. 6. 9
H. 3. 3

Paper, $8\frac{1}{4} \times 5\frac{3}{4}$, ff. 181 and flyleaves. Double columns of 37, 31 etc. lines. Cent. xv, in several hands; the first very neat, some of the rest disgraceful.

Old binding, black leather over wooden boards.

Lib. Acad. Marischall. Aberdon.

At foot of f. 1 Liber (two or three words erased): de Dee ex dono ven. viri mag. Alexandri Gallouay rectoris de kynkell a. d. milles. quingent. vicesimo.

Collation: a^2 (1 paste-down) b (two): 1^{12}–14^{12} 15^{10} 16 (three) c^2 (2 paste-down).

Among notes on the flyleaves is one in English of 1583 referring to linen, etc., and mentioning M. Andro Galloway.

Quaestiones super Summam Confessorum . . . . f.	I
Inc. tituli (of the four Books).	
Inc. prol. in priorem libellum questionum casualium com-penditer a fr. G. de Cayoto ord. fr. pred.	2
Licet doctores iuris cononici Raymundus Gaufr' Innocencius et alii	
Lib. II. 33. On 52 *b* the neat hand gives way to worse ones. The beginnings of III. and IV. are obscure.	
Ends 171: habet tantam ypotecam (?) hostiensis	
Expl. tract. de matrimonio et finitur per consequens quasi in quatuor libros diffinitum totum compendium extractum a fr. Guillelmo de Cayoto ord. fr. pred. de summa confessorum edita a fr. Ioh. teutonico lectore quondam in eodem ordine. deo gracias.	
A table follows	171
On 181 *b* late note on Prescriptio, and on the paste-down more memoranda like that at the beginning.	

198. N. DE TUDESCHIS ETC.
$\left\{ \begin{array}{l} \text{D}^2.\ 4.\ 35 \\ \Theta.\ 1.\ 11 \end{array} \right.$

Paper, $11\frac{1}{2} \times 8\frac{1}{4}$, ff. 84 + 58, two portions in double columns of 48 lines. Cent. xv. The first hand hideous, the second very pretty.

Binding, paper boards.

Liber Coll. Regii Aberdon.

The entry liber Willelmi de Elphinstoun is at each end of each part.

Collation: a^{12}–g^{12} | the rest (part II) impracticable.

I.	Lectura IV^{ti} Libri decretalium per Nicolaum (Panormitanum) .	f. I
	Rubrica de sponsalibus...Supra visum est in precedenti libro	
	—tantorum doctorum. Et ista sufficiant	
	Expl. lectura quarti lib. decret. sec. ven. d. Nicolayum abbatem Cicilie doctorem eximium. deo. gr. amen.	
	R. S. (This colophon in a better script.)	

II. 1. Panormitanus in Clementinas   I

       Inc. glose clementinarum cum quibusdam nouis questionibus occurrentibus etc.

       This leaf is torn and tender. At bottom in blue and red capitals is: LL DE E.

       The gloss on Lib. v ends f. 58 *a*: tenementi. deo gr.

       Expl. panormitanus super clementinis declarando glosam Johannis andree.

   2. In a similar hand.

       Constitucio ad regimen Benedicti XII   58

       Benedictus...Ad regimen ecclesie quanquam uniuersalis

       Dat. A[d]uiñion. tercia ydus Jan. pontif. nostri anno primo.

       Benedict. XII (Jacques Fournier) 1334—1342.

217. BIBLIA. $\left\{ \begin{array}{l} D^2.\ 6.\ 37 \\ II.\ 3.\ 8 \\ O.\ 3.\ 5 \end{array} \right.$

Vellum, 12 × 8½, ff. 271, double columns of 60 lines. Cent. xiii late, in very good hands of two or three scribes.

   Binding: old russia, gold tooling.   2 fo. passionem.

   Lib. Acad. Marischall.

   Collation: 1^{12}–5^{12} 6^{10} 7^{12}–9^{12} 10^8 | 11^{14} | 12^{12} 13^{12} (wants 5) 14^{10} 15^{12}–21^{12} (wants 1) 22^{16} (wants 16) | 23^{12}.

       At top of f. 1 (xv–xvi) John tyson.

       Proll. of Jerome.

       Gen—2 Paral. Prayer of Manasses in separate paragraph.

       Esdr. Neem. Tob. Jud. Esth. Job. 114 *b* blank.

       Psalter Gallican in another hand: with ps. 151 Pusillus eram.

       Parab.—Ecclus. Canticles divided among speakers.

       Isa.—Mal. The first hand resumes at Canticles.

       1, 2 Macc.

       Evv., Paul. Epp., Act., Cath. Epp., Apoc.

       At the end of Apoc. memorial verses on the Books and a note on the Twelve Stones.

       Interpretationes nominum. 4 cols. to page 260 Aaz—Zuzim.

       Two columns of notes. de sapientia in lege diuina. de multiplici effectu legis diuine etc.

It is a fine piece of writing, and in good condition with few gaps. The only storied initial is that to Genesis, which has seven vesica-shaped pictures of the days of Creation and the Sabbath rest. Gold occurs here, and there is whitish foliage pattern on blue ground.

The grounds of the pictures are pink draperies, green and white. English work. Other initials are in blue and red, some indented, with flourishing.

243. R. Hampole on the Psalter.

{ Old marks
D². 7. 35
II. 3. 14
O. 4. 11

Vellum, 11 × 7¾, ff. 2 + 160, double columns of 47 lines. Cent. xv (first half), very well written by a scribe, Walter Day.

Binding, old rough sheep (xvii) stamped in gold with arms and coronet of the Earl of Stamford: his library was dispersed in 1721.

Lib. Acad. Marischall.

On the paper flyleaf the names of: Stamford 1693: J. Ames 1733: J. Caborne.

Collation: 1 paper flyleaf, 1 vellum, 1⁸–12⁸ | gap | 13⁸–20⁸.

The vellum flyleaf is a piece of a roll—perhaps a muster roll— written on both sides, in reverse directions. It has a series of lists of names grouped under side headings : *e.g.* recto

> Mans' Joh. de la Pole.
> Mans'...Galfr Swinnerton.

On verso is only Mans' Thom. Morieux.

It is of cent. xiv.

Richard Rolle of Hampole on the Psalter   .   .   .   . f.   1
Without the prologue. Text begins:
Beatus vir etc. In yis psalme first he spekis of crist & of his folowers.
The Latin text is in larger script than the English.
A quire is missing after f. 96, containing part of Ps. 90 (91) 2 to 102 (103) 22.
The Psalter ends 133 *b*: Þarfor ilka spryte louue ye lord.
  Expl. psalt. dauid regis.
Canticles   .   .   .   . 133 *b*
ending with Quicunque: and tech it to men vnder yem. Amen. Expl.
In red : Ecce dies murus. hiis binis iungito terus. (*i.e.* Walterus Day).
Office of the dead with exposition 153
ending 160 with Benedictus (unfinished):
  Exaltabo—suscepisti me
  Deo gr. Q. Yad (i.e. Day)
  Ecce dies etc. ut supra.

The MS. was seen and described in 1900 by Miss A. C. Paues, and in 1921 Miss Dorothy Everett had extracts made. The editions of the text are (Psalter) by Bramley, Oxford, 1887; (Canticles) Arnold, *Select English Works of Wyclif*, Oxford, 1869, III. 3.

The MS. is mentioned and classed with uninterpolated copies in Hope E. Allen's *Writings...of R. Rolle*, p. 172. The decoration is not by a very skilled hand. It consists of borders full or partial to the Nocturnes and other principal divisions. Smaller initials are mainly in blue and red.

247. CATHEDRAL INVENTORIES ETC.   { Old mark D². 7. 47

Vellum, 11⅝ × 6¾, ff. 100 (86), various number of lines to page. Cent. xv and xvi, in many hands.

Wooden boards, re-covered with leather: clasp.

> Hic Inc. Inuentarium seu Registrum Thezaurarie ecclesie Aberdonensis. Quod fieri fecit ven. vir Mag. Henricus de Rynde eiusd. ecclesie thezararius. Ac Reu^di in cristo patris d^ni d^ni henrici de lichton utriusque iuris legum doctoris eiusd. eccl. tunc temporis episcopi huiusque presentis eccl. constructoris nepos. A. d. milles. quadring. trices. sexto.
>
> Inc. libri theologie . . . . f. 1
> Essentially the same as the catalogue printed at p. 80, but shorter. The divisions are the same. But on f. 5 are libri non reperti, libri decretalium absentes, followed by libri chori 5 b, libri in communi seruicio chori, missalia.
> Ornamenta magni altaris 7, Cappe, Panni pro ornamentis ecclesie 8 b.
> A stained leaf in another hand: De mitra et contentis in eadem .   10
> Inc. Jocalia. (See p. 78) with additions   11
> Pro altari nostre domine, b. Michaelis, b. Johannis, b. Katerine   12 b
> Carte et euidentie (f. 13 cut out)   14
> Signatures and additions (f. 16 gone)   17
> Obitus (f. 18 gone)   19
> De horis diuinis celebrandis . . . . .   21 b
> Facultas eccl. Aberdon. 23. Fundaciones 23 b.
> Capellani perpetui 24. 24 b blank.
> Statuta 25.
> Charters, Bulls, etc., in many hands . . . . .   31 b
> Visitacio Iocalium eccl. Aberdon. (1496) . . . .   68 b
> In the large hand of f. 1 (1436), list of Bishops of Aberdeen .   72
>   Tempore Malcolmi regis filii Kennach etc.
> continued to the 28th bishop, Blakburne.
> Charters, Bulls, etc., in many late hands follow.

On 96, 97 is The Inuentar' of all ye geyr left be bischope
Alexander Gordone,
followed by other documents, of Gawin Dunbar, etc.
Parts of the book are a good deal stained.

In the list of *Jocalia* above, on p. 80 this older copy shows plainly
that for pcia (l. 18) we must read prucia (*i.e.* spruce-wood). The
name of St Machar is uniformly given as Mauricius. (See Forbes,
Kalendars of Scottish Saints, s.v.)

This is MS. C in Cosmo Innes's *Registrum* (I. lxx) and was
called *Registrum Rubeum*. Facsimiles of the old hand are in
II. 127, and the Inventories of books and jocalia are printed on
127—153, and the other contents in various parts of the two
volumes.

256. PHILONIUS ETC.   { D². 7. 62 / Θ. 1. 12

Paper, 11¾ × 8⅝, ff. 226, double columns of 45 lines. Cent. xv
(1461), in a very decent rather sloping hand by Will. Umfra.
Liber Coll. Regii Aberdon.

Binding, old stamped leather over wooden boards. The principal
stamp: double-headed eagle displayed, deer, trefoil leaf, lamb and
flag. Five metal bosses remain. Second cover partly renewed.

First leaves defective at top. A shield cut out of lower border.
Collation: probably in tens, but difficult.

Beginning defective with the capitula of the
Quintus liber Philonii.
Deus cum tua summa et misericordia infinita inc. liber quintus
Philon(ii) in quo domino cooperante dicetur de passionibus
menbrorum secunde digestionis quia in quar[to]ta parte iam
diximus de passionibus membrorum in quibus prima digestio
celebratur .   .   .   . f. 1
Cap. 1. de anothomia epatis
Sicut scribimus (?) quarto.
f. 36. Expl. quintus liber philonii et inc. sextus eiusdem finitus
per me mag^{rum} Gill^m Vmfra pro tunc parisius residentem
Anno d^{ni} mill^{mo} quadr^{simo} sex^{mo} primo. mens vero apr. die
decima deo gr.
Lib. vi. 36 b. Capitula 25.
Lib. vii. part I, f. 132. Capp. 17.
    ,, part II, f. 169. Capp. 38,
ending 211 b.

Expl. septimus liber philonei completus per me gill^m Vmfra in
artibus mag^rum parisius residentem et in medicina pro tunc
studentem.

2. (Barthol. Putanensis de crisi)   212
Circa autem pronostica(ciones?) IIII^or sunt notanda,
ending: peccatorumque veniam tribuat ut ad ipsum peruenire
meriamur. Qui est bened. in sec. sec. Amen.
Expl. summula mag. bartholomei putanensis de cresi et creticis
diebus per me mag. Guill^m Vmfra rubricata et ad diuersa
notabilia reducta finitur a. d. mill. quadr. lx^mo nono xx^ma
die febr.

3. Sequitur aggregacio de cursu planetarum per me Gill^m Vmfra .   224 *b*
Omnes autem planete duplici mouentur sc. naturali et proprio,
ending imperfect in a chapter on comets, 226 *b*.

258. MEDICAL RECEIPTS IN ENGLISH. $\left\{ \begin{array}{l} \text{Old marks} \\ \text{D}^2.\ 7.\ 64 \\ \text{II. 6. 4} \\ \text{O. 4. 25} \end{array} \right.$

Paper, $11\frac{1}{4} \times 8$, pp. 331, 31 lines to page. Cent. xv, in a clear
ugly hand.

Lib. Acad. Marischall.

Stiff parchment cover.

Collation: 1 flyleaf (vellum): rest perhaps in twelves, but difficult.
Pp. 1, 2 gone: two vellum flyleaves at end.

On the flyleaf two receipts added in English.

Text begins imperfect .   .   .   . p.   3
    Whoso bereþ verueyne vpon hym he schal haue loue of
      grete maystres.
The next articles are on Vyolet & Camamille
—for many maner metes. here endeþ ye uertues of herbes aftur
      galyene ypocras & Socrates.
here bygynneþ for hed hache   6
    Take and seþe verueyne and bytonye.
On p. 13 crossed out: here is a charme for þe hawe in mannis
      eye or wommans.
Other charms are crossed out, *e.g.* pp. 16, 21, 22, 23, 33, etc.
Here men may see þe vertues of diuerse herbes whyche ben
      hote & whyche ben colde, etc.   39
Quynte foyle þat is fyue leefe
This section ends with Rosemarie, p. 52.
The receipts that follow seem to be quite miscellaneous.
On p. 103 are Unguenta.

8-2

On 105. Dilectissime frater ut intellexi multum times pro instanti pestilencia

—et sic preseruabis te deo mediante (107).

On 128 another tract on Virtues of herbs beginning with Quinfoyle and ending with Mint.

Receipts continue 140.

p. 167. Here begynneþ good medisines þat good leches han drawe out & foundyn in bokes þat ys to say galyen & asclepius & ypocras for þay were þe best leches in þe world.

for þe akyng of þ heed. Make lye of varuayne, etc.

p. 193. Apparently a third copy of the tract on herbs. Quinfoyle, etc., ending this time with Onion & Garlic.

Receipts, 207.

On 243–246 is a list of some part of the contents, the items numbered in a xvith-cent. hand.

Receipts, 246.

p. 257. A fourth copy of the tract on herbs, ending with Garlic.

Receipts, 273.

They continue to p. 325: on 318–324 they are in Latin.

ending 325: and alle these thyngis wytnesseth ypocras.

On the last pages, originally blank, are additions of various dates—pen-trials, etc., one in French: and, on p. 331,

The newyears gifts of the yeare of L. 1578 given vnto Thomas butevill of brinckleye bye the neighbours & tenants (?) as followeth Eliz. vicesimo:

Stephen Rooke of Weston	. .	one pigge
Giles dormant of brincklye	. .	one capone
Stephen Bentleye ,,	. .	,, ,,
Siluester Turner ,,	. .	1 dozen of larks & 1 woodcoke
Stublefild ,,	. .	1 capone
John dobitee ,,	. .	iij chikyns
,, ,, of Willingham	. .	one pigge
John Amye of Brincklye	. .	one capone
Rob. Rooke ,,	. .	one henne
Gilbert Rooke ,,	. .	one capone
The widowe rande ,,	. .	,, ,,
Will. Bye ,,	. .	,, ,,
Sherman ,,	. .	,, ,, & 1 henne
Mrs Barnwell	. .	a dishe of Aples
Jhon Knocke ,,	. .	one capone.

Brinkley, Willingham and Weston Colville are all in Cambridgeshire.

There is probably a great deal of repetition in this book, besides what has been noted here. I cannot detect any system in the arrangement of the receipts.

259. Avicenna.
$$\begin{cases} D^2.\ 7.\ 65 \\ \Theta.\ 2.\ 13 \end{cases}$$

Paper, $11\frac{3}{4} \times 8\frac{1}{4}$, ff. $1 + 241 + 2$, double columns of 54 lines. Cent. xv (1469), in an ugly current hand.

Old binding, wooden boards covered with leather.

Lib. Coll. Regis Aberdon.

A vellum flyleaf at beginning and two at end from a xiiith-cent. MS. de virtutibus. At foot of one at end is scribbled (xv–xvi), Mem. yat Jon. Mower aw me viis 11*d* ? ley*ſ*'.

Collation: 1^{16} apparently : the rest not worth making.

Pars Canonis Avicennae.
? F) en quarta primi canonis etc. . . . . . . f. 1
Capitula (30).
Text. Dicemus q' res medicas(?) 1
ending 240 *b* : secundum ipsius d. ... biles naturas.
Expl. quarta fen (?) primi canonis Avicenne cum comento ipsius
    quam compleui anno d^{ni} m^o cccc^o lx ix in vigilia s. jacobi.
    apostoli. Amen. deo gr.
Nota quod de corduba⟨que⟩ est ciuitas in hispania et de Osula
    andalasie fuerunt nati auicenna aueroys etc. ... ptholomeus de
    3° climate. amen.
Alyr hoc scripsit istum librum de natione scotus et de ? cuius
    una IIII d. venerabili viro et discreto magistro Guillermo
    umfra magister par*i*sien? fuit.

Umfra is the scribe of **256**.

Leaves at the ends are rather damaged, but the book is clean and little used, and very ugly.

278. Obit-book of the Grey Friars of Aberdeen.
$$\begin{cases} \text{Old marks} \\ C^2.\ 5.\ 61 \\ \text{II.}\ 5.\ 7 \\ O.\ 4.\ 28 \end{cases}$$

Paper, $7\frac{5}{8} \times 5\frac{1}{4}$, ff. 58, varying numbers of lines to page. Cent. xvi, the principal hand a fine Italic script.

Lib. Acad. Marischall.

The cover is a leaf of a service book, noted, of cent. xv, with part of the office for St Albert (the patriarch of Jerusalem and stablisher of the Carmelites). Inside the pad are two old stamped leather covers, pieces of xiv^th.-cent. law books and printed fragments (not early) of Plautus.

The book was transcribed in 1881 by R. Howlett, who pronounced it to be a fair copy of an older record: "the entries extend almost from the foundation of the convent by Vaus in 1450 to the year of the collapse of all the orders (1560)."

On f. 2 is Ex libris guilielmi keyth, and his name is on 2 *b*.

Collation: 1^{10} 2^8–7^8 (wants 6) 8 (parts of 4 and 5 left).

The book is in Kalendar form, 3 days to a page.

The entries of saints are few.

On Mar. 6. Thome confessoris.

Ap. 11 Vincentii C. May 20 Bernerdini C. 24 Tr. S. Francisci and other Franciscan feasts, but none of Scotland.

The leaves lost are in Nov. 22–27, Dec. 10–21, and 28 to end.

The book has been used for entering family records to the end of cent. xvi.

The main hand seems to be of near 1550.

364. PTOLEMAEI QUADRIPARTITUM CUM   { Old mark
          GLOSA HALY.   { M N. 3. 266

Paper and vellum, 12½ × 8¾, ff. 151 + 1, double columns of 44 lines. Cent. xv (1426), mainly in a decent German hand.

Binding, white skin, stamped (xvi?).

From the Library of Dr Melvin, presented to Marischal College 10th Sept. 1856.

Printed slip: Georg Kloss, M.D.

Like others of his books, it came from the abbey of St Maximin at Treves. On f. 1 is: N. 181.

Also: Ƶ. Codex monasterii s. maximini prope vrbem treverim situati,

and on f. 2: Ex libris Imperialis Monasterii S. Maximini.

On the last flyleaf: Dijs buegh jst der wurdiger vnd geistlicher hrn priors vnde convents zu sant maximine by Trier Vnn durch Gerhart plait von lonckwich zur ziit Iren (?) ober. scholtissen gegeben Im Jare xv^c(?) vnd ?dxii vff sant bartholomeus applen tagh vt kůnt syner handt. Gerhart manu propria.

Collation: 1 (three) 2^{14} 3^{16}–6^{16} 7^{10} 8^{16}–10^{16} 11^{12} 1 flyleaf.

1. Text: Dixit Egydius de tebaldis lumbardus de ciuitate Parmensi f.   1
   Scire et intelligere gloriosum est—temporibus immortalis
   Tract. primus glose haly abenrudiani super prima parte libri
        Quadripartiti Ptolomei Pheludiani.
   Uerba que dixit sapientissimus ptolomeus in arte Judiciorum etc.
   Glosare uolentes dicimus quod judicia
   —quod liber sit bene diuisus.
   Cap. 1. Primi Tract. etc.
   Propositio prima quadripartiti   4
        Res omizori quibus proficiuntur
        Ptolemeus inspexit in omnibus
   The text of Ptolemy is in larger script than the gloss.
   Lib. II. 39 *b*, III. 71.
   At foot of 91 is a date: 1425, 14 marcii.
   Lib. IV. 115, ending 148 *b*
        deus te dirigat in uiam rectam.
   Expl. quadrip. pthol. cum glosa haly.
   Scriptum aquis a. d. n. I. C. 1426 incompleto 8 die febr.

2. In a small neat hand   149
   Hyginus. m. fabio. plurimam salutem
        Et si te studio gramatice artis
   A portion of the tract de signis coelestibus (Lib. II. of the
        Poet. Astron.) ending in Arctofilax.
   qui adolescens factus cum uenaretur
   in margin : exemplari caret.

984. Ps. Athanasius etc.

Vellum, 10½ × 6½, ff. 1 + 108, 29 lines to page. Cent. xv, in a very
good Italian hand with slight slope, modelled on Carolingian
script.

Binding, stiff parchment.

Purchased 1929 with Carnegie Grant, of E. P. Goldschmidt
(no. 142 in a catalogue of his).

At foot of f. 1 of text and at the end of the text is an owner's
name in capitals erased, beginning with D.

Collation: 1 flyleaf 1⁸-8⁸ | 9¹⁰-11¹⁰ 12⁸ 13⁶.

Flyleaf blank but for erasures.

1. Inc. Questio Atanasii contra Arrium de filio Dei   .   .   . f.   1
   Title in faint red capitals.
   (Cum) Apud Niceam urbem a trecentis xviii episcopis. *P. L.*
        lxii. 155.
   Inc. gesta secunde cognitionis, 20 *b*.
   Inc. sententia iudicis, 56.

Apparently a library mark is erased in the inner edge of f. 61.

Ends : indubitata sorte capescant. Τέλοσ ἀμὴν.

2. Versus tiburtine sybille de iudicio .   .   .   .   .   .   63 *b*

    Iudicii signum—sulphuris amnis. Ἀμὴν.

The well-known Sibylline acrostic.

f. 64 blank.

3. Five spurious Epistles of Clement of Rome   65

    These five letters stand at the head of the Ps.-Isidorian collec-
      tion of Decretals : ed. Hinschius, 1863, pp. 30–66.

     1. To James. 65.   Clemens Iacobo...Notum tibi facio

     2.   ,,   85.   Clemens Romane...Quoniam sicut a b. petro

     3. To the Church. 90.   Clemens urbis...Urget nos

     4. To Julius & Julianus. 101.   Oportet fratres

     5. To the Church of Jerusalem. 106 *b*.   Communis uita

     —celebrari festiua.   Deus autem pacis sit cum omnibus
      uobis. Ἀμὴν.

    Erasure.

    Exp(l)iciunt epistolae Clementis Episcopus (!) urbis Romae.

The decorative initials in the first part are in the familiar Italian manner with white branch-work : in the second part plain gold on square patches of blue.

THOMAS REID (died 1624)
Latin Secretary to King James VI and I
Benefactor of Marischal College Library
From the portrait at Marischal College

HISTORICAL NOTE ON
ABERDEEN UNIVERSITY LIBRARY

By W. DOUGLAS SIMPSON, M.A., D.Litt., University Librarian

THE history of Aberdeen University Library is complicated by
the fact that for a period of more than two and a half centuries this
remote northern town, alone in all the world, possessed two complete
Universities, each perfect in all its faculties: "the University and
King's College" in Old Aberdeen, founded by Bishop William
Elphinstone in 1494/5; and "Marischal College and University,"
founded in the New Town in 1593 by George Keith, fifth Earl
Marischal. Until the final abolition of Episcopacy in 1690, King's
College was under the patronage of the Church, the Bishop of
Aberdeen being *ex officio* Chancellor. As such, King's College
inevitably became a stronghold of conservatism during the successive
religious changes of the sixteenth and seventeenth centuries. It
adhered first to the ancient faith, and thereafter to "Prelacy" as
against Presbyterianism: and drastic action was required in order
to bring it into line with the wishes of the party whose ideas of
church governance ultimately triumphed. Marischal College, on the
other hand, was conceived by its founder as a Protestant seminary,
a counter-check to the Roman Catholic influence that emanated
from the older University. Moreover, by a development the course
of which is not quite clear, the College in the New Town at an early
date came to be almost entirely under the control of the Magistrates
and Council. This divergent character of the two Universities has
left its mark on their Libraries, alike in history and contents. Since
the "Fusion" in 1860, when King's College and Marischal College
were united by Act of Parliament, the libraries have become one;
although as a matter of convenience the books in Law, Medicine,
and Science (except Botany and Forestry) are meantime shelved in
the Marischal College building. At present the total contents of the
Library number some 236,000 volumes and 14,000 pamphlets. There
are some 200 incunables, of which a catalogue was published in 1925[1].

[1] *A list of Fifteenth Century Books in the University Library of Aberdeen.* (Abd.
Univ. Studies, No. 98.)

King's College Library may be presumed to have taken its origin with the establishment of the University by Elphinstone, as it still contains a number of books bearing his signature, among them the MSS. nos. 12–17, 184, 198, 222, and 262 in the present catalogue, also books (including MS. no. 214)[1] autographed by Hector Boece, the first Principal (*circa* 1500–36), and by the Sub-Principal, William Hay (see MS. no. 239), who succeeded Boece and died in 1542. MS. no. 263 belonged to John Vaus, the first Humanist (1516–38). But the origin of the "bibliotheck" as a building appears to date from the time of Bishop William Stewart (1532–45). In the *Album Amicorum* or old register of the benefactors of King's College, compiled in 1640, it is stated that this Bishop "built the librarie hous, and with a number of bookes furnisht the same; as also he built the jewell or charterhous, and vestrie or chapter hous[2]." All these rooms were housed in a lean-to structure abutting on the south wall of the Chapel: although built a generation after the latter, some such annexe must have been intended from the outset, as the chapel windows on this side are kept high so as to clear the pentice roof. The "librarie hous" is shown in the earliest known picture of King's College, in James Gordon's *Aberdoniae Novae et Veteris Descriptio*, 1661. This first Library, having become ruinous, was replaced in 1725 by a new building on the same site, erected out of funds provided by a generous graduate, Dr James Fraser (donor of MS. no. 274), the first Secretary of Chelsea Hospital, and Librarian of the Royal Library under James II: but, in or about 1770, this building seems to have been burned[3], and thereafter the Library was removed to the western portion of the then disused Chapel[4]. The present fine library building dates from 1869–70, with subsequent extensions.

It is recorded that in the Reformation troubles many books perished: Protestant writers accused the Roman Catholics, and

---

[1] The signature on folio i of this MS. is that of Alexander Galloway, Prebendary of Kinkell, Official of Aberdeen, and Rector of the University. He served as master of works to Bishops Elphinstone and Dunbar in their architectural undertakings. *Cf.* also MSS. Nos. 108, 248, 250, and 261.

[2] *Fasti Aberdonenses*, p. 533.

[3] On this question see Dr Norman Macpherson, *Notes on the Chapel, Crown, and other Ancient Buildings of King's College, Aberdeen*, pp. 23–5.

[4] As shown in R. W. Billings' plate—*Baronial and Ecclesiastical Antiquities of Scotland*, vol. 1.

vice versa. At all events, whoever was to blame, "many goodlie volumes" were "ather robbed, or embasled, or purloyned by unfaythfull keepers[1]." Considering the stormy history of King's College throughout the sixteenth and seventeenth centuries, the wonder is that so many of the early books and MSS. remain. From pre-Reformation times a partial catalogue survives in the report of a Rectorial Visitation in 1542: the list, however, is concerned merely with the service books pertaining to the Chapel[2]. Among them may be mentioned a *myssale, capitalibus elementis aureis rubris et azureis, artificiosis picturis adiectis, habet in initio secundi folii "In nomine Sanctissimi," penultimi "Sancti Colmoci."* In 1637 there is mentioned a book entitled *Plenisching, Rentall, and Assignatioun of Stipends,* which contained amongst other items "ane catologue of the buikis of the kingis colledge of Aberdeine[3]"; but evidently it was unsatisfactory, as in that year enactment was made that "ane perfyte and exact Catalogue" should be prepared[4]. Progress however was slow. Ten years later it had to be ordered that the "Bibliothecar" should "tak paines to gett in good order all the books of the librarie, and to place them in most convenient manner that so ane formall Catalogue of them may be drawen wp[5]." The oldest written catalogue now preserved bears the date 1717: the books, 2857 in number, are classified under the six heads of: "Theological, Episcopal, Medical, Juridical, Philosophical, and Historical and Grammatical." The oldest printed catalogue (of books in Theology) was published in 1790.

Space forbids us to touch upon the numerous details of picturesque interest in the long history of King's College Library: but two quaint entries may be quoted. On 1st November, 1634

"it is ordainet be the rectour and memberis that the keeper of the bibliotheck sall, about the tyme of Michaelmese yeerlie, wpone fourtie-aucht houris advertisment, delyver the key of the bibliotheck to the rector of the universitie, that he may imploy tuo or thrie off the memberis for visitting the said bibliotheck to sie giff all the

---

[1] James Gordon, *Description of Bothe Tonns of Aberdeene,* 1661 (ed. Spalding Club, 1842), p. 24.
[2] *Fasti Aberdonenses,* pp. 568-71.   [3] *Ibid.* p. 406.
[4] P. J. Anderson, "Notes on the University Libraries," in *Aberdeen University Calendar,* 1893-4, Supplement, p. 79.
[5] *Ibid.*

buikis and instrumentis belonging therto be present in the librarie *ipsa corpora*; with certificatioun against the said keeper, that in caice aney be amissing without and nocht within the dooris of the said librarie at that tyme, he salbe lyable not onlie to furnische ane wther buik of the samen kynd upon his awen expenssis, bot also to pay for his negligence the sowme of ten merkis for ilk buik that bees wanting as said is, by the pryce of the samen[1]."

And on 20th December, 1639, it is

"ordanit that the Keeper of the Librarie in all tyme cumming sall make the librarie patent twyse in the weik, viz., Tuysday and Fryday, betwixt ane and twa houris efternoone; quhairin if he failzie, he sall pay two merkis *toties quoties* to the commoun pro-curator to the behooff of the Librarie[2]."

In 1720 books were allowed to be borrowed for periods deter-mined by their bulk: an octavo for a week, a quarto for a fortnight, and a folio for a month. The fines for undue detention were levied strictly on the same principle[3]!

Marischal College Library has in some respects a different, and in its benefactions a much more fortunate, history. The Town Council Minutes record that the founder had "promest" books for the equip-ment of "ane commoun Librarie," and a building was reconditioned to receive them[4]: but actually the first recorded books belonging to Marischal College were those bequeathed in 1613 by Dr Duncan Liddell, the one-time Professor of Mathematics in the University of Helmstadt. A much more important bequest—the MSS. items of which bulk large in the present catalogue (nos. 1–11, 24, 137, 205, 215, 218, 219, 240, 241, 244)—was that made in 1624 by Thomas Reid, Latin Secretary to King James VI. Reid, who in 1603 had been a regent at Marischal College, by his testament, dated 19th May, 1624, the original of which is still preserved in the University muni-ment room, "finding himselfe Sick of Body but perfect in Memory... for the Love I bear to the Town of new Abd and wishing the new College Schools thereof should flourish" granted "my whole Library of Books acording to a Catalogue written by Mr John Garden in an

---

[1] *Fasti Aberdonenses*, p. 398.
[2] Anderson, *ut supra*, p. 79.
[3] *Ibid.* p. 83.
[4] *Records of Marischal College and University*, vol. i, p. 112.

old Custome house Book and Subscryved by me...and acording to another Catalogue written by M[r] John Cheyne Parson at Kinkell... sicklike subscryved by me, Whilks Books acording to the s[d] Catalogues I ordain to be put in the Bibliotheck of the s[d] new College." He also bequeathed capital to provide a yearly salary of six hundred merks for a "Bibliothecar," "and the s[d] BIBLIOTHECAR his duty shall be to hold his Door open 4 days a Week for the Scholars and Clergy to have the use of the Books of the s[d] Bibliotheck, and NO WAYS to be astricted in NO further Duty[1]."

Reid's Catalogue, containing some 1350 titles, still exists, and so does his legacy in aid of the Librarian's salary, which in the financial year 1930–1 yielded a sum of £14. 0s. 4d. Reid died in London, and his books were duly shipped to Aberdeen, as appears from a Minute of the Town Council, whereby having in view the "long tract of tyme" before the monetary legacy would accumulate interest enough to enable it to be applied to the purpose stated, and "considdering, if the saidis buikis sall ly still in dry wairis, during all this Interim, not onlie sall the most pairt of thame mothe and consume, But lyikwayis the clergie of the towne and college sall be defraudit of the use and benefite of the saidis buikis," it was "thought meit and expedient....That the saidis haill bookes and manuscriptis sall be transported frome the keyheid, out of the sellar quhair thay are lyand for the present, in hogheidis, to the college of this burghe, and thair set wp in the college librarie, be Catalog and Inventar[2]." The earliest Catalogue of Marischal College Library, compiled about 1670, contains a list of the printed books and MSS. bequeathed by Reid. Among them is the entry "*Isidorus de natura hominis bestiarum, etc.—perg.*" This is the "Aberdeen Bestiary," the *pièce de résistance* of the University's collection, described as no. 24 in the present volume (pp. 18–25)[3].

A portrait of Thomas Reid is in the possession of the University, and is reproduced here. His famous bequest is described by a contemporary annalist as "the best Library that ever the north

---

[1] *Records of Marischal College and University*, vol. 1, pp. 194–7. Reid's library cost him "neere vpon Three hundred pound sterling money," *ibid.* p. 174.

[2] *Ibid.* p. 198.

[3] See paper by Mr Walter Menzies, B.A., Superintendent of the Marischal College Library, on the Aberdeen Bestiary, read to the Edinburgh Bibliographical Society, 13th Feb. 1921, as reported in *The Scotsman* next day.

pairtes of Scotland saw[1]." A century later we have an account of
Marischal College Library from the pen of Principal Thomas
Blackwell, who clearly brings out the importance of Reid's legacy.

"The excellent Library of the Marishal College...was indeed
originally begun upon no greater Stock than that belonging to the
Convent of the *Grey-Friars*, which contained most of the School-men
and Monkish Writers; and particularly a good Number of the *Latin*
Fathers in Vellom MSS. and some few of the Classics, *Horace, Lucan,
Martial*, etc., likewise in MSS. Then Dr Duncan Liddel enriched
it with the antient *Physicians* and *Mathematicians, Greeks, Latins,*
and *Arabs,* and with the most eminent Moderns who had wrote in
either Science before his Time: but Mr *Thomas Reid* Secretary to
K. James VI for the *Greek* and *Latin* Tongues was the great
Benefactor. In his Travels thro' the greater Part of *Europe* he
bought up the fairest and largest Editions of all the *Classics* that
were printed from the Time of *Aldus Manutius* until the year 1615,
including the Philosophers, Lawyers, Greek and Latin *Fathers,* with
the works of the chief Critics, *Scaligers, Casaubons, Lambins*, etc.
that flourished in that Period, and many valuable and curious MSS.
among which is the curious *Hebrew-Bible*, the fairest and most
correct Book of that kind in *Britain*[2]....Since that Time, the additions
of the Libraries of the Revd. Mr. *Dunlop*[3], of Dr. *Alexander Reid*[4],
of the Revd. Mr. *Lorimer*[5], and many other private Donations of
Noblemen, Gentlemen and others, with the Books yearly published
from *Stationers Hall,* have considerably increased it, and contributed

---

[1] James Gordon, *History of Scots Affairs* (ed. Spalding Club, 1841), vol. III, p. 89.

[2] Listed as no. 23, *infra*, p. 129.

[3] John Dunlop, alumnus, Marischal College, 1671–5; Minister of Skene, 1686;
deprived as a non-juror, 1695; died, 1714.

[4] Alexander Reid or Read (1581–1641), the distinguished surgeon, and elder brother
of Thomas Reid. He graduated M.A. at Marischal College in or after 1600, and endowed
his Alma Mater not only with his "bookes of divinitie and philosophy" but also with
a valuable bursary. His "medicinall Bookes," strangely enough, he left, together with
certain moneys, to the "Colledge of Auld Aberdeine." (Will in *Records of Marischal
College*, vol. I, p. 234, and cf. *Fasti Aberdonenses*, p. 534.) See Mr Menzies' paper on
Reid in *The Library*, vol. XII (1931), pp. 46–74.

[5] Rev. William Lorimer, of London (alumnus, Marischal College, 1657), by his will
in 1722 left money to Marischal College for a bursary, and also his books, which "are
not very considerable for many of them were taken by the French in time of War and
carried to Dunkirk and I could never recover them nor my manuscripts which were taken
with them." *Records of Marischal College*, vol. I, p. 404.

to make it, if not the most numerous, one of the best chosen Collections in the Kingdom[1]."

The seventeenth century was marked by a spasmodic dispute between the Town Council and the College authorities as to which had the right to appoint the Librarian. A far more serious crisis arose after 1709, in which year "the four Universities of Scotland" received the right to obtain copies of every book registered at Stationers' Hall. King's College treated the privilege as applying solely to itself, and challenged the right of Marischal College to call itself a University. A settlement was reached in 1738, when the House of Lords decided that the books should be shelved at King's College, but that Marischal College should have the right to consult them. This did not entirely obviate friction, however, and on one occasion, in 1805, the Sacrist of Marischal College intercepted a case of books destined for King's! In 1836 the Stationers' Hall privilege was withdrawn, in return for very meagre pecuniary compensation.

A few particulars may be added about certain of the donors of MSS. described in the present Catalogue. Gilbert Burnet, Bishop of Salisbury (1643-1715), the famous ecclesiastical statesman and historian of the Reformation, who bequeathed to Marischal College the sumptuous Psalter no. 25, belonged to the Aberdeenshire family of the Burnets of Crimond, a branch of the house of Leys. He graduated M.A. at Marischal College in 1657, being then not yet fourteen years of age. To his Alma Mater he gifted 20,000 merks Scots for founding scholarships.

Of Dr Samuel Guise, the donor of items 106, 107, 156, 161, 216, 242, 275, 276, as well as of other items not dealt with here, nothing seems to be known beyond the fact that he received the honorary degree of LL.D. from Marischal College on 14th February, 1809, being on that occasion described as "late of Surat; now resident in Montrose."

The Necrology of the Cathedral, no. 248, was gifted to King's College, as the inscription on the flyleaf records, by Mr George Leslie, of Eden, Banffshire, whose grandfather, Sir Patrick Leslie, had attended classes at Marischal College in 1617 and 1618, and in 1634

---

1 *An Account of the Erection of the Marishal College and University in the City of Aberdeen* [1736], p. 3.

was chosen Provost of Aberdeen—a "wehement Covenanter." His politics were so obnoxious to Charles I that the king sent down a strongly worded letter to the Magistrates, complaining of "seditious convocatiounes" and of the way in which the Provost had "wrongit your trust in his careage at our late parliament"; and concluding with the intimation that "it is our pleasur for that effect that you remove the said Patrik Leslie from being your provest[1]." He was Provost again in 1639–40, 1642–3, and 1647. Leslie's "seditious" principles did not prevent him from accepting a knighthood at the hands of Charles II on the "Merry Monarch's" visit to Aberdeen in March, 1651. His grandson's gift to King's College Library was deemed of sufficient importance to require a special entry in the College Minutes[2]:

"12th December, 1727. The said day, Lesley of Iden having sent to the college as a present a curious manuscript on vellum relating to the cathedral church of Aberdeen, containing the necrologie thereof and other valuable papers, a letter of thanks to be written him."

"The Scougals," who gifted to King's College the Inventory of the Cathedral Plate (no. 250), were Patrick Scougal, Bishop of Aberdeen from 1664–82, and his son, Henry (M.A., King's College, 1668, and Professor of Divinity there from 1673–8), the author of *The Life of God in the Soul of Man*—one of the few religious classics that Scotland has produced. The gift of books by the Scougals is referred to in a College Minute of date 24th November, 1684.

The MSS. nos. 139 and 148 were gifts to Marischal College from the Governors of Gordon's Hospital, Aberdeen, founded in 1730 by Robert Gordon, a Danzig merchant, to whom the MSS. may originally have belonged.

*   *   *

It may be added that since Dr James wrote his descriptions the Bestiary (no. 24) has been rebound at the British Museum, and Gilbert Burnet's Psalter (no. 25) in Aberdeen.

---

[1] A. M. Munro, *Memories of the Aldermen, Provosts, and Lord Provosts of Aberdeen*, pp. 138–9.
[2] *Fasti Aberdonenses*, p. 445.

HAND-LIST OF MANUSCRIPTS
NOT INCLUDED IN THE
DESCRIPTIVE CATALOGUE

18. Gordon, J. History of Scots affairs, 1637–41.

19–20. Spalding, J. Memorials of the troubles in Scotland and England, 1624–44. Transcribed by J. Dalgarno. 2 copies. 1778–9.

23. Bible. Old Testament. Masora: various readings by Rabbi Asher, and others.

34. Maclaurin, C. Dissertationes mathematicae Academicae; Letters to him on mathematical subjects; Miscellaneous mathematical papers.

35. Instructions in navigation.

36. Hamilton, R. Miscellaneous papers.

37. Skene, D. Miscellaneous papers.

38. —— Correspondence. With index by Professor Trail.

39. —— Correspondence. [*Typewritten.*]

40. —— Correspondence. [*Duplicate.*]

41. Aberdeen. Old Aberdeen. Gardener fraternity. Account book, 1821–64.

42. —— Old Aberdeen merchant society. Sederunt book, 22 July 1700 to 15 December 1729. (Subscriptions to 12 Nov. 1792.)

44. —— Old Aberdeen. Sederunt book, 7 Nov. 1796 to 2 June 1840.

45. —— Old Aberdeen. Sederunt book, 25 Sept. 1840 to 12 Dec. 1901.

46. —— Old Aberdeen. Rules and regulations, 1813.

47. —— Old Aberdeen. Annual payment book, 1841–99.

48. —— Bon Accord society. Register, 1778–1810.

—— —— Rules, 1794, with list of members. [*Printed.*]

49. —— Gordon's Mill. Minutes of farming club at Gordon's Mill.

50. Mackintosh, P. Minutes of trustees under deed of settlement, 30 Sept. 1837. 1840–52.

51. Clark, T. Experiments on phonetics.

52. French, G. Collection of letters and papers concerning Dr G. French, 1767–1830.

53. Dutton, T. Hymns and odes, 14 Nov. 1710—6 Aug. 1712.

54–55. Gordon, J. Lunar tables arranged by eighty-four year cycles. 2 copies. 1775.

56. Walker, J. Syllabus of a course of lectures on rural oeconomy.

57. Aberdeen. Stent roll of the burgh of Aberdeen, 1748–49.

101. Liturgy of the Coptic church. Second month. Coptic-Arabic.

102. Liturgy of the Coptic church. Fourth month. Coptic with Arabic notes.

103. Colvill, S. Mock poem; or, Whigg's supplication.

104. Mitchell, W. Notes of sermons by Nisbet, Semple, Walker, etc., 1708–21, etc.

109–110. Buscoducis, G. de. Lecturae in Aristotelis Physica, De coelo et mundo, De meteoris, [etc.], 2 vols.

111. Physica generalis et particularis in Harcurio sub auspiciis Lemonnier, physicae professoris. 1731.
112. Gleageus, T. Cursus logicus ab eo dictatus et a T. Ogilvie scriptus. 1648-9.
113. Dun, P. Dictata logica, etc. 1610.
—— Dictata in Aristotelis Acroamatica, De coelo, etc. 1611.
114. Jamesoun, W. The description of the proportional ruler and other instruments. 1628.
115. Tractatus physico-theologicus de oculo et visione.
116. Forbes, T. Notae quaedam in Aristotelis Ethica, in Demosthenis Orationes quasdam et in Homeri Iliados libros 1-2. 1602-3.
117. Richardson, A. Sermons on Mark xi. 22; Exod. xx. 3; Ps. cxi. 2; Chas. Hay, Inverkeithing, 1785.
118. Henley, J. On Chronicles x. 16; One reason to give up Gibraltar. 1749.
120. Scot, *Sir* John. The staggering state of the Scottish statesmen, 1550-1650.
121. Keith, R. Catalogue of coins and medals of the kings of Scotland, preserved in the Advocates' Library, Edinburgh.
122. Jamesoun, W. Of the logarithmal trigonometria of Baron Napier. 1621.
123. Commonplace Book. Versus super Christum crucifixum; Bred and mylk for chyldryn [etc.].
124. Fraser, W. Notes on English silver and copper coins.
125. Turkey. Travels in Turkey, 1773, translated from Dutch.
126. Fraser, W. Notes on Scotch silver and copper coins.
127. —— Notes concerning the silver coins of Scotland. With a catalogue of the copper and mixed coins and notes on it. 1783.
128. Physica generalis.
129. Cullen, W. Clinical lectures in R. Infirmary, Edinburgh, 1769-70. Taken by G. French.
  Gregory, J. Notes of clinical lectures in R. Infirmary, Edinburgh, 1769-70. Taken by G. French.
130. Stuart, J. *the Pretender*. Memorials addressed to him, about 1717-20, by some astrologer.
131. Blair, H. Synopsis of lectures on rhetoric. 1765.
132. Gordon, J. Cursus juridicus IV libros Justiniani Institutionum comprehendens, in usum Collegii Regii studiosorum. 1701.
—— Positiones juridicae quas in Collegio Regio juris studiosi sub ejus praesidio variis temporibus publice propugnabant.
133. Millar, J. Course of lectures on government. 1782.
134. The Myroure of our Ladye. [Cent. xv-xvi: owner Eliz. Mentoun.]
135. Exercitatio parasceuastica de quadruplici hominis statu, etc. 1675-6.
136. Baron, R. Disputationes theologicae quaedam, etc., 1687.
140. Orem, W. Description of the Chanonry, King's College, and the Cathedral in Old Aberdeen, for 1724-5. Transcribed by J. Dalgarno, about 1770.
  Scougal, H. Morning and evening service of the Cathedral church in Old Aberdeen.
141. Physicae generalis enchiridion, 1701.
142. James I. A Paraphrase of the Revelation of the apostle John; historical table.
143. Scotland. Catalogue of the Lords of Session, 1532-1789, with notes.
—— Forms of address used by Charles II and William III to Sovereigns, states, nobility, clergy, universities, colleges, etc.

144. Spotswood, J. The form of process before the Lords of Council and Session.
145. Rules of Aberdeen philosophical society, with questions proposed, 1758–72.
146. Mitchell, W. Diary. 9 Feb.—16 April, 1717.
147. Orem, W. Description of the Chanonry, King's College, and the Cathedral in Old Aberdeen.
149. Stella, T. Tafel oder Calendar mit Erklärung; Bericht von den Theilen und von dem Gebrauch des Compasses. 1569.
150. Moir, J. Annot. in Aristotelis Libros De coelo et De anima; Partium corporis humani descriptio, etc. 1619.
151. Aristotle. Annot. in ejus Praedicamenta, Postpraedicamenta, Analytica priora et posterioria, etc. 1622–3.

    Moir, W. Annot. in Aristotelis libros acroamaticos et de ortu et interitu. 1619.

    Cursus logicus, viz.—Compendium logicae; De natura logicae, etc. 1622–3.
153. Clerus, G. Compendium humanitatis constipatum. 1616.
157. Robertson, J. Eighteen sermons. 1713–15.
158. Row, J. Ane Overture and humble adwyse hou the leatter translatione of the Byble 1612 may be much bettered, 1657.

    M'Kinnon, W. Ane Musick book of tones, with the rudiments of musicke, wreyten ye 18 May 1657.
159. Gillespie, T. Sermons on Job xxxvi. 18; II Chron. xvi. 9; Heb. xii. 22–24; John xvi. 8–9.
160. Collectanea e variis de Veteris Testamenti textu et codicibus hebraicis de versionibus eiusdem, de Talmud, de antiquitatibus hebraicis, etc.
162. Officia quaedam, Litania, etc., translated.
166. Abu Bakr Mohammed Ben Assim. Poems. [*Arab.*]

    Ishak, B. J. The treasure of gems. [*Arab.*]
167. Khosru, A. Matlah al Anwar. [*Persian.*]
168. Nuzhat. Works. [*Persian.*]
169. Mohammed. The conquests of him and the three caliphs. [*Arab.*]
170. Hafiz. Diwan. [*Persian.*]
171. Nekhsheby, H. Tooti nameh. [*Persian.*]
172. Sadi. Gulistan. [*Persian.*]
173. —— —— ——
174. Jami. Sikander Nameh. [*Persian.*]

    Nizami. Makhzan al Asrar. [*Persian.*]
175. —— —— ——
176. —— Khosru u shirin. [*Persian.*]
177. Jam. Jami Jam.
178. Mohammed. On the legitimate successors of Mohammed. [*Persian* fr. *Arabic.*] *Imperf.*
179. Hafiz. Diwan. [*Persian.*]
180. Koran. [*Arab.*]
181. ——
182. Bahar-i-Danish. [*Persian.*]
183. The Wonders of nature. [*Persian.*] [With miniatures.]
185. Concordantiae Veteris et Novi Testamenti conscriptae per manus Roberti Perkini. 1551.

De nominibus et intitulationibus LXX discipulorum Christi per manus R. Perkini. 1555.

More, *Sir* T. Treatise to receive the blessed body of Our Lord sacramentally and virtually. Copied by R. Perkins. 1555.

Perkins, R. On prayer, fasting, almsgiving, the four lives [etc.] 1555.

Staphylus, F. Apology for right understanding of the Scriptures. Trans. T. Stapleton and copied by R. Perkins. 1555.

186. Angelis, G. ab. Comment. in Aristotelem De interpretatione. 1607.

Aristotle. Comment. in ejus Praedicamenta, de interpretatione, Analytica priora, Topica, De Sophisticis elenchis.

—— Comment. in ejus Praedicamenta, Postpraedicamenta, Analytica priora et posteriora. 1605.

Hunnaeus, A. Prodidagmata in logicam. 1607.

Disputationes VI de gratia, de justificatione, et de merito. [1607.]

187. Aristotle. Arnoldi comment. in ejus De physica auscultatione, De anima, Metaphysica, De coelo [*etc.*] *Imperf.*

Arnoldus. Dictata et tractatus in sphaeram.

189. Greenfield, W. Notes of lectures upon Belles lettres delivered in Univ. of Edinburgh; Notes of four philological lectures by Aw. Dalziel. 1786. Taken down by R. E. Scott.

190–191. Stewart, D. Notes of lectures on moral philosophy, delivered 1785–86. Taken down by R. E. Scott. 2 vols.

192. Chronicle of the kings of Scotland from Fergus Ferchard to 1346.

193. Chronicle, 6 June to 27 Aug. 1642. Transcribed by J. F.

194. Tractatus de propositionibus, de syllogismis, de praedicabilibus, de praedicamentis, etc.

195-7. Reterus, H. Relata super libri XXIV digestorum titulo de soluto matriminio, scripta per W. Elfynston.

—— Relata super libri XLV digestorum titulo de verborum obligationibus, scripta a W. Elfynston, Lovanii, 1433.

Justinianus. Lecturae Grosbeli, Reteri, Ricardi de Turnaco et aliorum in titulos selectos codicis institutionum [etc.], Scriptae per W. Elfynston, Lovanii studentem, 1433. 3 vols. [Paper.]

Grosbelus, J. Relata super libros XII–XIII digestorum scripta per W. Elfynston, Lovanii, 1433.

Ricardus de Turnaco. Lectura super libri VI digestorum titulo de rei vindicatione. Scripta per W. Elfynston, Lovanii, 1433.

199. Comment. in Decretalium libri II titulos XXIII–XXX. [*Imperfect.*] [xvi early.]

200. Clemens V. Comment. in Clementinarum Constitutionum Lib. I–V. 3. [xvi early.]

201. —— Comment. Joan.' de Imola in Clementinas Constitutiones.

202. Lexicon juridicum. [From Bp. Elphinstone, with 201.]

Horborch, W., *Alemannus.* CCCCLI conclusiones, seu Determinationes aut decisiones dominorum de rota, usque ad a.d. 1381.

203. Leslie, J. Armageddon, a poem. Aberdeen, 1816.

204. Baxter, A. Histor, a dialogue in favour of the English method of estimating the forces of moving bodies and against Leibnitz's method.

206. Maclaurin, C. Letters to Sir A. Cumming, A. Malcolm, etc. 1720–43.

207. —— On fluxions.

208-209. Maclaurin, C. An Account of Newton's Philosophical discoveries, etc., 2 vols.
210. The officers of honour appertaining to the Army Royal.
211. French, G. Historical tracts concerning geographical discoveries, etc.
212. Lindsay, R. History of the affairs of Scotland, 1436-1565. Transcribed by J. Hunter. 1727.
213. Mémoires touchant l'Ancienne Alliance entre la France et l'Escosse, et les priviléges des Escossois en France.
   Dares *Phrygius*. De bello Trojano.
220. Myln, A. Vitae episcoporum Dunkeldensium ad annum 1515.
221. Revenue. Brief state of the income and issues of the public revenue, 5 Nov. 1688 to 29 Sept. 1691.
224. Balfour, *Sir* J. A Gehealogical account of several dukes, marquesses, and earls of Scotland.
225. De unione regnorum Britanniae tractatus. 1703.
226. Vemius, P. N. de. Caledonia; seu, Dissertationes de primis Caledoniae incolis. Vol. I. Aberdeen, 1726.
227. Church of Scotland. Acts and proceedings of General Assembly. 1560-1602.

228.	——	——	——	——	1690, 1692.
229.	——	——	——	——	1702-05.
230.	——	——	——	——	1706-10.
231.	——	——	——	——	1711.
232.	——	——	——	——	1712-17.
233.	——	——	——	——	1718-21.
234.	——	——	——	——	1722-25.
235.	——	——	——	——	1726-28.
236.	——	——	——	——	1729-30.
237.	——	——	——	——	1731-33.
238.	——	——	——	——	1734-36.

251. Registrum assedationum Cathedralis ecclesiae Aberdonensis.
257. Lectura super libros III Decretalium. [Cent. xvi early.]
264. Irlandus, J. Quaestiones in libros III-IV Lombardi sententiarum. [From Hector Boece.]
277. Pybrac, M. de. Quatrains escrit en diverses sortes de lettres par Esther Anglois francoise, a Lislebourg. 1600.
301. Gordon, T. Moral philosophy; Logic.
302. Melvin, J. Latin grammar, supplementary to the Rudiments. Second edition. Aberdeen.
303. Schraderus, J. Dictata in Suetonium. 1753-4.
304. —— Fundamenta styli cultioris.
305-14. Burmannus, P. Dictata in Tursellini Hist. Epitomen, cum continuatione ad 1650. 10 vols.
315-19. Burmannus, P. Dictata in Tursellini Hist. Epitomen, cum continuatione ad 1650. 5 vols.
320. Burmannus, P. Dictata in Tursellini Hist. Epitomen, cum continuatione ad 1650. Vol. I.
321. Burmannus, P. Animadversiones in Epistolas Ciceronis ad familiares, cum formulis Epistolae bene scribendae.

322–323. Burmannus, P. Dictata in Suetonium. 2 vols.

324. —— Dictata in Terentii Andriam et Eunuchum.

325. —— Dictata in antiquitates Romanas. Leide, 1720.

326. —— —— —— Vol. 1. Leide, 1724.

327. —— —— —— Vol. 2. Leide, 1725.

328. Haitsma, A. Antiquitates Romanorum haustae ex ore P. Burmanni.

329–331. Saxé, C. Dictata ad antiquitates Romanas. 3 vols. [Bd. with Burmannus' Antiq. Rom. brev. descrip. Lugd. Bat. 1743.] 1758.

332–333. Saxé, C. Praelectiones et illustrationes in antiquitates Romanas. 1778-9.

334–335. Rulaeus. Adversaria. Partes III–IV.

336. Bos, L. Excerpta quaedam ex ejus ore in antiquitates Graecas, etc.

337–338. Ruckerus, J. C. Dictata in Institutiones Justiniani. 2 vols.

339–340. Struchtmeyer, J. C. Dictata in Suetonium. 2 vols.

341–342. —— Compendium historiae recentioris. 2 vols.

343. Arntzenius, H. J. Dictata in Tursellini Epitomen.

344. Gronovius, J. Comment. in Sallustium Crispum.

345. Lives of saints. Translated from Jerome and others. [Cent. xviii.]

346. Bosscha, H. Dictata in Suetonium et ad antiquitates Romanas. 1809-10.

347. Ernesti, J. A. Archaeologia literaria.

348. Valcknaer, L. C. Antiquitates græcæ.

349. Oudendorpius, F. Dictata in antiquitates Romanas. Lugd. Bat.

350. Goudœrer, A. Annotatio ad Livii librum XXI. 1823-25.

351. Bos, L. Dictata in antiquitates Graecas.

352. Havercampus, S. Dictata in antiquitates graecas.

353. Graevius, J. G. Notae et observationes in Taciti Annales.

354–358. Saxius, C. Notae in Tursellini Romanarum historiarum epitomen. 5 vols.

359. Wassenberg. Antiquitates græcæ.

360–361. Historiae novi foederis compendium brevissimum. 2 vols.

362. Pollius, M. Compendium historiæ universalis. 1721.

363. Bos, L. De scriptoribus latinis; De necessitate disciplinæ militaris.

365. Stuart, J. Notes on Greek grammar written on interleaved copy of " Linguae graecae institutiones grammaticae, 1728," used by him in Marischal College.

366. Optica.

367. Gronovius, J. Dictata in Matthæum et Lucam.

368. Scheltingha, G. Prælectiones ad Justiniani Digesta, vol. IV.

369–373. Wesseling, P. Dictata in Tursellini epitomen historiarum. 5 vols.

374–375. Russell, J. Complete and perfect index to Holland's translation of Livy's History. 2 vols. 1744.

376. Suetonius. Dictata in Suetonium.

377–378. Libri II de officiis et de juribus. 2 vols.

379. Notes from various authors. 1730.

380. Isagoge Biblica, 1598.

381–383. Perizonius. Annotata in Tursellinum: S. Greg. 3 vols. 1708.

In **383.** —— Refutatio historiæ de Joanna Papissa. 1708.

384. Brown, J. A View of Old Testament types. 1774.

385. Bunyan, J. Peregrinantis progressus. Vita—Massey.

386. Sibodo. Carmen metricum de Sibodone.

387. Bruner. Hortus regius Blesensis.

388. Waldenses. Amica et fraterna adnotatio naevorum et verborum minus recte positorum in Confessione Valdensium.
389. Eginhardus. Vita Caroli Magni. [Cent. xvii.]
390. Melvin, J. Manuscript notes on Latin syntax.
—— Notes on Latin syntax.
391. Turretinus, F. *Appendix*. Notes on his De satisfactione Christi.
401. Allen, M. On the animal economy.
411. Buonarroti, F. Osservazioni sopra alcuni frammenti di vasi antichi di Vetro; Osservazioni sopra tre dittici antichi d'Avorio.
Fabrettus, R. Memoriae veteres ex ejus operibus extractae.
Ficoroni, F. de. Le memorie ritrovate nel territorio della prima, e seconda Citta di Labica.
Ficoroni, F. de. Raccolta di Maschere Sceniche e di figure comiche di antichi Romani.
Guarnacci, M. Breve trattato delle specifiche monete etrusche, o Italico-Antiche.
Lupi, P. Dissertatio ad nuper inventum Severae martyris epitaphium.
412. Colville, S. The Whig's supplication, a poem. Part 2.
413. Wilson, R. Travels and sketches in Greece and Sicily, in 1818-19, and 1825-26.
414. —— Tour through Norway, in 1830.
415-419. —— Journey through Egypt, Nubia, Palestine, Syria, Arabia, Mesopotamia, Babylonia, Persia and India, in 1820-22. 5 vols.
420. Wilson, R. Descriptive tour through Switzerland and Italy, in 1816.
421. —— Remarks on punishments, crimes, etc.
422-423. —— Duplicates of some of his letters, 1820-25. 2 vols.
424. Wilson, A. St A. Verses, 1823-58.
425. Wilson, R. Autobiography; Miscellanies.
426. —— Album for literary contributions by his friends.
427. —— Hugo Conwaie, a novel.
428. —— Descriptive tour through France, in 1816, with remarks on the specimens of sculpture and painting in the Louvre, in 1814.
429. Wilson, R. Duplicates of some of his letters, 1812-15.
430. —— Remarkable surgical cases on board the "Glory," 1805-7.
431. —— On the preservation of health on board; on remittent fever; on dysentery.
432. —— Notes on various subjects.
433. —— Remarkable events. 1804-14.
434. —— Extracts from letters to his brother during travels in Greece, Palestine, Asia Minor, Sicily and Egypt, in 1819-26.
435-437. Wilson, R. Notes during travels, 1854-5.
438-439. Copland, P. Notes on lectures on Natural philosophy in Marischal College, 1803. 2 vols. Taken down by R. Wilson.
440. Wilson, R. Portraits of Turkish sultans.
441. Lomax, G. De fluxu marino, an essay; An essay on St Paul's thorn in the flesh. Caerleon, 1730.
442. Wilson, R. Coloured sketches of the principal Turkish officers of state.
443. Catalogue of the Wilson Studio.
451. Hamilton, R. Commonplace book, 1764-
452. —— Essays.
453. —— Finance; statistics.
454. —— Journal, 1812-21, etc.

455. Hamilton, R. Lectures on natural philosophy, 1779–80.
456. —— Letters, 1766–1829.
457. —— Mathematical problems, etc.
458. —— Miscellaneous papers.
459. —— National debt.
460–461. —— Notes from various books. 2 vols.
462. —— Notes of sermons.
463. —— Progress of society.
464. —— Summaries of books.
471. Skene, D. Botanical descriptions.
472. —— Chemistry.
473. —— Cryptogama and algae.
474. —— Entomological descriptions.
475. —— Literary essays.
476. —— Medical cases.
477. —— Medical essays.
478. —— Mineralogy, coals, etc.
479. —— Miscellaneous.
480. —— Natural history discourses.
481. —— Zoology.
482. —— Miscellaneous descriptions and observations.
483. —— Letters to and from him.
484. Johnstone, J. F. K. Bibliographia Aberdonensis 1472–1640. *Printed proofs with MS. notes.*
485–485². New Spalding Club. Minutes I and II. 1886–1915.
486. —— Minute-book of Editorial Committee, 1886–1900.
487–498. Littlejohn, D. Calendar of deeds registered in Sheriff Court of Aberdeenshire, 1606–1658. Compiled 1909–20. 12 vols.
499. Maclachlan, E. Transcript of Dean of Lismore's MS. 1814.
500. Forbes, W., v. Skene, G. Queries and answers of Counsel.
501. Lexicon of medical terms.
502. Perreau, M. C. Letters, 1773–75.
503. Aberdeen. Extracts from burgh records anent Chanonrie, etc.
504. Mackay, A. Astronomical observations made in observatory in 1785, '86, '87, '88.
505. Fordyce, G. Miscellanea from lectures, 1778–79.
506. Aberdeenshire. Names of individuals extracted from the Poll-tax book, 1696. By A. Dingwall Fordyce.
507. Aberdeenshire. Valuation book of lands in Aberdeenshire. 1802.
508. Caithness, J. A., *Earl of.* Genealogical notices of the Dukes of Normandy and their successors from the 9th to the 16th century. 1888.
509. Grant, L. M. Protomantis, and other poems.
510–511. Cheyne, P. Adversaria and Scintillae. 2 vols.
512. Bourignon, A. Antichrist discovered. Done out of French. 3 pts.
513. Collection of sermons, 1714.
514. Mowat, J. Latin versions, and notes of sermons. 1709.
515–517. Aberdeen. Breviarium Aberdonense. Pars aestivalis (pars hyemalis). 3 vols. Copied for Spalding Club.
518. Aberdeen. Literary debating society. Minute book, 1836–37.

519. Robb, W. Poems and songs, Aberdeen, 1876. [Remarks by T. P. N., 1876.]

520. Persius. The English Persius, by me, Alexander Cuming, was written in Aberdeen under William Smith in the yeir 1707.

521. Suther, T. G. Notes on passages of the New Testament. 1836.

522. Bain, A. The senses and the intellect.

523. —— The emotions and the will.

524. —— On the study of character.

525-527. Robertson, J. Collections for a Biographia Abredonensis. 1833-35. 3 vols.

528. —— —— —— —— Index. By Jean E. Kennedy.

529-530. —— Biographia Abredonensis. 2 vols. 1837.

531. Lauder, *Sir* T. D., *bart.* Remarks on the geology of the River Findhorn. 1827.

532. Aberdeen. Very curious extracts from the records of the city of Aberdeen, 1398-1658. Made by J. Man.

533. Rorison, W. P. Story of the Scottish metrical psalter. 1909.

534. [Cruickshank, J.] Newhills book list, 1910.

535. Black, J. Notes of reports on schools inspected between 1 September 1861 and 31 Aug. 1862.

536. Braemar. St Andrew's Catholic church. Register of baptisms, 1703-57. Abstracted 1910.

537. Braemar. St Andrew's Catholic church. Index locorum. Index nominum. 1910. By Jean E. Kennedy.

537². Gordon, P. Description of the Mission of Braemar.
Farquharson, C. Short account of change of religion in Braemar.

538. Glengairn and Braemar. Register of baptisms, 1782 (to 1845).

539. Aberdeen. Philosophical society. Minutes, 1758-71.

540. Skene, D. Notes of discourses in Philosophical Society.

541. Aberdeen. Society of probationers for advancing the interests of the Church of Scotland. Minutes, 1834-38.

542. Dutch system of education from the King's decree, Aug. 1815.

543. Aberdeen. Union perseverance society. Minute book, 1 May, 1818—20 June, 1840.

544. Aberdeen. Natural history association. Minute-book, 1845-51.

545. Anderson. Marriages, deaths, and baptisms in the families of Anderson belonging to Rayne. Extracted from registers, 1672-1820.

546. Aberdeen. Lyceum. Rules, revised 1833 [printed]. Papers contributed to it, 1831-33.

547. Sermons, 1730-32.

548. Broekhuisen, J. van. Jani Broukhusii Carminum nunquam antea editorum appendix nova.

549. Gospel of St Barnabas. [Transcript of Italian MS. in Vienna Library for Canon Ragg's edition: date 1902.]

550. Scotland. Roll or list of the claims to heritable jurisdiction, entered in the Court of session in Scotland, November 1747.
Scotland. Intromissions of the Receiver-general relative to estates forfeited.

551. Anderson, J. History of the Highland clans. 1835.

552. Ogilvie. Abstract of the writs of the Regality of Ogilvie, etc., deposited within Cullen House. Copied by W. Cramond. 1888.

553. Bulloch, J. M. Aberdeenshire and Banffshire volunteer muster-rolls, 1797-1803, from the Public record office.

554. Trail, S. Notes on the Confession of faith.

555. Lectures on philosophy.

556. Essays on conveyancing.

557. Rose, A. Minutes of trustees under deed of settlement 16 April, 1845, 1850-65.

558. Spalding, A. Notes on Scots law, 1673.

559. Ogilvie, G. Treatise on law, 1675.

560. Turner, A. M., *Mrs*. Album of original and selected verses, commenced by Mrs Turner *c*. 1798; continued by family to 1889.

561. Aberdeen. Dr Tulloch's academy. School register, 1852-73.

562. —— W. Grahame Walker's academy. School register, 1873-86.

563. Gordon, P. Short abridgement of Britain's distemper, 1639-49.

564. Hope, *Dr*. Lectures on botany. 1774.
Middleton, M. Directions for planting forest trees.
Cullen, *Dr*. Of Marle.

565. McIntosh, E. S., *of Borlum*. Criminal letters, H.M. Advocate against E. S. McIntosh of Borlum, and others.

566. Inverness. Decreet of modification and locality 7 July 1827 and 1 Mar. 1828.

567. Aberdeen. Don-fishings. Decreet of valuation of the teinds of the half netts salmon fishing. 1709.

568. Aberdeenshire. Book off poleable persons. 1696.

569-584. Thucydides. Works. Edited by F. T. Rickards. 16 vols. 19...

585-586. Brown, J. Phrase book at Gymnasium, Old Aberdeen, 1850. 2 vols.

587. Aberdeen. Chanonry House cricket club. Minutes, 1858-80.

588. Forbes, W., *Lord*. Rentale, made in the year 1552.

589. English-Gaelic vocabulary.

590. Leigh, G. Extract of Gerarde Leighe his Avidence of armorye. 1642.

591. Bible. Johannis Theologi Apocalypsis Taoduni scripta. Anno 1780.

595. Aberdeen. Alphabetical index to first 67 vols. of Council Register, 1398-1800. Compiled W. Kennedy. 1815.

601. Anderson, G. Essay on the early descents and settlements of the Norsemen on the Northern and Western coasts of Scotland. 1827.

602. Anderson, J. A Magistrate's recollections in St Vincent's in 1836.

603. Anderson, P. Miscellanies.

604. Ancient monuments bill. [Print.], and relative letters.

605. Deer. Book of Deir. [Transcript for Stuart's edition.]

606₁₋₉. Stuart, J. [Letters addressed to Dr John Stuart with reference to the Spalding Club 1837-85.]

607. Spalding Club. Minute book, 1839-70.

608. —— Treasurer's list, 1840-69.

609. —— Letter book. No. 1. 1851-72.

610. —— Cash book, 1840-46.

611. —— —— 1846-59.

612. —— —— 1858-72.

613. Aberdeenshire. Bibliography of Aberdeen, Banff and Kincardineshires. Correspondence anent bibliography, 1893-1902.

614. Historical notes to 1748.

615. Historical notes of Scotland to 1757.

616. Danson, J. M. Considerationes modestae on "Heraldry British and foreign" by Drs Woodward and Burnett. [1892.]

617. Hardy, T. An Imaginative woman. *Original MSS.*

618-627. Terry, C. S. Claverhouse notes. 10 vols.

628. Bible. Old Test. Proverbs. New translation from the Hebrew of the Proverbs, or Parables of Solomon. 1798.

629. Baillie, R. Notes of sermons preached at Inverness 1704(-1705).

630. Fraser, J. Homelies and exercises theological and moral. 1662.

631. Grahame, T. Collectanea anent Temple superiorities of the county of Aberdeen now belonging to Alexander Macdougal, etc. Made 1830.

632. Gordon, A. Treatise on the epidemic puerperal fever of Aberdeen.

633. Aberdeen. Grammar school. Records of annual dinner of those who joined Mr Nicol's class in October 1807.

634. MacPherson, *Sir* Aeneas. The Loyal.dissuasive. London, 1701.

635. Forbes, John, *of Corse.* A Diary, or spirituall exercises. Copied 1687 and 1690.

635 A. —— —— Spirituall exercises in Old Aberdeen. Copied 1687.

636. Monro, A. Lectures on surgery. Taken by Alexander Gordon.

637. Reid, P. Compt book. 1693.

638. Aberdeen. Old Aberdeen savings bank. Minutes. (April 1816–February 1860.)

639. Fordyce, A. D. Abstract made in 1833 or 1834 of old documents then in hands of W. Smith, Union Street, Aberdeen.

640. Letters on religion.

641. Anderson, C. Ane Styll book. Begun 1726 and ended 1727.

642. Chalmers, G. Aberdeenshire—Etymologies of names. 1799.

643. Gordon, A. The Practice of physick. Vol. 1.

645-646. —— —— —— Vols. 3 and 4.

647. Corbet, J. Sketch of the opium trade in India. 1857.

648. Dey, W. Grammar School, Old Aberdeen. Register of pupils from Autumn quarter 1870 to October 1885.

649. Campbell, G. Theological tracts. Tract 1. Of implicit faith.

650. —— Strictures on Dodwell's Paraenesis.

651-655. —— Defence of the doctrine contained in the foregoing.sermon "The spirit of the Gospel." 5 vols.

656. Fraser, W. The spirit of the times—In three discourses; to which is subjoined another On the love of country. 1820.
—— The duty of subjects to the King and other rulers. 1821.

657. Fraser, A. Medical notes on reading.

658. Burnet, D. Pourtrait of true loyalty exposed in the family of Gordon. 1691.

659. Hadden, G. Collection of geometrical problems and theorems. 1796.

660. Reid, (?). Poems.

661. —— Collection of unsigned letters from Aberdeen, in one handwriting. 1778-87.

662. Gordon, A., *4th Duke.* Poems.

663. Boerhaave, H. Part of Dr Boerhaave's Practical aphorisms. Translated from the last edition.
Monro, A. Practical corollaries from ye essay on ye nutrition of foetuses.

664. Bible. Psalms, translated in metre by Francis Davison, etc. [*17th century*].

665. Sermons. Two sermons from Luke viii, 18; Two sermons from Gen. i, 27, etc., etc.

666. Orem, W. Description of the Chanonry in Old Aberdeen. 1724–25.

667. ——   ——   ——   ——

667^2. [——]   ——   ——   ——

668. Aberdeen flora.

669. Barclay, J. Description of Roman Catholic church, 1679.

670. Campbell, *Sir* H. Essay upon the Lord's prayer.

671. F., W. Lords decisions and acts of sederunt. 1713–15.

     ——   ——   ——   1714.

     Edinburgh. Form of process of Commissar Court of Edinburgh. 1687.

     Progress of the securities made use of in Scotland.

     Practica forensis. 1662.

     Alstedius, J. Observationes quaedam geographicae.

     Ignorantia literarum morbus et medicina.

     Musicæ encomiolum.

     Introductio ad astronomiam.

     Reasons against the pressed bond asserted to be by the pastor of Pennicook.

     Forbes, W. Theses philosophicae de natura possibilitatis.

     Menzies, J. Character of William Forbes, student.

     Skene, W. [Letter to D. H. Cockburn, *Lat.*] "Viro amplissimo" D. H. Cockburn.
         1673.

     Wishart, G. De rebus ad Jacobo Marchione Montisrosarum comment. 1650.

     Arithmetica practica.

     Tractatus arithmeticus.

     Oaths. [On oaths.]

     Bramhall, J. Speech.

     Livingston, J. Life. Written by himselfe. Copied and compared 1666. (Short
         breife relation of some of the ministers of Scotland.)

     Livingston, J. A Papper continuing a brife relation of severall predictions, and
         prophesies of famouse ministers and profesors.

     Grame, J. To the Reverend the minrs. of Presbry of Dunfermline to be delivered to
         their Moderator. Dunfermline, 1709.

     Grame, J. Answer to libel against Mr James Grame. 1700.

     Skene, W. Vestibulum eloquentiae.

     Buchanan, G. Epithalamium upon the marriage of Marie, Queen of Scots to the
         Dauphin of France. Done from Latin.

672. Gregory, D. Tractatus de geometria practica.

673. Diary of a voyage. March 10—October 14.

674. Leightonian library. Catalogue. Edin. 1843.

675. Bible. The Psalter. Paraphrased by F. Forbes.

676. Institutiones physicae generalis.

677. Aberdeen, W., *2nd earl*. Decreet absolvitor, Earl of Aberdeen and Patrick Duff of
         Premnay against Alexr. Irvine of Drum, 1741.

678. Taylor, W. Decreet of modification and locality against the heritors. 1763.

679. Petrarca, F. Liber triumphorum. [Vellum, cent. xv, with decorations.]

680$_{1.2}$. Stewart, J. List and glossary of some Oriental place and other names.
         2 pts.

     $_{3.4.5.}$ Stewart, J. List of place names in Spain, Portugal and S. France. 3 pts.

680₆. Stewart, J. Some unfinished notes on tribes and peoples connected with Afghanistan but not Afghans.

681₁₋₄. Stewart, J. Some Oriental place names. 4 pts.

   ₅₋₇. Perceval, C. de. Essai sur l'histoire des Arabes. Vol. 2. pp. 1–313. Trans. into English by J. Stewart (*and two other items*).

682–685. Stewart, J. Collections on place and other names. [*Arranged under sources.*] 4 vols.

689. Peterkin, A. The Club. 1813.

690. Jamesone, G. Collection of pencil sketches of his portraits. By J. Bulloch.

691–696. Vaux, Charles Grant, *Vicomte de.* Histoire des Ecossois. 6 vols. 1799 etc.

697. Gordon, A. Poems. Collected by W. P. Smith.

698. Terry, C. S. Bibliography of literature relating to Jacobite history.

701–703. Greig, G. Folk songs. Index to words and tunes. 3 vols.

704. —— Folk music. Index. Compiled by W. Walker.

705–708. —— Folk music. 4 vols.

709–710. —— Folk songs. Words. Index. 2 vols. Compiled by W. W.

711–774. —— Folk songs. Words. 64 vols.

775. —— Folk songs of the north. Collected 1906. Book 1.

776–780. —— Traditional versions of old ballads. 5 vols.

781–784. —— Transcripts of old Scottish ballads and songs. 4 books.

785. Duncan, J. B., and Greig, G. Traditional ballad tunes. Collected 1913.

787. Duncan, J. B. Folk songs. Complete list of contents. Compiled by W. Walker.

789. —— —— Index. Compiled by W. Walker.

790¹–790³. Greig, G. Greig and Duncan MSS. 3 parcels.

791. Thomson, W. Orpheus Caledonius: collection of best Scotch songs set to music by W. Thomson.

792. Kinloch, G. R. Airs from Kinloch's Ancient Scottish ballads—Appendix.

793. Christie, W. Original MS. of Scottish music.

794. Christie, A. Miscellaneous and critical observations on Hebrew tongue.

795. Marshall, J. Music book. 1835.

796. [Treatise on armorial bearings.]

797. Meldrum, J. *Appendix.* Trial for burning of Frendraught. 1633.

798. Fountainhall, *Sir* J., *Lord.* Diary, 1665-6.

799. Commonplace book.

801. Ree, S. Extracts from Scots Magazine. 1732–1825.

802. —— Notes on schools.

803. —— Inventory of charters in Gordon Castle. *c.* 1802–3.

804. —— Copy—"Memoirs of the origin and descent of several families of the surname of Gordon." 1901.

805. —— Copy of "Origin of the familie and sirname of Leslie."

806. —— Extracts from Burke's Landed gentry. 1898.

807. —— Notes on family of Innes.

808. —— Extracts from Lord Rosebery's List of persons concerned in the Rebellion

809. —— Extracts from Register of Privy Council of Scotland.

810. —— Extracts from Exchequer Rolls.

811. —— Extracts from Great Seal Register.

812. —— Schoolmasters, Presbytery of Aberlour.

813. —— Notes on family of Forbes.

814. Ree, S. Notes on family of Gordon.

815. —— do.

816. —— do.

817. —— Notes from Chalmers' Caledonia.

818. —— Notes on family of Duff.

819. —— Extract minutes from Presbytery.

820. —— Report of Schoolmasters' widows' fund for year ending 19 Sept. 1823. Edinburgh, 1824.

821. —— Notes on Schools.

822–836. Ree, S. [Fifteen miscellaneous notebooks.]

837. Aberdeenshire. Abstract of Register of Seisins, 1599–1606.

838. Mackintosh, *Family of.* De origine et incremento Makintoshiorum epitome.

839. Craig, J. *Appendix.* Collections as to the life of Mr John Craig.

840. Gordon, *Family of.* Letters (47). 1694–1814.

841–842. Hasan, Abu'l-Kasim, *called* Firdausi. Shahnāmah. 2 vols.

843. Mackintosh, The, *of Inverness.* Lawyer's case book. [*19th cent.*]

844–47. —— —— Letter-book. 1833–1850. 4 vols.

848. Chapman, J. Genealogy of the Grants, 1729.

Lumsden, M. Genealogie of the name of Forbes, 1580–1706.

Arbuthnott, A. Continuation of the genealogie of Arbuthnott.

Leslie, *Family of.* Genealogy.

Ross, *of Arnage, Family of.* Genealogical notes on family of Ross.

Achinbreck, *Family of.* Genealogie. 2d. Aprile 1741.

Strachan, *Family of.* Memorial of Strachans.

Seton, *Family of.* Notes on family of Seton.

Lumsden, A. Pedigree.

851–853. Trail, J. W. H. Journal of voyage to Parà, etc. 3 vols.

854–857. —— Genealogies of Trail family. 4 vols.

858–859. —— Ancestry of Trail family. 2 vols.

860. —— Sources for Trail descents.

862. —— Autobiographical reminiscences.

863. —— Catalogue of specimens, Amazon valley 1873–75.

864. —— Colours of flowers. Record begun 1915.

865. —— Data of botany specimens. 1916–18.

866. —— Manuscript of Trail Memorial volume.

867. —— Distribution of flowering plants and fern allies. 1906.

871. Trail, S. Abstract of genealogy of family of Trail. Enlarged upon by J. W. H. Trail.

872. Burr, H. A. Notes on Schivas. [*Typewritten.*]

873. Inverness lawyer's account book, 1792–93.

874. Ledger of an Inverness W. S. 1807–38.

875¹. Bedingfield, A. L. Miscellany of the family of Lumsden. 1927. [*Typewritten.*]

875². —— Genealogical records of the family of Lumsden. 1928. [*Typewritten.*]

876. Jamesone, G. *Appendix.* Correspondence relating to George Jamesone, the Scottish Vandyck. Addressed to John Bulloch. 1886.

877. Simpson, H. F. Morland. Translations—English into Latin and Greek; Latin and Greek into English.

877₁. Simpson, H. F. Morland. Diary of events in the years 1649–50—Montrose's proceedings.

878-880. Dallas, *Family of.* Calendar—Dallas, etc., 1262–1870. 3 vols.

881-882. Webster, J. Autograph letters regarding College. 2 vols.

883. Cooke, E. W. Correspondence addressed to J. Webster. 1851–64.

884-888. Webster, J. Autograph letters addressed to J. Webster. 5 vols.

889-890. ——— Private correspondence 1857–59 addressed to J. Webster. 2 vols.

891. Terry, C. S. Bibliography of Jacobite history, 1689–1788. [With MS notes and additions.]

892. Smith, J. Book of generations of families related to Rev. Jas. Smith.

893. Brodie, A. Sermons.

894-895. Session record of S. Ronaldshay and Isle of Burray, 1657–69 2 vols.

896. Craven, J. B. Collections and studies on Trithemius.

——— Doctor Heinrich Khunrath.

897-898. Carson, W. E. Through the Hebrides, 1897. 2 vols.

899. Lectures and sermons, Arbroath, 1792–96.

900. Hay, A. Ad Cardinalem D. Betoun gratulatorius panegyricus. [Transcript.]

981₁. Glennie, J. Journal of a tour thro' part of Scotland, 1825.

₂₋₄. Glennie, M. Journals. 1825, 1828, 1835.

982. Aberdeen—Old Aberdeen. Description of ye Chanry, 1725 & 1724.

983₁. [Sermons. Dissertations on the ten commandments.]

₂. [Sermons. 1759 etc.].

1005-1006. Several Canarese, Cingalese, and Pali MSS. on leaves and cloth.

Yang Gan. [*Burmese.*]

1007. Bhagavad Gita. [*Sanskrit.*]

Commentary of Raghavendrapati. [*Sanskrit.*]

1008. Burmese oath taken in court of justice by witnesses. Scratched on palm leaves.

1009¹–9². Mr Secretary Bale's papers.

NOTE.—A series of manuscripts dealing exclusively with University affairs is omitted in the above list.

INDEX I

CHRONOLOGICAL LIST OF MSS. DESCRIBED

INDEX II

AUTHORS OF MSS. DESCRIBED

INDEX III

PROVENANCE OF MSS. DESCRIBED
(FORMER LIBRARIES, PRIVATE OWNERS, SCRIBES, ETC.)

Hereford, William, 154
Hinton, Carthusian monastery, 154

Irving, Andrew, 261
—— Richard, 254

Jackson, John, 216

Kalman, John, notary, 248
Keith, William, 258
Kerr, John, Professor of Greek, King's College, 239
Kloss, Dr Georg, 364

Laurence, William, Archdeacon of Brechin, 163
Lesley, Andrew, 223
Leslie, George, of Eden, 248
—— Patrick, of Eden, 248
Little Comberton, 271

Mawnshull, Master J., Fellow of Oriel, Oxford, 218
Melvin, Dr James, 364, 688
Morris, of Cologne, scribe, 263

Orcamp, Cistercian Monastery, 156
Oriel College, Oxford, Master J. Mawnshull, Fellow of, 218

Phillipps Collection, 687

Reid, Thomas, Regent, Marischal College, 1, 2, 3, 4, 5, 6, 7, 8, 9, 10, 11, 24, 137, 205, 215, 218, 219, 240, 241, 244, 271, 272

Royal Library of England, 24

St Andrews, Archibald Whitelaw, Archdeacon of, 214
St Paul's Cathedral, 1, 2, 3, 4, 5, 6, 8, 9, 10, 137, 205, 219, 240, 241, 244
Salisbury, Bishop Gilbert Burnet of, 25
S. Maria de Caritate, 106, 242
Sapidus, Villelmus, 262
Scenan (? Shennan), William, Carmelite, scribe, 239
Schagen, Helena van der, 274
Scortus, Andreas, scribe, 164
Scougal, Henry, Professor of Divinity, King's College, 250
Scougal, Patrick, Bishop of Aberdeen, 250
Sheffield, Edward, 276
Stamford, Earl of, 243

Treves, Monastery of St Maximin, 364
Tyson, John, 217

Umfra, William, scribe, 256, 259

Vaus, John, Humanist, King's College, 263

Wallace, William, scribe, 263
Warmyngton, A., 148
Whitelaw, Archibald, Archdeacon of St Andrews, 214
Winterbottom, J., 154
Woodall, George, 154

Yester, John Hay, Lord of, 21

CAMBRIDGE: PRINTED AT THE UNIVERSITY PRESS BY WALTER LEWIS, M.A.

www.ingramcontent.com/pod-product-compliance
Ingram Content Group UK Ltd.
Pitfield, Milton Keynes, MK11 3LW, UK
UKHW030902150625
459647UK00021B/2673